MW00450498

ATLANTIC COASTAL PLAIN
WILDFLOWERS

A Field Guide to
the Wildflowers of the Coastal Regions of
Virginia, North Carolina, South Carolina,
Georgia, and Northeastern Florida

For Carolyn —
Happy
botanizing!

GIL NELSON

9 Apr 08

FALCONGUIDE®

GUILFORD, CONNECTICUT
HELENA, MONTANA
AN IMPRINT OF THE GLOBE PEQUOT PRESS

*A***FALCON**GUIDE®

Copyright © 2006 by Morris Book Publishing, LLC

Falcon and FalconGuide are registered trademarks of Morris Book Publishing, LLC.

Text design: Nancy Freeborn
Maps created by Multi Mapping Ltd. © Morris Book Publishing, LLC
All photographs © Gil Nelson unless otherwise noted.

Library of Congress Cataloging-in-Publication Data is available.

ISBN 0-7627-3433-7

Manufactured in China
First Edition/First Printing

IN MEMORY OF MY GRANDMOTHER,

Bessie Pettus, with deep appreciation for her love of wildflowers,

birds, and all of nature's creatures.

CONTENTS

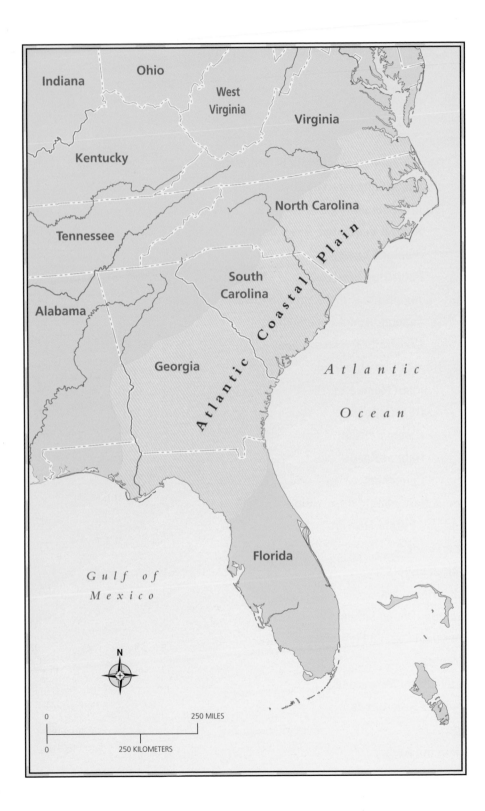

ACKNOWLEDGMENTS

Numerous people have helped me with the research and writing of this book. Most important among them is Wilson Baker. Wilson has been helpful in the development and completion of this and all of my previous books. He made many suggestions about which species should be included in the present volume, contributed suggestions for numerous excellent wildflowering locations, and regularly alerted me to good locations for photography and field research. Our many hours in the field and subsequent discussions constitute one of the most enjoyable parts of writing this book. Wilson also suggested many important human resources who could aid in my fieldwork across the region and reviewed a number of my photographs. He is ranked by many biologists among the most knowledgeable and important naturalists in the Red Hills region of northern Florida and southern Georgia. This expansive knowledge of the ecology, natural history, and botany of our region has made a significant contribution to my understanding of our flora. His expertise and his friendship are highly valued.

Bruce Sorrie has been my Carolina guide and field companion throughout this project. Bruce's knowledge of the southeastern flora is extensive and his willingness to share it and his time has been invaluable. He took me to locations for many species in the North Carolina Sandhills that I would not have had time to find for myself, and he has been most gracious and accommodating. He reviewed and added to the accuracy of flowering dates for many of the North Carolina species and made numerous invaluable suggestions about what species to include in the book, including a number of species that I had not previously considered for inclusion.

I owe a great debt to my good friend and field companion, Angus K. Gholson Jr., field botanist and expert on the flora of southern Georgia and northern Florida. Angus helped with me with difficult identifications, kept track of my photographic progress, and regularly alerted me to good localities for my photography. His extensive records of flowering times, excellent private herbarium, and expansive knowledge were invaluable resources. Our time in the field is always both inspirational and educational, and I thank Angus for both his direct and indirect contributions to this book.

I wish also to thank Dr. Austin Mast, professor of botany at Florida State University and director of the Robert K. Godfrey Herbarium, and Sarah Braun, curator of the Godfrey

Herbarium. Austin's generosity with herbarium resources and his support of my work there have been immensely helpful. Sarah's unselfish assistance with herbarium resources, especially with helping me find and review specimens, as well as her delightful company in the field is very much appreciated. I spent many hours at the herbarium checking distribution data, morphological characters, measurements, flowering times, and plant descriptions, all of which was made easier by Austin and Sarah's interest.

I thank Todd Engstrom for his help with both this and the companion volume, *East Gulf Coastal Plain Wildflowers.* His willingness to allow me free rein at Greenwood Plantation near Thomasville, Georgia has been very helpful. I owe a debt to Virginia Craig and Dan Miller for alerting me about plants in flower and alerting me to photographic locations.

Pam and Bill Anderson have been very helpful field companions, photographic and image consultants, and field observers. Bill and Pam's photographic expertise has been invaluable and Pam's talents with digital image processing are unsurpassed. Together they encouraged my transition to digital photographic format, which has been much appreciated. Pam also contributed the author photograph that appears at the end of this volume, for which I am grateful.

My daughter, Hope Nelson-Pope, has contributed enthusiasm and both personal and technical support. I often relied on her skills as a professional editor, asking many questions about usage, grammar, and punctuation. Her professional success and personal character constitute a tremendous source of pride.

Finally, I thank my wife, Brenda Nelson. Brenda was an early and persistent advocate of my writing this and the previous Falcon wildflower field guide. Her unwavering encouragement and support of my work are without equal. She is my best friend and biggest fan, and is an incomparable lifetime companion.

INTRODUCTION

The Atlantic Coastal Plain Wildflowers

The South Atlantic Coastal Plain is an elongated 25-million-acre subunit of the more expansive Southeastern Coastal Plains, a collection of physiographic subdivisions of eastern North America that stretches from extreme southeastern Virginia southward across northern Florida and west to easternmost Texas. The boundaries of the South Atlantic Coastal Plain have been variously defined, with some authorities dividing it into upper and lower units segregated by an east-west line through the approximate center of South Carolina, and other authorities limiting its western extent only to extreme southeastern Georgia and northeastern Florida east of the Suwannee River. As envisioned by the Bureau of Land Management (BLM) for the Partners in Flight initiative, the region is considered to include an area that originates at the Great Dismal Swamp in extreme southeastern Virginia and extends southward along the Atlantic coast to just north of Daytona Beach, Florida. According to BLM's definition, the region's western boundary is defined by a southwesterly trending line that follows along the Piedmont and Fall Line Hills southwestward to the Georgia and Alabama state line, then southward along the Chattahoochee and Apalachicola Rivers to the Gulf of Mexico. The southern boundary follows the Gulf Coast to about Cedar Key, Florida, then northeastward across the northern Florida peninsula to the Atlantic Ocean. Given the homogeneity of the flora across this region, this somewhat expanded circumscription has been adopted for the purposes of this book.

The South Atlantic Gulf Coastal Plain is a predominately flat, weakly dissected, gradually eastward and southward sloping plain, bordered on the northwest by an abrupt change in elevation that transitions into the Piedmont plateau. On the east it is bordered by the active Atlantic coastline. The soils are primarily fine to coarse, unconsolidated silts, sands, and clays of Pliocene-Pleistocene origin. According to botanists Bruce Sorrie and Alan Weakley in their consideration of coastal plain endemics *(Castanea,* Vol. 66, p. 70), eight of the world's ten soil orders are represented in the Southeastern Coastal Plains, with pH values ranging from 3.0 to 9.0. Sorrie and Weakley suggest that the divergent origin of the region's soils from both ancient Appalachian erosion and marine deposition during periods of higher sea level at least partly account for the considerable soil diversity in such a geologically young landscape.

This soil diversity has contributed to an interesting array of vegetative assemblages, especially given the region's relatively uniform terrain. In the flatlands fine sands often retard surface water percolation, resulting in mesic, pine-dominated forests pocked with standing water wetlands such as swamps, pocosins, Carolina bays, cypress domes, and shallow, shrub-filled depressions. On drier upland sites coarse sands encourage rapid drainage, creating xeric sandhill environments well known for their floristic diversity. In still other areas, the combination of fine sands and steep slopes that retard natural fire give rise to rich, organic soils that support upland hardwood hammocks and slope forests.

Endemism and Floristic Diversity

The South Atlantic Coastal Plain is well recognized for the richness, uniqueness, and diversity of its flora and is widely considered an important area for endemism. Of the more than 1,600 vascular plants that are endemic to the greater Southeastern Coastal Plains, approximately ninety are restricted primarily to the Atlantic Coastal Plain, and many more of the 1,600 occur there. A sizable number of these regional endemics are restricted to pine-dominated wetlands and sandhills, two ecosystems that have dwindled significantly in extent over the last 150 years. The dramatic losses to Longleaf Pine-dominated communities and the suppression of natural fire have been accompanied by dramatic losses in the abundance of what are now our rarer species, leaving many of our endemics critically imperiled and struggling for survival. Important examples of regional endemics that are featured in this book include Southern Colicroot *(Aletris obovata)*, Largeflower Milkweed *(Asclepias connivens)*, Carolina Wild Indigo *(Baptisia cinerea)*, Skyflower *(Hydrolea corymbosa)*, Sandhills Lily *(Lilium pyrophilum)*, Pineland Leatherroot *(Orbexilum virgatum)*, and Honey-Cups *(Zenobia pulverulenta)*.

At least part of the reason for the Atlantic Coastal Plain's large number of regional endemics is attributed to the occurrence of at least three smaller centers of endemism within it borders. The first of these regions encompasses part of the Fall Line Hills, the geographic dividing line between the Atlantic Coastal Plain and the Piedmont. The Fall Line is defined by a meandering and sometimes disappearing line from north of Southern Pines, North Carolina, southward and westward through Columbia, South Carolina, and Augusta, Macon, and Columbus, Georgia. From the Carolinas into eastern Georgia, the Fall Line is

Old growth longleaf pines, like these 300-plus-year-old trees at the privately owned Greenwood Plantation in Thomasville, Georgia, once covered much of the Southeastern Coastal Plains but are now limited in extent to only a few thousand acres scattered across the region.

associated with the Fall Line Sandhills, a region of deep sand that supports stands of Longleaf Pine *(Pinus palustris)* and provides habitat for such specialties as Sandhills Milkvetch *(Astragalus michauxii)*, Sandhill Thistle *(Cirsium repandum)*, Sandhills Lily *(Lilium pyrophilum)*, Dwarf Bristly Locust *(Robinia nana)*, and many more.

The second region of endemism stretches from southeastern Virginia to northeastern Georgia and includes the terrestrial portions of the Cape Fear Arch, a crescent-shaped region of geological uplift extending offshore of the Carolinas from about Cape Lookout, North Carolina, to Cape Romain, South Carolina. According to Richard LeBlond *(Castanea,* Vol. 66, pp. 83–97), twenty-two plants are strictly endemic to the region associated with the Cape Fear Arch, including Georgia Indigo-Bush *(Amorpha georgiana* var. *confusa)*, Venus Flytrap *(Dionaea muscipula)*, Sandhills Blazing Star *(Liatris cokeri)*, and Spring-Flowering Goldenrod *(Solidago verna)*. In addition, another twenty-two plants are nearly endemic to the region, making this portion of the North and South Carolina coastal plain a center of speciation and exceedingly rich in unique and interesting wildflowers.

The third area of high endemism spans southeast Georgia and northeast Florida and includes such species as Bartram's Ixia *(Calydorea caelestina)*, Hartwrightia *(Hartwrightia floridana)*, and Pineland Leatherroot *(Orbexilum virgatum)*. Only recently have botanists turned considerable attention to this region. In the last decade explorations by Dr. Loran Anderson, professor emeritus in botany at Florida State University, have resulted in records of range expansion for several species and discoveries of new populations of several known rarities.

In addition to endemic species, an impressive number of plants also find the limits of their ranges in the region, most of which fall into one of three general patterns of distribution. The first pattern includes those species that are better known to the north of the region, or are species with primary distributions in the Piedmont or southern Appalachians. Examples include Pinebarren Gentian *(Gentiana autumnalis)*, Small Green Wood Orchid *(Platanthera clavellata)*, Carolina Lily *(Lilium michauxii)*, Turk's-Cap Lily *(Lilium superbum)*, and Indian Pink *(Spigelia marilandica)*. Another group includes species that are mostly of the East Gulf Coastal Plain but find the eastern terminus of their ranges in the northern parts of the Florida peninsula or extreme southern Georgia. One of the best examples is Night-Flowering Wild Petunia *(Ruellia noctiflora)*. This and other species that fall into this category can be found in the companion volume *East Gulf Coastal Plain Wildflowers*, also published by Falcon. A third group includes species that are widespread in the middle and southern portions of the Florida peninsula, but the ranges of which also expand northward along the coast into Georgia and southernmost South Carolina. Tarflower *(Bejaria race-mosa)* and Saw Palmetto *(Serenoa repens)* are good examples.

Plant Communities

Plants occur in or colonize all sorts of places, from the natural, relatively undisturbed vegetative communities that are sometimes found in our publicly protected lands, to radically altered or disturbed areas such as lawns, roadsides, pastures, and urban parks. Learning which plants occur in what types of habitats, and where such habitats might be found, is essential to studying a region's wildflowers.

For the purposes of this book, I have divided our dominant natural vegetative assemblages into four broad categories: pineland systems, temperate hardwood forests, palustrine wetlands, and coastal strand. The first two categories include mostly inland communities, whereas examples of the third group are spread across the region. The fourth group, as its name implies, includes those assemblages that lie within a few miles of the coast. I have also included a discussion of several types of ruderal, or disturbed, habitats that sometimes prove to be rewarding places to search for wildflowers.

Natural Vegetative Assemblages

Plants often occur in distinctive natural vegetative assemblages, each of which is typically characterized by a handful of dominant species in conjunction with few to numerous associate species. Some plants are extremely limited in habitat preference and are found solely within a particular community type, while others enjoy wide latitude in the types of communities in which they occur. Such assemblages are variously referred to as natural communities, plant communities, ecosystems, and habitats. Though the use of the latter term first centered on animal ecology and was used mostly by ecologists to connote an environment that provides the food and shelter required for an animal to make its home, its definition has been more recently widened to also include the home environments of plants and other organisms. It is used here and in the accounts that follow as a shorthand designation for vegetative assemblage or plant community.

Many of our vegetative assemblages are relatively stable in both community structure and species composition and are easily distinguished in the landscape. Learning to recognize them insures an excellent foundation for learning the region's flora and is essential when attempting to search out rare or endemic species. The species accounts presented in this guide include detailed notations about each species' preferred habitats.

The Carolina Sandhills Gamelands near Southern Pines, North Carolina, provide an excellent example of Fall Line Hills pinelands and are rich in both woody and herbaceous wildflowers, many of which are endemic to this unique landscape.

Pineland Systems

In her classic 1950 book *Deciduous Forests of the Eastern North America,* Lucy Braun included the Southeastern Coastal Plains within what she called the Southeastern Evergreen Forest Region. Her name for this expansive area is an obvious reference to the extensive pine-dominated woodlands that once clothed its landscape. No vegetative assemblage is more representative of the Coastal Plains.

Some estimates suggest that more than 90 million acres of the Longleaf Pine-Wiregrass ecosystem dominated the coastal plain during presettlement times. When the first European settlers arrived in the region, they were treated to a landscape characterized by 200- to 500-year-old pine trees towering above an herbaceous ground cover that was nearly devoid of shrubs and other small trees. In fewer than 300 years, the extent of these old-growth forests has been reduced to fewer than 20,000 acres, eliminated primarily by intense forestry, the naval stores industry, fire suppression, development, and a burgeoning human population. In the early 1900s botanist and naturalist Roland Harper was already lamenting the loss of these forests to the ax, reflecting the destruction wrought by "cut and run" lumbermen who preferred quick profits over sustainable forestry. What remains of old-growth timber in our region today are primarily small-acreage tracts on an ever-shrinking system of public and private lands. About 2,500 acres of old growth occur in Georgia, 5,000–10,000 in Florida (much of which is west of our region), fewer than 500 acres in North Carolina, and none in South Carolina and Virginia. By today's standards, rejuvenated forests with eighty-year-old trees are considered old. Only future generations will be able to appreciate these new forests in their maturity.

The pinelands of our region can be categorized into several types, based primarily on a combination of soil moisture, ground cover, and shrub layer, in conjunction with their dominant pine species. Dry, sandy, well-drained uplands that are dominated by an over-story of Longleaf Pine *(Pinus palustris)*, a midstory of Turkey *(Quercus laevis)* and Bluejack *(Q. incana)* oaks, and a ground cover of grasses and forbs, including conspicuous popula-tions of Wiregrass *(Aristida stricta)* and/or Pineywoods Dropseed *(Sporobolus junceus)*, are referred to as xeric **sandhill** communities. These communities cap the region's higher hills and are noted for containing coarse sands that encourage rapid surface water percolation. In some parts of the region, subsurface clay and hardpan deposits retard the flow of under-ground water, redirecting it laterally so that it emerges near the bottom of the slope, form-ing boggy seepages and wet-weather streams. Wildflowers common to the sandhill community include Sandhills Wild Petunia *(Ruellia ciliosa)*, Fringed Bluestar *(Amsonia cili-ata)*, Pinewoods Milkweed *(Asclepias humistrata)*, Clasping Milkweed *(Asclepias amplexi-caulis)*, Rose-Rush *(Lygodesmia aphylla)*, Sandhills Milkvetch *(Astragalus michauxii)*, Butterflyweed *(Asclepias tuberosa)*, Hairy Angelica *(Angelica venenosa)*, Pineland Silkgrass *(Pityopsis aspera)*, and several species of Gayfeather or Blazing Star (*Liatris* spp.).

The extensive Fall Line Hills region of North Carolina, South Carolina, and northeast-ern Georgia offers excellent examples of xeric pinelands. This region takes its name from the Fall Line, an abrupt change in elevation that separates the Piedmont from the coastal plain. The Fall Line Hills probably deserve recognition as an independent topographic province, distinct from either the Piedmont or the coastal plain. However, the extensive Longleaf Pine forests and wetland depressions and drainages that characterize its land-scape are distinctly coastal plain in character. Wildflowers found in the Fall Line Hills region, some of which are unique to it, include Sandhill Thistle *(Cirsium repandum)*, Puc-coon *(Lithospermum caroliniense)*, Grassleaf Roseling *(Callisia graminea)*, Sandhills Blazing Star *(Liatris cokeri)*, Sandhill Chaffhead *(Carphephorus bellidifolius)*, Dawnflower *(Stylisma*

patens), Dwarf Bristly Locust *(Robinia nana),* Sandhill Goldenaster *(Pityopsis pinifolia),* and many others.

Mesic (moist), less well-drained communities consisting of fine sandy soils and dominated by Longleaf and/or Slash Pine *(P. elliottii)* with a shrub layer of Saw Palmetto *(Serenoa repens),* Gallberry *(Ilex glabra),* and/or Fetterbush *(Lyonia* spp.) are called **flatwoods** or **pine-palmetto flatwoods.** The shrub layer of wetter flatwoods also often includes other shrubby members of the heath family (Ericaceae), including blueberries *(Vaccinium* spp.) and staggerbushes *(Leucothoe* spp.), intermixed with numerous herbs. On wetter sites, especially along the edges of swamps and drainages, such communities may include, and are sometimes dominated exclusively by, Pond Pine *(P. serotina)* in conjunction with a larger number of predominantly wetland trees and shrubs. Littleleaf Titi *(Cyrilla racemiflora),* Black Titi *(Cliftonia monophylla),* and Sweetbay *(Magnolia virginiana)* are examples. Common names for Pond Pine-dominated flatwoods include **wet flatwoods, Pond Pine flatwoods,** or **pine pocosin.** The acid soils of flatwoods support a large and varied assortment of showy wildflowers, including white and pink sabatias *(Sabatia* spp.), Yellow Star Grass *(Hypoxis* spp.), and numerous species of blazing stars *(Liatris* spp.), goldenrods *(Solidago* spp.), meadow beauties *(Rhexia* spp.), and milkworts *(Polygala* spp.).

Palustrine Wetlands

Pinelands often encompass and grade into a number of less extensive vegetative assemblages, including bogs, savannas, shrub bays, baygalls, pocosins, and cypress swamps. Though such assemblages are distinct systems with their own unique ecological parameters and processes, they can also be viewed as integral parts of the greater pineland mosaic.

Baygalls are peat-filled seepage wetlands that are also referred to as bay swamps, bayheads, or simply swamps. These areas occur in wetter depressions within pinelands, often at the base of a seepage slope, and contain standing water and saturated soils much of the year. The primary flora of baygalls consists of woody shrubs and a variety of wetland trees, including the Sweetbay *(Magnolia virginiana),* Loblolly Bay *(Gordonia lasianthus),* and Swamp Red Bay *(Persea palustris),* from which these wetlands take their generic name. Baygalls typically have few herbaceous wildflowers but numerous flowering shrubs, many of which are in the heath or blueberry family (Ericaceae). Baygalls occur mostly in northern Florida and southern Georgia.

Pine flatwoods occur widely from Florida northward to South Carolina and are typically dominated by an overstory by Slash Pine above a shrub layer of Saw Palmetto.

Carolina bays and pocosins are also shrubby wetlands found mostly in the Carolinas and northeastern Georgia. Both are characterized as much by their geology and morphology as by their constituent and often variable plant communities. **Carolina bays** are essentially elliptical or teardrop-shaped depressions that are variously filled with evergreen shrubs, bay trees, open marshes, small lakes surrounded by a dense shrubby border, or swamp. They are consistent in form, shape, and geographic orientation. Though they vary dramatically in size—some may be less than 200 feet long while others may span up to 5 miles—all are oriented along a northwest to southeast axis and, when seen from the air, display a similar outline and remarkably parallel arrangement in the landscape. Several theories have been advanced to explain the origin of Carolina bays, including ancient meteor showers, the presence of upwelling springs in the ancient landscape, the action of wind and waves, the formation of pools by spawning fish, and the creation of coastal sandbars during the retreating Pleistocene seas. To date, however, no universally favored theory has emerged and considerable disagreement still exists about the conception of these once-abundant landforms.

Carolina bays often overlap with or contain pocosins. **Pocosins** are broad-leaved evergreen shrub-filled depressions, mostly of the outer Atlantic Coastal Plain, and are similar in many respects to Florida's baygalls. Like baygalls they typically occur on poorly drained, inundated organic soils and are composed of a variety of evergreen shrubs, often with an overstory of Pond Pine *(Pinus serotina)*, Loblolly Bay *(Gordonia lasianthus)*, and Sweetbay Magnolia *(Magnolia virginiana)*. Characteristic pocosin shrubs featured in this book include Titi *(Cyrilla racemiflora)* and Honey-Cups *(Zenobia pulverulenta)*. Pocosin wetlands are often divided into high pocosins and low pocosins, modifiers that describe the height of the vegetation rather than the elevation and relief of the land. Use of the word pocosin, or one of its numerous derivatives or predecessors, extends back to at least the mid 1600s and probably came from the Algonquian word for a wooded valley. Early settlers sometimes referred to such places as "dismals," a name that survives today as part of the name for Virginia's and North Carolina's Great Dismal Swamp.

For wildflower enthusiasts, the margins of Carolina bays and pocosins present excellent territory for exploration. Many are surrounded by broad, wet ecotones that contain numerous herbaceous species. White-Topped Sedge *(Rhynchospora latifolia)*, Colic Root *(Aletris* spp.), Yellow-Eyed Grass *(Xyris* spp.), Savannah Iris *(Iris tridentata)*, Pipewort *(Eriocaulon* spp.),

Bayside beaches of coastal barrier islands and inland saltwater bays are not subject to the high-energy waves of the Atlantic Ocean.

Sweet Pepperbush *(Clethra alnifolia)*, and Virginia Willow *(Itea virginica)* are examples.

Also floristically interesting are the region's **pitcher plant bogs,** variously called **herb bogs, flats, savannas,** and **wet prairies.** Pitcher plant bogs are characterized as wet, treeless plains that lack overstory, understory, and shrub layers, but support a moderate to dense covering of grasses and other wetland herbs. Such prairies may be only inches lower in elevation than adjacent pinelands, and only inches higher than adjoining drainages, and are usually wet or boggy much of the year. These open, sunny habitats are filled from spring to fall with numerous showy wildflowers, as well as tiny hidden treasures that must be searched for under the dense ground cover.

The South Atlantic Coastal Plain harbors an assortment of carnivorous or insectivorous species, many of which occur in bogs, savannas, and wet pinelands, and along the margins of pocosins and Carolina Bays. Some of the better locations to search for these fascinating plants include the Apalachee Scenic Byway in the Apalachicola National Forest (Florida), Jennings State Forest (Florida), Francis Marion National Forest (South Carolina), Croatan National Forest and Holly Shelter Game Lands (North Carolina), and Great Dismal Swamp National Wildlife Refuge (Virginia).

All of our native pine communities and their associated bogs, savannas, Carolina bays, and pocosins are **fire-influenced ecosystems** that rely heavily on periodic fire to maintain their health and character. In prehistoric times lightning-set fires burned frequently, perhaps even as often as once per year, and typically swept across thousands of acres. These fires reduced the encroachment of woody species, released soil nutrients, and favored the establishment and maintenance of pine-dominated uplands and savannas. As a result of its fire-dependent nature, the pine-dominated ecosystem is often called a fire-subclimax community, meaning that its character and composition depend on regular conflagration. Modern land managers now better understand this process and attempt to replicate it. Almost all of the Atlantic Coastal Plain's national and state forests use prescribed fire to simulate natural fire regimes. Some of these intentionally set fires (also called controlled burns) are started in winter and result in a very showy spring flora in the burned area. Growing season, or summer, burns are often followed within days or weeks of cooling by numerous flowering herbs, many of which are typically spring-flowering species seemingly blooming out of season. Wildflower enthusiasts who keep an eye out

Beaches along the Atlantic shore are composed of wind-blown and wave-washed sands and are harsh communities populated by only the hardiest of salt-tolerant plants.

for freshly burned pinelands, then visit them regularly during the year following the burn are likely to be rewarded with a wildflower wonderland.

Temperate Broad-Leaved Forests

Temperate broad-leaved forests, also called **southern mixed hardwood forests,** are among the southeastern United States' more structurally complex natural communities. Unlike southern pinelands, which are essentially two-tiered communities with overstories that are dominated by only one or two species, broad-leaved forests are multilayered, closed-canopied ecosystems with diverse overstories, dense understories, sparse ground covers, and sometimes rich shrub layers. Characterized mostly by a mixed assortment of deciduous and evergreen hardwoods, they are closely related to the deciduous forests of the Piedmont and southern Appalachians, but extend well southward in the Southeastern Coastal Plains. At their northern limit they are primarily deciduous woodlands. Farther south and east, their overstories are increasingly dominated by evergreen trees. This changing character with concurrently decreasing latitude and increasing longitude, coupled with their unique position along the southeastern edge of the North American continent has led at least some ecologists to regard them as a transitional link between eastern North America's cool temperate and warm tropical biomes. Given their temperate character and northern aspect, southern mixed hardwood forests are the most likely locations to find the northern elements in our flora.

Temperate hardwood forests often occur along ravine slopes, where they grade into sandhill pinelands at their upper edge, and floodplain woodlands at the bottom of the slope. **Floodplain woodands** occur along large rivers and their tributaries. A variety of hardwood trees and shrubs grow in floodplain or bottomland forests, including Red Maple *(Acer rubrum)*, Sweetgum *(Liquidambar styraciflua)*, American Hornbeam *(Carpinus caroliniana)*, Water Oak *(Quercus nigra)*, and Wax Myrtle *(Myrica cerifera)*. A few showy wildflowers also occur here.

Good examples of temperate hardwood forests are scattered across our region. Santee State Park in Orangeburg County, South Carolina, preserves a good example of an American Beech *(Fagus grandifolia)* forest, and the floodplains of our larger rivers often include excellent hardwood and floodplain forests. Locations along the Apalachicola River in Florida, the Chattahoochee River in Georgia, the Savanna River in Georgia, and the Congaree River in South Carolina are good examples. Congaree Swamp National Park encompasses several thousand acres of old-growth, floodplain and bottomland timber traversed

Coastal hammocks like this one on Jekyll Island, Georgia, are often dominated by an overstory of Live Oak (Quercus Virginiana) *and were considered by ecologist B. W. Wells as a "salt-spray climax" community.*

by a network of boardwalks and is an excellent place to see what may have once been a more common occurrence in our region.

Coastal Strand Communities

The extensive coastline that serves as the South Atlantic Coastal Plain's eastern boundary consists of several distinctive plant associations, many of which support unique and interesting collections of wildflowers. The more obvious of these habitats include **beaches and dunes, saltwater and freshwater marshes,** and **maritime hammocks.** As might be expected, the coastal zone can be a harsh environment. Salt spray, intense sun, and saline conditions impose significant challenges for plants. Hence, the plants that occur here are often adapted to specific stresses that help them compete and survive under difficult circumstances.

The beach-dune system occurs on high-energy shorelines that directly border the Atlantic Ocean. These are xeric, well-drained habitats characterized by wave-deposited beaches that often slope abruptly up to wind-deposited foredunes. Some of these beaches

Some of the more extensive and beautiful examples of floodplain woodlands can be seen along the boardwalks and trails at Congaree National Park, South Carolina, which preserves the largest intact tract of old-growth floodplain forest in North America.

occur on offshore barrier islands, like Cumberland, Jekyll, and St. Simons Islands along the Georgia coast; Little Talbot Island in northeast Florida; and North Carolina's Outer Banks. On active and mostly undisturbed beaches, foredunes may be backed by low, coastal meadows, dune fields, or maritime hammocks dominated by wind-pruned Live Oaks *(Quercus virginiana)*. Due to the harsh coastal environment, dunes and beaches are sparsely vegetated communities, consisting mostly of a handful of species that include Sea Oats *(Uniola paniculata)*, Bitter Panicum *(Panicum amarum)*, Railroad Vine *(Ipomoea pes-caprae)*, Beach Morning Glory *(Ipomoea imperati)*, and several species of grasses. Several of these plants, especially Sea Oats and the other grasses are ecologically advantageous to dune establishment and stabilization.

Low-energy shorelines along the inland margins of protected saltwater bays often support a densely vegetated **salt marsh** or **tidal marsh** composed of a limited number of plant species, especially Needle Rush *(Juncus roemerianus)* and at least two species of *Spartina*. Between the low energy inland coastlines of barrier islands and the mainland, like those of Florida and Georgia, Needle Rush marshes sometimes cover vast expanses along a gradual, almost imperceptible, gradient from the edge of coastal uplands to the edge of the sea. Though the inner marsh is mostly a monoculture of Black Needle Rush, its bayside border is usually lined with Salt-Marsh Cordgrass *(Spartina alterniflora)* or Marsh-hay Cordgrass *(Spartina paten)*.

Few wildflowers, except the perennial Salt-Marsh Aster *(Symphyotrichum tenuifolium)*, occur within the depths of a salt marsh, but numerous species occur along its inland edges, especially where it grades into coastal hammocks, pinelands, or freshwater marshes. Some of the more showy species include Seashore Marsh-Mallow *(Kosteletzkya virginica)* and Sweetscent Seaside Oxeye *(Borrichia frutescens)*.

Maritime hammocks, also called **coastal hammocks,** are essentially Live-Oak *(Quercus virginiana)*-dominated woodlands characterized by dry to moist, well-drained sandy soils and a sparse shrub layer. Ecologist B. W. Wells, whose 1932 *The Natural Gardens of North Carolina* continues to be a standard reference for Carolina ecology, recognized at least some of these hammocks as "salt spray climax" communities, in deference to the continual onslaught of salty winds that favor the development of Live Oak over other mainland species. Understory trees and shrubs of maritime hammocks include Red Bay *(Persea borbonia)*, American Holly *(Ilex opaca)*, Wild Olive *(Osmanthus americanus)*, Yaupon *(Ilex vomitoria)*, Red Cedar *(Juniperus virginiana)*, and Wax Myrtle *(Myrica cerifera)*. This community is subject to the same harsh conditions as most coastal habitats. It contains few species of herbaceous wildflowers, but constitutes one of the coastal zone's more picturesque landscapes and is an extremely important resting and foraging habitat for neotropical birds before and after their long migrations across the Gulf of Mexico and along the western Atlantic Ocean.

Non-Natural Assemblages

In addition to the foregoing natural systems, the South Atlantic Coastal Plain also encompasses several ruderal, or disturbed habitats, at least a few of which provide enticing haunts for wildflower enthusiasts. Two of the most important include road shoulders and roadside ditches, especially along highways that traverse what is otherwise natural terrain. Regular roadside mowing somewhat simulates natural disturbance, often favoring the establishment of both native and weedy species. Throughout the spring, summer, and fall, this mixing of native and non-native species makes ditches and road shoulders productive places to search for wildflowers.

Extensive saltwater marshes along the coastal zone of Georgia, the Carolinas, and northeastern Florida are dominated by black needle rush and several species of cordgrass.

Some of our woodlands might appear natural, but are actually artifacts of human disturbance. Where the natural covering of pines and hardwoods has been removed, Loblolly Pine *(Pinus taeda)* often dominates, intermixed with hickories *(Carya* spp.) and other upland hardwoods. Loblolly Pine is also sometimes called "Old Field Pine" due to its tendency to rapidly colonize untended fields, clearings, and untended clear-cuts. Stands of Loblolly Pine are often indicative of major environmental disturbance and are not considered to represent natural assemblages. Nevertheless, wildflowers that are typical of natural communities can also be found in these disturbed pinelands. Loblolly Pine has become an important component in the timber and paper industry, and is often the major tree in pine plantations.

How to Use This Guide

Included in this guide are photographs and descriptions of more than 300 wildflowers that occur within the South Atlantic Coastal Plain. In many ways the present volume is a

The borders (or ecotones) of Carolina bays, like this one at the edge of Wambaw Bay in Francis Marion National Forest, South Carolina, are typically rich in wildflowers.

companion to *East Gulf Coastal Plain Wildflowers,* also published by Falcon. With some exceptions the East Gulf Coastal Plain and South Atlantic Coastal Plain are homogeneous landscapes with many species in common, meaning that the two volumes referenced here are useful far beyond their stated geographic extents. Moreover, fewer than one hundred species are duplicated between the two books and many of the unduplicated species range widely across both regions. When used together, these books become useful guides to more than 500 coastal plain wildflowers from Virginia to Louisiana.

Species accounts are arranged by color, and organized within each color section alphabetically by botanical family, genus, and species. Though the use of Latinized scientific names as an organizing tool may seem daunting at first, such names provide a level of standardization that cannot currently be achieved through the use of common, or vernacular, names. Most species have only one generally accepted scientific name, whereas the same species may have numerous common names that vary from region to region. Moreover, a single common name may sometimes be used for several, often-unrelated species.

Nearly 8,000 species of vascular plants occur within the Southeastern Coastal Plains, including the numerous species of ferns, conifers, grasses, sedges, and rushes that are typically not encompassed within the commonly understood definition of "wildflower." Given such a large and diverse flora, I have chosen to limit this guide mostly to a combination of herbaceous wildflowers and woody shrubs, and to those species that best represent the families and genera that are common in or endemic to the region. Few predominantly aquatic plants are featured and about 75 percent of the plants are widespread. The other 25 percent either enjoy restricted ranges, sometimes being narrowly endemic to a particular locale within the region, or represent species that may be more common in adjoining floristic provinces, but the ranges of which extend into the South Atlantic Coastal Plain from the north, west, or south. Though some of the species may be featured in other plant guides, I have made efforts to feature species for which few good photographs have been published.

Grouping plants by flower color has advantages and disadvantages. Though flower color often provides a convenient and efficient method for narrowing one's choices when attempting to identify plants in the field, the flowers of many plants are extremely variable. Flower color for a single species may range across many shades, depending upon

The National Audubon Society's 11,000 acre Francis Beidler Preserve, which lies in the heart of Four Holes Swamp, South Carolina, encompasses the world's largest remaining virgin Cypress-Tupelo swamp forest.

sunlight, time of day, soil nutrients, the age of the flower, and the health of the plant. It is not atypical to find a white-flowered individual of a typically blue- or pink-flowered species. Plants with bicolored flowers are also common. Hence, it is important not to limit your search to a single color section when attempting to identify a plant in the field. Look for blue-flowered plants in the pink section and vice versa, and always check the white section.

Plant Names

Each account begins with one or more common names, followed by the currently preferred scientific name. Botanical nomenclature is governed by an international code that attempts to assure that every plant is uniquely named and that the names of plants are appropriately devised, applied, and published. The earliest name validly applied to a species takes precedence over later names. Nevertheless, in some cases the appropriate scientific name for a species is in dispute or may have only recently been changed. For example, virtually all of the species in the South Atlantic Coastal Plain that were previously included within the genus *Aster* have recently been reclassified and are now included within several genera, mostly notably the genera *Eurybia* and *Symphyotrichum.* In such cases I have included a notation of the species' most recent synonym (the scientific name by which the plant was previously known). These are shown in parentheses and preceded by the designation "Syn." This will help you cross-reference the plants featured in this book to those featured in older guides or references.

Family names are also included. The common name of the family is given, followed by the Latinized name in parentheses. According to the rules of nomenclature, Latinized family names are constructed by concatenating the suffix *aceae* to the name of the family's largest, most important, or type genus (the first genus in the family to be scientifically recognized and described). For example, the botanical name of the Aster Family is Asteraceae. However, a few older botanical family names have been in use for so long that they predate the rules of nomenclature and have been conserved. Hence, the name Compositae is also sometimes used for the Aster Family, the name Leguminosae for the Bean Family (Fabaceae), and the name Labiatae for the Mint Family (Lamiaceae). Such names are not incorrect, but are not as often used by modern botanists as the newer names. Several of the families represented in this guide have conserved family names. These are included within the parentheses following the more commonly used family name. For example, the botanical family names for the Aster Family are given as (Asteraceae or Compositae).

Complete scientific names are composed of a Latinized binomial, which includes a genus name followed by a specific epithet, followed by one or more additional indicators. The genus name is analogous to an English sir name, and the specific epithet to the given name. Following the epithet is an indication of the author or authors who named the plant, and when appropriate, the name of the author who most recently changed or updated the name. Some species are further divided into varieties or subspecies. These are taxonomic subdivisions that recognize stable differentiations below the species level. Varietal and subspecific names are also followed by the names of their authors. Only a few varietal or subspecific designations are included in this book.

Generic names and specific epithets often provide informative clues that serve as important reminders of particular morphological characters that distinguish a given species. Such names as *angustifolius,* which means "with long, narrow leaves," and *hirsutus,* which means "hairy with coarse, stiff hairs," are examples. Where possible, and for species where salient morphological characters aid in identification, I have provided the essential meaning of such descriptive nomenclature within the text. More complete definitions of some of this terminology can be found in the glossary.

Generic names and specific epithets also often commemorate the contributions of well-known or particularly influential botanists, naturalists, scientists, or personages of the day. A few of these individuals figure so prominently in the botanical history of the southern United States that their names appear often as authors, or as Latinized components of scientific names. The more important of these, and those whose names you will see regularly in the pages that follow, include Stephen Elliott, Alvan W. Chapman, John K. Small, Roland M. Harper, John and William Bartram, Andre and Francois Michaux, Bertram Whittier Well, Robert K. Godfrey, Wilbur Duncan, and Albert E. Radford.

Stephen Elliott (1771–1830) is one of the best-known and most commemorated names in South Carolina botany. He was the author of *Sketch of the Botany of South Carolina and Georgia,* a two-volume work completed between 1821 and 1824. He helped establish the Medical College of South Carolina and in 1824 became its first professor of botany and natural history. Like many early botanists, Elliott's interests extended beyond his scientific discipline. He was the co-founder of the *Southern Review,* and served in the South Carolina State Senate from 1812 until his death in 1830. His name appears in the epithets of numerous southern plants and is further commemorated in the genus name *Elliotia,* which contains the endangered species Georgia Plume.

Alvan W. Chapman was a physician who lived at separate times in both Quincy and Apalachicola, Florida, and whose botanical career spanned much of the nineteenth century. The three editions of his *Flora of the Southern United States* (the last one published in 1897) constituted the first complete and respectable botanical manual for our region. The third edition, in particular, is still regularly referenced in scientific literature. Several dozen plant species are named for or by Chapman.

John K. Small's voluminous works include three complete floras of the southeastern United States, the third of which *(Manual of the Southeastern Flora,* 1933) was long considered the standard botanical reference for the Southeast, including the subtropical tip of the Florida peninsula. Small was a tireless field botanist and keen observer who described numerous new species and for whom many species are named. His works include many smaller floras and numerous papers about his travels and discoveries.

Roland M. Harper was a botanist at the University of Alabama who traveled extensively in the Southeastern Coastal Plains, including many trips along the eastern seaboard from Virginia south through the Carolinas and Georgia and into Florida. He produced many botanical papers and publications, including several that recount his travels to the Fall Line Hills and through the Carolinas and Georgia. He was a friend to and regular correspondent with John K. Small. Harper was a meticulous naturalist and ecologist with many important insights into the phytogeographical, botanical, and ecological relationships of our region.

John and son, William, Bartram were eighteenth-century botanical explorers across much of the Southeast. They were avid plant collectors who found and described numerous new plant species. John was the king's botanist in America and William is best known for the 1773 volume recounting his travels, published today under the name *Travels of William Bartram.*

Andre Michaux and his son, François, were French botanists who visited North America in the late 1700s and catalogued and described many new species. Their names appear in many plant names, or as authors. The life of Andre Michaux and several of the other explorers mentioned here are chronicled in Gail Fishman's *Journeys Through Paradise: Pioneering Naturalists in the Southeast,* 2000.

Bertram Whittier Wells was the head of North Carolina State College's botany department from 1919 to 1949, but remained on the faculty until 1954. Wells authored numerous

A typical brackish stream threads through the tidal marsh at Harris Neck National Wildlife Refuge, one of seven national wildlife refuges managed as part of the Savannah Coastal Refuges Complex.

scientific papers, most of which betrayed an abiding interest in ecology and in understanding the functioning of healthy ecosystems. He was especially interested in the habitats of the coastal zone and the formation of Carolina bays, and was one of the earliest eastern scientists to earn the moniker, ecologist. His classic work *The Natural Gardens of North Carolina* has been reprinted and is a testimony to his penchant for understanding and preserving North Carolina's natural lands.

Robert K. Godfrey, late professor of botany at Florida State University (FSU) and for whom the university's Robert K. Godfrey Herbarium is named, was one of the twentieth century's most influential southern botanists. His two-volume work *Aquatic and Wetland Plants of Southeastern United States* (1979, 1981), co-authored with Jean W. Wooten, continues to be regarded as the leading reference for our wetland flora, and his *Trees, Shrubs, and Woody Vines of Florida and Adjacent Georgia and Alabama* (1988) is unsurpassed in detail and coverage. Godfrey published numerous papers and described several species. His name is commemorated in the specific epithets of a number of southern plants.

Loran Anderson, who followed Godfrey at FSU has been an avid collector, mostly in Florida. He is professor emeritus in botany at FSU and is the former director of the Godfrey Herbarium. He is responsible for describing several new species within our region of coverage, and within the last decade has discovered populations of numerous species in northeast Florida whose southern range limits were previously thought to lie in southern Georgia.

Wilbur Duncan was professor of botany at the University of Georgia for forty years. His first photographic wildflower guide, *Wildflowers of the Southeastern United States*, co-authored with Leonard Foote in 1975, was for many years the only readily available reference for southern wildflower enthusiasts. This early work was updated in 1999 with the publication of his more expansive *Wildflowers of the Eastern United States*, co-authored with Marion Duncan. Two other of his notable works, also co-authored with Marion Duncan, are *Seaside Plants of the Gulf and Atlantic Coasts* and *Trees of the Southeastern United States*.

Other recent botanists include Albert Radford, retired plant taxonomist and emeritus director of the herbarium at the University of North Carolina. Radford is the leading co-author, with Harry Ahles and C. Ritchie Bell, of the 1968 *Manual of the Vascular Flora of the Carolinas*. This was one of the first modern floras for our region and has been used widely by botanists and plant taxonomists well beyond the geographical boundaries of North and South Carolina. It still serves as a standard reference for the Carolina flora but is now being updated and expanded by Alan Weakley, administrative curator and curator of vascular plants at the University of North Carolina herbarium. Weakley has made successive drafts of his work available for download online at http://www.herbarium.unc.edu/flora.htm.

Descriptions

The descriptions included in each account detail the prominent morphological features that help distinguish one species from another. The form, shape, and size of leaves, flowers, and stems are universally included, with descriptive statements regarding fruit and roots added when such features have special significance to the plant or might prove an aid to identification. Insofar as possible, I have tried to use nontechnical language, except in instances where a technical term fits too well to ignore. Sometimes I have enclosed technical terms in parentheses adjacent to nontechnical terms. In other instances I have chosen to insert short, parenthetical definitions adjacent to what might be an unfamiliar word. A glossary has also been included that includes all of the technical terms that appear in the text. Accompanying figures also show what is meant when such terms as "elliptical in outline" or "lance-shaped" are used to describe a leaf. Also included in the figures are drawings of a typical complete or perfect flower (a bisexual flower that contains both male and female reproductive structures). Drawings are also included for the specialized flowers common to the aster family (Asteraceae), milkweeds (of the genus *Asclepias*), and members of the orchid family (Orchidaceae). Study these drawings carefully when attempting to decipher descriptions of plants in these groups.

It should be noted that the descriptive language of botany is exceedingly rich and extremely helpful to the process of plant identification. Though mastering this language might seem overwhelming at first, learning its rudiments and at least some of its intricacies is a richly rewarding experience that will add immeasurably to your study of plants.

Measurements are described in feet, inches, and fractions of inches. In most instances a range of values is given. Hence, leaves may be described as being 1–4" long, even if their predominant length is 2". These maximum and minimum figures are intended to encompass the variation that is inherent in most plant parts. Sometimes only a single measurement is given, as in "½" flowers." Single measurements are used mostly when variation is slight, or when most specimens are likely to reflect or closely approximate the stated value. All measurements used in the book were arrived at from taking numerous measurements of pressed and mounted plant specimens housed at the Robert K. Godfrey Herbarium at Florida State University in Tallahassee, Florida. It should be noted that the actual measurements of some live plants might vary from the measurements given here. Shade leaves, the parts of injured or disturbed plants, and the parts of poorly situated plants sometimes take on proportions atypical of a species. Suffice it to say that variation should be expected.

Some accounts include descriptions of the hairs or glands that often appear on plant parts. Such structures are often very small and extremely difficult or impossible to see clearly without magnification. It is recommended that readers purchase and carry with them a 10X or 14X loupe. High quality loupes are available for under $50.00 and may be purchased at biological supply companies, hobby shops, and even bookstores. Being able to magnify plant parts will add immeasurably to your enjoyment of learning and studying wildflowers.

Bloom Season

The blooming season for each species is given in whole months and has been determined by examining the reproductive condition of numerous herbarium specimens, also at Godfrey Herbarium, as well as from literature reports and personal field notes. These ranges are designed to encompass the typical flowering period of the species for the entire region. The fact that plants at the more northern parts of the region might flower later than those at the southern end of the region should be taken into account. Further, it is not unlikely to encounter plants flowering outside of these stated extremes. Such extralimital records are often associated with natural or artificial disturbance. Wild or prescribed fire, roadside mowing, unusual weather patterns, and human-engineered alteration to a landscape can trigger flowering at what might otherwise seem to be an odd time of year.

Habitat/Range

The habitat and range section provides information about the ecosystems, vegetative assemblages, and general geographic regions in which a species is likely to be found. A species' geographical distribution or preferred growing conditions often provide important clues to its identification. Species that are morphologically similar may differ markedly in habitat preference. Others are highly restricted to certain soil, moisture, or sunlight regimes, or are found almost exclusively in association with a particular vegetative assemblage or plant community.

Range is given by state, south to north, as Florida, Georgia, South Carolina, North Carolina, and Virginia. Plants with ranges that are described as "throughout the region" have been documented in all states within the South Atlantic Coastal Plain. It should be understood that the designation "throughout the region" is not intended to imply that a particular species is to be found in all plant communities. Plants so listed may also be rare, uncommon, or highly restricted to a single community type. Moreover, the distribution statements presented here come from a variety of sources, including personal field experience and expert opinion, as well published floras, lists, reports, and scientific papers. Due both to unpublished records and recent discoveries of species previously unknown to a state, the reader should not view statements of range as immutable.

Additional remarks in this section as well as in the comments section that follows sometimes offer extended information about the species' rarity, range, or protected status (see explanation below under Comments). Unless otherwise noted in the account, all species are considered to be native, or indigenous, to the region.

Comments

The comments section offers additional information about featured species, often including the derivation of their scientific and common names, notes on toxicity, or known or reported folk and medicinal uses. More importantly, since the book is designed primarily as a field guide, special emphasis is given to detailing critical clues to identification. This is especially true for plants that represent large genera, or that might be easily confused with "look-alike" species in other genera or families. Since the expansiveness of our flora makes it impossible to include a complete account for all species within the region, this section helps readers learn how to differentiate the featured species from others featured in the book as well as from those that could not be included.

This section also sometimes includes general statements about a particular species' rarity or abundance, or its inclusion on NatureServe's list of imperiled species. For such statements, a caveat is in order. Words and phrases like "endangered," "rare," "uncommon," "threatened," and "of special interest" are used informally and are not meant to convey official designations or to suggest inclusion on federal or state lists of endangered species. The terms "critically imperiled," "imperiled," and "vulnerable," on the other hand, have consistent meanings from account to account and are based on precise definitions. Species designated critically imperiled include those with five or fewer occurrences or fewer than 1,000 individuals within a state, or those that are extremely vulnerable to extinction due to some natural or man-made factor. Imperiled species are those with six to twenty occurrences or fewer than 3,000 individuals within a state, or that are vulnerable to extinction due to some natural or man-made factor. Vulnerable species are defined as those that are very rare and local throughout their range (twenty-one to one hundred occurrences or fewer than 10,000 individuals), or that are found only locally or within a restricted range.

A Note about Conservation

Wildflower enthusiasts should practice sound conservation ethics and should be activists for the protection of our native wildflowers. During wildflower forays, be mindful of the delicacy of the habitats you visit and be sure to practice low-impact recreation. Don't dig or collect plants from the wild, and try not to disturb the landscape in which they occur. When on public lands, commend land managers and conservation personnel for good management and conservation practices and let them know how much the public appreciates their efforts. If you find imperiled or unusual species on public lands, let the park manager know of your discovery, or report it to the state's or heritage program's botanist to insure that new populations of imperiled species are adequately managed and protected. If you are not sure of an identity, seek help from the herbarium curator at one of the region's state universities, or contact the leaders of your state's native plant organization or botanical society.

Wildflowers constitute an essential part of our natural heritage. Protecting the habitats in which they grow is an important conservation activity and one that will insure both the perpetuity of our wildflowers and the enjoyment of those who stalk them.

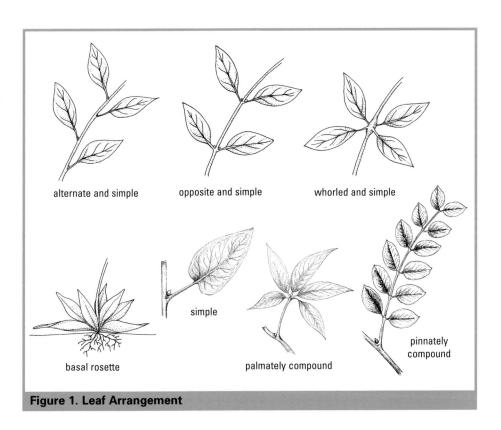

Figure 1. Leaf Arrangement

alternate and simple

opposite and simple

whorled and simple

basal rosette

simple

palmately compound

pinnately compound

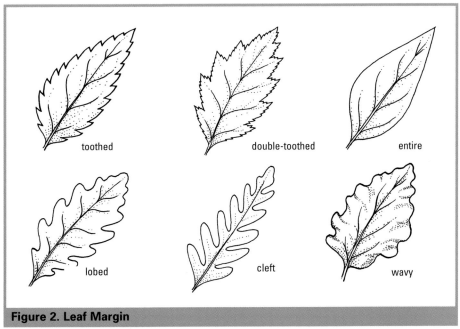

Figure 2. Leaf Margin

toothed

double-toothed

entire

lobed

cleft

wavy

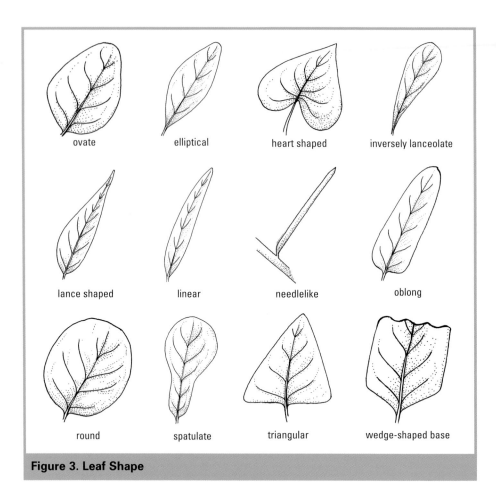

Figure 3. Leaf Shape

ovate

elliptical

heart shaped

inversely lanceolate

lance shaped

linear

needlelike

oblong

round

spatulate

triangular

wedge-shaped base

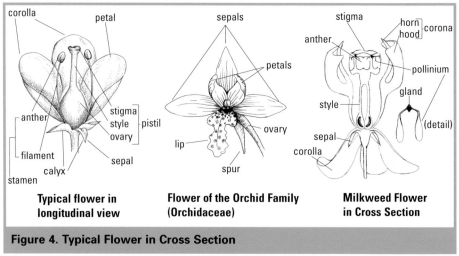

corolla

petal

sepals

stigma

horn ⌉
hood ⌋ corona

anther

petals

pollinium

gland

style

anther

stigma
style ⌉ pistil
ovary

ovary

(detail)

filament

lip

sepal

calyx

spur

sepal
corolla

stamen

Typical flower in longitudinal view

Flower of the Orchid Family (Orchidaceae)

Milkweed Flower in Cross Section

Figure 4. Typical Flower in Cross Section

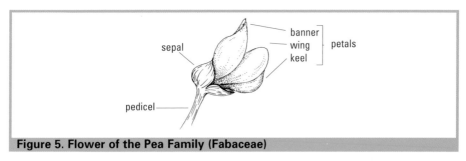

Figure 5. Flower of the Pea Family (Fabaceae)

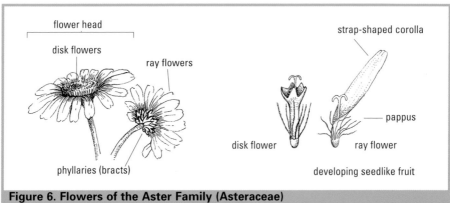

Figure 6. Flowers of the Aster Family (Asteraceae)

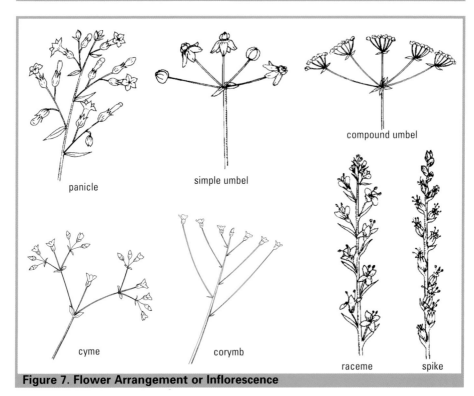

Figure 7. Flower Arrangement or Inflorescence

BLUE AND PURPLE FLOWERS

This section includes flowers that vary in color from pale blue to deep indigo and violet. Since these colors grade into pink and lavender and since some plants produce flowers that vary across all of these colors, you should check the pink section if you don't find the flower you are looking for here.

SANDHILLS WILD PETUNIA OR CILIATE WILD PETUNIA
Ruellia ciliosa Pursh
Acanthus Family (Acanthaceae)

Description: Several blue-flowered wild petunias occur in our region, only 2 of which are fairly common and widespread. Sandhills Wild Petunia is a dwarf, hairy, low-growing plant of sandy pinelands. Its leaves are 1–3" long, more often widest near the tip than at the base, and are arranged in a flattened, basal rosette. The flowers are funnel-shaped, pale blue, and about 1–2½" long.

Bloom Season: May–September.

Habitat/Range: Sandhills. Florida, Georgia, South Carolina, and North Carolina.

Comments: The similarly flowered and much more common Wild Petunia *(R. caroliniensis)* is a taller, erect plant with a leafy stem and no basal rosette. Some experts consider *R. ciliosa* to be a subspecies of *R. caroliniensis*. Sandhills Wild Petunia is more common in the southern parts of our region and is considered critically imperiled in North Carolina. Like many sandhill species, Sandhills Wild Petunia responds rapidly to fire and may be one of the more common plants in the ground cover following a controlled burn. It produces new leaves within a few weeks following a blaze and often flowers profusely in temporary, fire-generated clearings with only freshly charred ground as a backdrop. The more northern Limestone Wild Petunia *(R. strepens)* occurs rarely in calcareous forests in Virginia and the Carolinas and is distinguished by its wider, linear, blunt-tipped sepals that may be a little more than ⅛" broad.

PINELAND WILD PETUNIA

Ruellia pinetorum Fernald
(Syn: *R. pedunculata* Torrey ex A. Gray subsp.
pinetorum (Fernald) R.W. Long)
Acanthus Family (Acanthaceae)

Description: Pineland Wild Petunia is an erect,
leafy perennial that is 6–18" tall. The leaves are
mostly lance shaped or elliptic, up to about 1¾"
long, and borne on short stalks. The flowers are
funnel shaped, 1–2" long, and arise singly from
the axils of the stem leaves. The subtending
sepals are very narrow, usually measuring less
than ⅟₁₆" wide.

Bloom Season: May–September.

Habitat/Range: Dry to wet pinelands. Florida and
South Carolina.

Comments: Known occurrences of this species in
the Atlantic Coastal Plain are rare and are
currently recorded only from 2 counties in South
Carolina and at the western edge of our region in
Florida. The species is more common westward,
from the Florida panhandle and Alabama to
Louisiana. It should probably be more diligently
searched for in both Georgia and North Carolina.
Pineland Wild Petunia is most similar to the
common and widespread Wild Petunia *(R.
caroliniensis)* but is distinguished by its flowers
arising only from the axils of the stem leaves
rather than at the top of the plant.

CREEPING ERYNGO

Eryngium prostratum Nuttall ex Augustin de
Candolle
Carrot Family (Apiaceae or Umbelliferae)

Description: This low-growing to nearly prostrate
herb has a slender, creeping, diffusely branched
4–28" stem. At first glance plants look like a
mass of tangled vines. Ovate to lance-shaped
basal leaves are ¾–1½" long and entire or bluntly
toothed along the margins. Stem leaves are
narrowly linear and ½–1½" long. Dense, rounded
¼" heads of bluish flowers terminate a short stalk
that arises from the leaf axils.

Bloom Season: May–October.

Habitat/Range: Ditches, pinelands, moist
meadows, and disturbed places; often in moist to
wet sites. Throughout the region.

Comments: The name Eryngo was an early name
for Sea Holly *(E. campestre* or *E. maritimum),* a
European medicinal herb. Though Sea Holly's
effectiveness has never been tested, the Greek
scholar Dioscorides recommended it as a
treatment for gas. Several species of *Eryngium*
occur in our region, including the very similar *E.
baldwinii.* The bracts subtending the flower heads
of *E. prostratum* extend well beyond the base of
the head, whereas those of *E. baldwinii* do not.

FRINGED BLUESTAR
Amsonia ciliata Walter
Apocynum Family (Apocynaceae)

Description: Two species of bluestar are common in our region but are easily distinguished from each other. Fringed Bluestar is a branched upright upland herb, confined mostly to dry sandy woodlands. The stem is copiously pubescent and bears alternate, filiform to narrowly linear 1¼–3¼" leaves. Numerous blue 5-petaled flowers are borne in a terminal panicle. The flowers are hairy on the outside. The fruit is a long, narrow 4–8" follicle and is characteristic of the Apocynum family.

Bloom Season: April.

Habitat/Range: Sandhills and sandy roadsides. Florida, Georgia, South Carolina, and North Carolina.

Comments: Fringed Bluestar takes its common name and scientific epithet from its hairy stems and hairy flower petals; *ciliata* means "fringed with hairs" and derives from the Latin word for "eyelash." The hairy flowers and stem, xeric habitat, and narrowly linear leaves distinguish it from Eastern Bluestar *(A. tabernaemontana)*.

EASTERN BLUESTAR
Amsonia tabernaemontana Walter
Apocynum Family (Apocynaceae)

Description: Eastern Bluestar is an erect 2–4' perennial herb with narrowly lance-shaped to elliptic 2½–5" leaves. The stem is topped by a pyramid-shaped cluster of pale blue, star-shaped 5-petaled flowers. Both the stem and outer side of the flower petals are glabrous. The fruit is a narrow 2–4" follicle.

Bloom Season: March–April.

Habitat/Range: Floodplains, mesic hardwood forests, and rich slopes. Throughout the region.

Comments: The genus *Amsonia* includes about 20 species distributed in Europe, Asia, Japan, and North America and was named in honor of Dr. Charles Amson, an 18th-century Virginia physician and scientific traveler. Several bluestars, especially Eastern Bluestar, are well-known garden herbs that require very little care once they are established. The specific epithet *tabernaemontana* commemorates Jakob Theodore von Bergzabern, a German physician and herbalist who Latinized his name to Tabernaemontanus. He was the author of a celebrated herbal that was popular in the late 1500s.

CLASPING MILKWEED
Asclepias amplexicaulis J. E. Smith
Apocynum Family (Apocynaceae)

Description: The common name of this robust, conspicuous milkweed references one of its most important field identification characters. The large, wavy-edged leaves clasp the stem, making it our only upright opposite-leaved milkweed with clasping leaves. Pinewoods Milkweed *(A. humistrata)* occurs in similar habitats and also has clasping leaves. However, the leaves of Pinewoods Milkweed are shaped like an arrowhead and have a pale green background that is adorned with numerous pinkish veins, whereas the leaves of Clasping Milkweed have a single cream-colored central vein against a dark green background. The rose-purple or lavender flowers of Clasping Milkweed are composed of 5 strongly reflexed sepals subtending 5 conspicuous upright hoods. The protruding horns are about 1½ times as long as the hoods. Plants of Clasping Milkweed produce as many as 3, 1–3' stems from a single root crown. The fruit is a conspicuous 3–6" follicle that splits at maturity to expose numerous seeds decorated with cottony appendages.

Bloom Season: May–July.

Habitat/Range: Sandy roadsides, sandhill pinelands, typically in dry, open locations. Throughout the region.

Comments: The epithet *amplexicaulis* means "stem-clasping." This is a widespread milkweed across most of the eastern United States. Like many milkweeds, it typically does not produce large colonies and is more often encountered as single, widely spaced plants. Though it is purportedly somewhat common in our region, its scattered occurrences lead to the conclusion that Clasping Milkweed is much less abundant than it actually is, making finding one a special pleasure.

ANGLE POD OR ANGULAR POD MILKVINE

Gonolobus suberosus (Linnaeus) R. Brown
(Syn: *Matelea gonocarpos* (Walter) Shinners and *M. suberosa* (Linnaeus) Shinners)
Dogbane Family (Apocynaceae)

Description: Few of our herbaceous climbing vines have the combination of opposite heart-shaped leaves and milky sap. Angle Pod is a twining, perennial high-climbing herb with a mostly hairy stem. Leaves may be up to 8" long and 6" wide but are often slightly smaller. Flowers are borne in a 7–12-flowered inflorescence and have 5 spreading petals that are yellowish at the tip but deep purple at the base. The fruit is a large, light brown tapering follicle up to about 5" long with conspicuously angled sutures (hence the common name). Follicles split at maturity to release numerous seeds.

Bloom Season: April–August.

Habitat/Range: Southern mixed hardwood forests, bluffs, floodplains, calcareous hammocks, and rich woods. Throughout the region.

Comments: Angle Pod is one of our region's more common and widespread climbing milkweeds. It was formerly included within the genus *Matelea,* all species of which have spiny rather than angled seed pods. Two species were formerly recognized. *G. suberosus* and *G. gonocarpus* are now considered by at least some authorities to constitute a single species. However, there is still disagreement about whether this species constitutes a single species with no varieties, a single species with 2 varieties, or 2 distinct species. The old epithet *gonocarpus* derives from the Greek root *gonio* for "angled" and *carpos* for "fruit." *Suberosus* means "cork-barked." Although the former epithet seems to be the better fit, the rules of botanical nomenclature require that *suberosus* be the accepted epithet.

SANDHILL CHAFFHEAD
Carphephorus bellidifolius (Michaux) Torrey & A. Gray
Aster Family (Asteraceae or Compositae)

Description: Two species of *Carphephorus* are endemic to the Atlantic Coastal Plain, both of which are multistemmed herbs with several erect to ascending stems that arise from a tuft at ground level. Sandhill Chaffhead grows to about 1½' tall and produces mostly glabrous stems, although the stems of some plants may display short hairs that are appressed to the stem surface. The leaves vary from oblanceolate to more or less elliptic and are also glabrous to minutely hairy. Basal leaves may be up to about 12" long and are much the larger. Stem leaves reduce abruptly in size and become sessile up the stem. Flowers are borne in conspicuous, showy heads near the branch tips. Each head consists of several tubular, pink to purplish lavender disk flowers. There are no ray flowers. The stems of the closely related and somewhat similar *C.*

tomentosus, the other Atlantic Coastal Plain endemic, have conspicuous, spreading hairs, and the surfaces of at least the basal leaves are tomentose.

Bloom Season: August–October.

Habitat/Range: Sandhills and xeric woodlands. Georgia, South Carolina, North Carolina, and Virginia.

Comments: Though Sandhill Chaffhead sometimes occurs with other members of its genus, it tends to be in the driest sites. It is not uncommon within its restricted range and is in some places abundant in the Carolina sandhills. The epithet means "with leaves like *Bellis,*" the genus of the true daisies that occur in Europe, North Africa, and Turkey. The name derives from the Latin *bellus* for "pretty" or "charming."

VANILLALEAF OR DEER'S TONGUE

Carphephorus odoratissimus (J. F. Gmel.) H. Hebert
Aster Family (Asteraceae or Compositae)

Description: The solitary stem of Vanillaleaf is erect, 2–5' tall, and glabrous. Upper leaves are sessile, clasping, usually less than 2" long, and strongly ascending, while those on the lower third of the stem are much longer (to about 1½'), whitish below, and have a somewhat succulent appearance. Most leaf surfaces bear tiny glandular depressions that require magnification to see clearly. The branches of the inflorescence are terminated by compact heads, each consisting of 5–15 purplish, tubular ¼" disk flowers. There are no ray flowers.

Bloom Season: August–November.

Habitat/Range: Sandhills, flatwoods, bogs, pond margins, moist to dry roadsides. Florida, Georgia, South Carolina, and North Carolina.

Comments: Vanillaleaf is somewhat similar to Hairy Chaffhead *(C. paniculatus)* and Florida Paintbrush *(C. corymbosus)* but is easily distinguished from both by its glabrous stem. The inflorescence of Vanillaleaf is more or less open and flat topped whereas the inflorescence of Hairy Chaffhead is broadly cylindrical and that of Florida Paintbrush is typically more tightly clustered. The common name Vanillaleaf derives from the presence of coumarin, which imparts a fragrant, vanilla-like order from crushed herbage and has sometimes been used to flavor tobacco. The large basal leaves resemble a deer's tongue in form and outline, hence the alternate common name. Vanillaleaf often occurs in large, very showy colonies with hundreds of plants all flowering at the same time. Such colonies are especially responsive to fire and are particularly attractive during a fall that follows a summer burn.

SANDHILL THISTLE
Cirsium repandum Michaux
Aster Family (Asteraceae or Compositae)

Description: The sandhill habitat, erect stature, thorny leaves, and naked flowering stalk of this 1–3' perennial herb help distinguish it from all of our other thistles. Numerous spreading, narrow, thorny, sessile 2–9" leaves are crowded along the stem and are usually separated from each other by less than ½". Basal leaves are absent, at least at flowering time, which is another helpful field identification character. Flowers are borne in conspicuous, purplish ¾–1½" wide heads at the tips of short terminal branches.

Bloom Season: Predominantly May–July.

Habitat/Range: Sandhills, pinelands, usually in dry sandy soils. Georgia, South Carolina, North Carolina, and Virginia (reports of occurrences of this species in Florida are unsubstantiated).

Comments: Sandhill Thistle is endemic to the Atlantic Coastal Plain. It is relatively common in the sandhills of both South and North Carolina but is extremely restricted in distribution outside of these states. The epithet *repandum* means "with slightly wavy margins," and refers to the undulate edges of the leaf blades. At least 11 species of *Cirsium* occur in the Atlantic Coastal Plain, only 2 of which are not native to the region. Pasture Thistle *(C. pumilum)* also has spiny leaves and is similar to Sandhill Thistle. However, plants of Pasture Thistle typically have well-developed and persistent basal leaves and the leaf nodes are generally at least ¾" apart, whereas plants of Sandhill Thistle usually lack well-developed basal leaves and the leaf nodes are usually less than ½" apart.

SAVANNAH GRASS-LEAVED ASTER
Eurybia paludosa (Aiton) Nesom
Aster Family (Asteraceae or Compositae)

Description: This is an erect to leaning perennial herb with a 1–2½' glabrous or hairy stem. Leaves are often described as "grasslike" because they are long (to about 8") and linear, with an evident midrib and a sheathing base. Several flower heads are borne in an open inflorescence. Up to 35 lavender to purplish ½–⅞" ray flowers surround a dense cluster of more than 30 disk flowers.

Bloom Season: July–October.

Habitat/Range: Sandhills, wet savannas, and pocosin margins. Florida (where reported only for Nassau County, in the extreme northeast corner of the state), Georgia, South Carolina, and North Carolina.

Comments: This species is endemic to the Atlantic Coastal Plain with a center of distribution mostly in the Carolinas, though it is not uncommon in extreme southeastern Georgia. Taken in combination the linear, sheathing stem leaves and blue ray flowers distinguish it in our region. The common name references the fact that this species was once assigned to the genus *Aster*. The epithet *paludosa* means "marsh-loving."

THREE-NERVED JOE-PYE-WEED
Eupatorium dubium Willdenow ex Poiret
Aster Family (Asteraceae or Compositae)

Description: Several species of *Eupatorium* in the eastern United States are called Joe-Pye-Weed. The name apparently comes from that of an American Indian who reportedly concocted numerous cures from plants of this genus. The present species is an erect 2–5' herb with 2–6" coarsely toothed leaves that are borne in whorls of 2–5 at the node. The leaves have 3 linear, parallel veins, all of which arise near the base of the blade. Numerous purplish to pinkish flower heads are borne in a conspicuous and very showy inflorescence at the top of the stem.

Bloom Season: July–October.

Habitat/Range: Swamps, pocosins, and other wet habitats with sandy, acid soils. South Carolina, North Carolina, and Virginia.

Comments: Several species in this genus have been used medicinally as diuretics and astringents. *E. dubium* is similar to *E. purpureum* and *E. fistulosum*, both of which are also called Joe-Pye-Weed. The present species is most easily distinguished from the latter 2 by its mostly 3-nerved leaves that are covered below with tiny, resinous dots that require magnification to see clearly.

HOLLOW-STEM JOE-PYE-WEED
Eupatorium fistulosum Barratt
(Syn: *Eupatoriadelphus fistulosus* [Barratt] King & H. E. Robinson)
Aster Family (Asteraceae or Compositae)

Description: The common name of this species derives from its hollow stem, which when cut in cross section resembles a soda straw. It is quite similar in form, size, and appearance to *E. purpureum*, which is similarly distributed in our region, but has a solid stem. The erect, leafy stem is generally purplish and may be up to about 9' tall but is usually closer to 6' tall. Stem leaves are 6–10" long and borne in whorls of 4–7 at the node, and have bluntly toothed margins. The large, branching inflorescence is composed of numerous purple to pinkish flower heads, each with 4–7 flowers.

Bloom Season: July–October.

Habitat/Range: Bottomland woods, ditches, and marshes. Throughout the region, though mostly west and south of our region in Florida. This species is actually less common in the coastal plain than in the Piedmont.

Comments: The epithet *fistulosum* means "hollow, like a pipe," and alludes to the hollow stem. The genus name honors Mithridates VI Eupator (132–63 B.C.), king of Pontus, and includes about 40 species in North American, Europe, and Asia. There is still considerable disagreement about the nomenclature and taxonomy of this group, with some experts "lumping" species within the genus *Eupatorium* and others dividing them among several genera. Consequently, it is not uncommon to find the same species listed differently among several books or botanical manuals.

FLAXLEAF ASTER

Ionactis linariifolia (Linnaeus) Greene
Aster Family (Asteraceae or Compositae)

Description: The narrowly linear, 1-nerved leaves and violet-blue flowers distinguish this aster from most of its closest relatives. Several somewhat wiry, finely hairy 4–28" stems arise from a woody knotlike base. Numerous ½–1¾" leaves alternate on the stem, each with entire margins and a single, central vein. The lowermost leaves often fall off by peak flowering time, leaving the lower ⅓ of the stem nearly bare. The flower heads consist of 10–20 blue to violet rays surrounding a yellow disk.

Bloom Season: September–November.

Habitat/Range: Sandhills and flatwoods, typically in drier sites. Throughout the region.

Comments: The genus name, *Ionactis,* means "with violet rays," in reference to the ray flowers. *Linariifolia* refers to the shape of the leaves. The common name derives from the similarity between the leaves of the present species and those of the fiber-producing (or flax-producing) members of the genus *Linum,* several of which are called Flax.

ROSE-RUSH OR FLOWERING STRAWS

Lygodesmia aphylla (Nuttall) Torrey & A. Gray
Aster Family (Asteraceae or Compositae)

Description: The epithet *aphylla* means "without leaves." The slender, sparingly branched 16–32" stems of this species ordinarily produce only inconspicuous, scalelike leaves, although a single linear leaf may be present near the base of the plant. Solitary flower heads are borne at the ends of the stem and branches. Flower heads lack a central disk and are composed instead of up to about 12 bluish to lavender or sometimes white 1" ray flowers that have conspicuous stamens and pistils. The stems of this species exude a milky sap when broken.

Bloom Season: April–July.

Habitat/Range: Dry sandhills, flatwoods, and disturbed sites. Florida and Georgia.

Comments: The flower heads of this species do not immediately suggest that it is a member of the Aster Family, most of which have a densely flowered central disk, numerous rays, or both. Rose-Rush is common in many parts of Florida but decreases in abundance north of southeastern Georgia.

GRASSLEAF BARBARA'S BUTTONS
Marshallia graminifolia (Walter) Small
Aster Family (Asteraceae or Compositae)

Description: The name Barbara's Buttons probably derives from the dense ¾–1¼" heads of purplish to pale lavender or nearly white flowers. The leaves are up to 10" long and about ⅝" wide. Most leaves are at least 7 times longer than wide and have an evidently 3-nerved blade. Small colonies of solitary or loosely clustered 1–3' stems may cover several square feet.

Bloom Season: July–October.

Habitat/Range: Wet pinelands and savannas. Georgia, South Carolina, and North Carolina.

Comments: The range of Grassleaf Barbara's Buttons overlaps in eastern Georgia with that of *M. tenuifolia*, which is also called Grassleaf Barbara's Buttons and ranges southward into Florida and west to eastern Texas. Some experts consider these 2 forms to represent a single species. However, the 2 are not particularly difficult to distinguish in the field. The basal leaves of *M. graminifolia* are erect or ascending and similar in form to the stem leaves (although the basal leaves are often larger). The basal leaves of *M. tenuifolia* are spreading and are conspicuously different in form than the stem leaves. In addition the basal leaves of *M. graminifolia* are persistent and often leave fibrous remains at the base of the plant, whereas those of *M. tenuifolia* do not. The name *Marshallia* honors Humphry Marshall, a cousin of the American botanical explorer John Bartram. The epithet *graminifolia* means "with grasslike foliage," in reference to this species' long, narrow leaves.

GRASSLEAF BARBARA'S BUTTONS
Marshallia tenuifolia Raf.
Aster Family (Asteraceae or Compositae)

Description: The erect solitary stems of Grassleaf Barbara's Buttons arise from a basal tuft of soft, spreading 3–6" leaves that are borne in a well-developed horizontal basal rosette. The numerous stem leaves lack stalks, are erect or ascending, linear in outline, and much narrower than the basal ones. Flowers are borne in a single congested head at the tip of the stem well above the uppermost leaves. Flower heads are ¾–1½" wide and consist of numerous, pale pink to nearly white or lavender disk flowers.

Bloom Season: July–September.

Habitat/Range: Moist pinelands, flatwoods, bogs, savannas, roadside ditches, and dry meadows. Florida and Georgia.

Comments: The redundancy in common names of the present and previous species stems from differing interpretations about whether these plants constitute 1 species or 2 species. The differences between them are outlined in the account for *M. graminifolia. M. tenuifolia* could equally well be placed with the pink flowers but was placed here as an aid to field identification.

TALL IRONWEED
Vernonia angustifolia Michaux
Aster Family (Asteraceae or Compositae)

Description: The stems of Tall Ironweed may be up to about 4' tall and are usually minutely hairy, especially along their upper extent. The crowded leaves are linear, to about 4½" long, and much longer than wide, as suggested by the epithet *angustifolia,* which means "narrow leaves." The disk flowers are purple, tubular, about ⅜" long, and borne in numerous long-stalked heads in a branched inflorescence. There are no ray flowers.

Bloom Season: June–September.

Habitat/Range: Sandy pinelands, sandy ridges, and dry roadsides. Florida, Georgia, South Carolina, and North Carolina.

Comments: Two varieties of Tall Ironweed occur in our area. Variety *angustifolia* is by far the more widespread in the region and is distinguished from other ironweeds by having 16–19 flowers per head. Variety *scaberrima* is found in only a single county in southeast Georgia as well as a few counties in South Carolina. The very narrow leaves help distinguish *V. angustifolia* from other ironweeds in our region.

NEW YORK IRONWEED
Vernonia noveboracensis (Linnaeus) Michaux
Aster Family (Asteraceae or Compositae)

Description: Three large-leaved ironweeds occur in the Atlantic Coastal Plain, all of which are tall, robust plants with at least some stem leaves wider than 1½" and no basal leaves. New York Ironweed is a 3–6' perennial herb with numerous lance-shaped stem leaves that may be nearly 1' long. The flower heads are ½–¾" tall and consist of 30–65 tubular, purplish disk flowers. There are no ray flowers.

Bloom Season: July–September.

Habitat/Range: Stream edges, moist meadows, low roadsides. Throughout the region.

Comments: New York Ironweed is similar in most respects to *V. glauca,* which has 32–48 flowers per head. The upper and lower leaf surfaces of New York Ironweed are uniform in color whereas the leaf surfaces of *V. glauca* appear 2-toned, with the lower surfaces being much paler than the upper surfaces. Giant Ironweed *(Vernonia gigantea)* is similar in form, but its flower heads typically have fewer than 30 flowers. The epithet *noveboracensis* means "of New York."

GLADE LOBELIA
Lobelia glandulosa Walter
Bellflower Family (Campanulaceae)

Description: The glabrous, weakly erect, unbranched stem of Glade Lobelia may be up to 3' tall or a little taller. The 1–6" leaves are sessile, linear, and mostly erect or ascending. The margins of the leaves are entire or lined with callous-tipped teeth. Up to about 20 (or more) flowers are borne in an elongated raceme at the top of the stem. Individual flowers are pale blue with a white spot, ¾–1½" long, and borne on a comparatively stout pedicel. The corolla is subtended by conspicuous lance-shaped sepals that are lined along the margins with gland-tipped teeth that are best seen with at least 10X magnification. The specific epithet *glandulosa* alludes to these glandular teeth.

Bloom Season: September–October.

Habitat/Range: Wet savannas, wet ditches, flatwoods, bogs, and the margins of bays and pocosins. Throughout the region.

Comments: Several species of blue-flowered *Lobelia* occur in the region. The robust size, relatively large and mostly linear stem leaves, and glandular calyx lobes help distinguish Glade Lobelia.

NUTTALL'S LOBELIA
Lobelia nuttallii Schult.
Bellflower Family (Campanulaceae)

Description: Several small-flowered *Lobelia* with threadlike stems occur in our region. Only 2 have narrow leaves disposed mostly along the stem. In Nuttall's Lobelia the stem leaves are less than ⅛" wide, the lowermost to about 1¼" long and narrowly lance shaped, becoming progressively shorter and linear above. Basal leaves are oval, up to about ⅝" long, and present mostly prior to flowering. The 8–30" stem is solitary or with long, ascending branches. Flowers are 2 lipped, about ⅝" long, and blue with a white throat spot.

Bloom Season: April–October.

Habitat/Range: Bogs, savannas, flatwoods, ditches, roadsides, seepage areas, and low woods. Throughout the region.

Comments: Nuttall's Lobelia is most similar to Boykin's Lobelia *(L. boykinii)*, a rare species listed as critically imperiled throughout much of its mostly North Carolina to Mississippi range. Boykin's Lobelia occurs mostly in standing water and has very fine leaves that are about ¼ the width of those of Nuttall's Lobelia. Its leaves usually fall off by flowering time and its flowers are borne on long, thin, dangling stalks.

SMOOTH SPIDERWORT
Tradescantia ohiensis Rafinesque
Spiderwort Family (Commelinaceae)

Description: The stems of this perennial herb are 8–32" tall. The leaves are 4–16" long, up to about ⅞" wide, and sheathed at the base. When opened and flattened, the sheath is wider than the leaves. Flowers are bright blue to purple and are borne in conspicuous showy clusters. Individual flowers have 3 petals and 3 sepals, the latter of which are mostly glabrous, except for a few hairs at the tip. The fruit is an oblong ¼" capsule.

Bloom Season: April–July.

Habitat/Range: Roadsides, disturbed areas, bottomlands, and moist or dry woodlands. Throughout the region.

Comments: Several species of spiderwort occur in our region. The most common include Ohio Spiderwort and the somewhat similar Hairy Spiderwort *(T. hirsutiflora)*. The mostly glabrous sepals that have at most only a few hairs at the tip provide the best clue for identifying Ohio Spiderwort. Some species of *Tradescantia* were reportedly used by American Indians as laxatives and treatment for kidney and stomach distress.

GEORGIA INDIGO-BUSH
Amorpha georgiana Wilbur
Pea Family (Fabaceae or Leguminosae)

Description: Georgia Indigo-Bush is a low herbaceous subshrub 1–3' tall. The pinnately compound leaves have 13–39, ¼–1" leaflets. The petiole is less than ¼" long. The inflorescence consists of a conspicuous congested 1¼–2½" raceme of tiny flowers. Individual flowers are about ¼" long with a reddish purple standard (upper petal). The fruit is an erect ¼" legume.

Bloom Season: May–July (but mostly during the earlier part of this period).

Habitat/Range: Sandhill pinelands. Georgia, South Carolina, and North Carolina.

Comments: There are 2 varieties of this species, though some authorities think they are different enough to warrant 2 distinct species. The plant featured here is *A. georgiana* var. *georgiana,* an Atlantic Coastal Plain endemic found primarily in the Fall Line Hills and sparingly eastward. Variety *confusa,* which is sometimes called Savanna Indigo-Bush, has bright blue flowers and longer petioles and occurs mostly in pine savannas. Both are rare and declining in abundance throughout their restricted ranges.

DWARF INDIGO-BUSH
Amorpha herbacea Walter
Pea Family (Fabaceae or Leguminosae)

Description: This conspicuously hairy, moderately shrubby legume can be nearly 5' tall but is often shorter. Its common name is a comparison to the more widespread Tall Indigo-Bush *(A. fruticosa),* which may be 16' tall. The common name notwithstanding, Dwarf Indigo-Bush can be about the same size as or even larger than the Georgia Indigo-Bush *(A. georgiana).* The violet-blue to whitish flowers are borne in clusters of conspicuous slender 4–12" racemes. The leaves are compound, to about 1' long, with up to about 45, ½–1" leaflets.

Bloom Season: May–July.

Habitat/Range: Sandhills, savannas, and flatwoods. Florida, Georgia, South Carolina, and North Carolina.

Comments: This species is endemic to the Atlantic Coastal Plain. Florida plants often have fewer hairs and are sometimes treated as variety *floridana.* The flowers of Georgia Indigo-Bush are more deeply colored and the central vein of each leaflet extends beyond the leaflet tip (mucronate); leaflets of Dwarf Indigo-Bush are tipped by a distinctive, usually stalkless gland.

SPURRED BUTTERFLY PEA OR CLIMBING BUTTERFLY PEA

Centrosema virginianum (Linnaeus) Benth.
Pea Family (Fabaceae or Leguminosae)

Description: This is a trailing or twining perennial herb with 3' stems and 3-parted leaves. The 1–2" leaflets are mostly ovate or lance-shaped but are sometimes linear and longer. The 1–1½" flowers range from blue to lavender or violet, usually have a creamy white spot in the center, and are egg-shaped to nearly round in outline due to the large, spreading upper petal (standard). The fruit is a flattened 2–5" linear pod.

Bloom Season: June–September.

Habitat/Range: Roadsides, fields, fence lines and other disturbed sites; dry woodlands, sandhills, margins of swamps, and open pinelands. Throughout the region.

Comments: White-flowered forms are sometimes encountered. Butterfly Pea is similar in appearance to another species often called Butterfly Pea *(Clitoria mariana)*. In *Centrosema* the sepals are at least as long as the flower tube and the legume is 2¾" long or longer, whereas in *Clitoria* the sepals are distinctly shorter than the flower tube and the legume is less than 2½" long. Once learned, these 2 species are easily distinguished at a glance. The name *Centrosema* comes from the Greek words for "spur" and "standard," in reference to the short spur behind the standard. Butterfly Pea ranges widely across the eastern United States and expresses a somewhat variable morphology. Because the leaflets of some southern plants are uniformly narrower than northern plants, some authorities recognize a variety of the present species designated as *C. virginianum* var. *angustifolium* (the varietal epithet means "having narrow leaves").

ATLANTIC PIGEONWINGS, BUTTERFLY PEA, OR BLUE PEA
Clitoria mariana Linnaeus
Pea Family (Fabaceae or Leguminosae)

Description: This 3' trailing or twining perennial vine sometimes forms dense tangles on low vegetation. Long-stalked compound leaves are divided into 3 ovate or elliptic ¾–3" leaflets. Attractive light blue or lavender flowers are borne from the leaf axils in a short-stalked, 1-flowered or 2-flowered raceme. Each flower is composed of a strongly in-curved keel petal flanked by 2 small winged petals, all of which are nested within a 1½–2½" standard. The standard petal in many species in the Pea Family is upright. However, the orientation of the corolla in the present species gives the appearance that the standard is at the bottom of the flower, a condition described as resupinate. The fruit is a 1–2½" legume.

Bloom Season: June–August.

Habitat/Range: Dry woods, sandhill pinelands, roadsides. Throughout the region.

Comments: This species also produces cleistogamous flowers, which are closed, self-fertile flowers that, in this case, lack petals, are less than ¼" long, and have the appearance of undeveloped buds. The genus name *Clitoria* is from the Latin word *clitoris*, which the flowers are said to resemble. *Clitoria mariana* is superficially similar in appearance to *Centrosema virginianum*, which is also called Butterfly Pea. Though it takes only a little practice to quickly distinguish between these 2 species, they are often confused. A summary of their differences is included with the description of *Centrosema virginianum*.

PINELAND LEATHERROOT

Orbexilum virgatum (Nuttall) Rydberg
Pea Family (Fabaceae or Leguminosae)

Description: Several species of *Orbexilum* occur in our region; most were previously included within the genus *Psoralea*. Pineland Leatherroot is easily distinguished as the only species in the genus with unifoliolate leaves, meaning that its compound leaves have only a single leaflet, thus appearing to be simple. The single leaflet is linear to narrowly oblong and 1–3" long. Numerous tiny flowers are borne in a congested ¾–2" raceme from the leaf axils. Individual flowers are violet to bluish purple and about ¼" long. The fruit is a brown or black legume.

Bloom Season: May–July.

Habitat/Range: Sandhills and the edges of wet prairies and savannas. Florida, Georgia, and possibly South Carolina.

Comments: Pineland Leatherroot enjoys a restricted distribution and is essentially endemic to northeastern Florida and southeastern Georgia. It has reportedly been collected in South Carolina, but its status there is uncertain. It is considered critically imperiled in Florida and possibly extirpated in Georgia. Plants with 3-parted lower leaves have been reported.

SANDHILL BEAN

Phaseolus sinuatus (Nuttall) Torrey & A. Gray
(Syn: *Phaseolus polystachios* (L.) Britton et al. var. *sinuatus* (Nutt. ex Torr. & A. Gray) Marechal et al.)
Pea Family (Fabaceae or Leguminosae)

Description: Sandhill Bean is a trailing perennial vine with stalked, compound leaves. Leaflets are triangular to ovate in outline, ¾–2" long, and often 3 lobed and sinuate along the margins. The flowers are lavender to purplish at maturity and about ⅜" long. The fruit is a flat, 1¼–1¾" legume.

Bloom Season: July–September.

Habitat/Range: Sandhills, dry pinelands. Florida, Georgia, South Carolina, and North Carolina.

Comments: Some authorities treat this species as a variety of Wild Bean *(Phaseolus polystachios).* The two may be distinguished by habit. Wild Bean is typically a climbing and twining herb that scrambles on supporting vegetation, whereas Sandhill Bean is a prostrate, trailing vine that produces extended aboveground runners that may be up to 16' long. The genus name *Phaseolus* is an ancient name for a modern group of American plants that include the Lima Bean and String Bean. Food plants of this genus enjoy worldwide cultivation.

COMMON VETCH
Vicia sativa Linnaeus
Pea Family (Fabaceae or Leguminosae)

Description: About 20 species of vetch occur in the greater southeastern United States, about ½ of which are non-native species that were introduced to the region largely for forage, cover, and soil improvement. About 140 species make up the genus *Vicia* worldwide. Common Vetch is an erect or more often sprawling annual herb, 12–40" long. The leaves are pinnately compound with 2–14, ½–1¼" leaflets. Flowers are sometimes white but become purple or pink. The fruit is a 1–2½" legume. Plants with 4–10 leaflets per leaf are sometimes treated as variety *nigra,* while those with 2–7 leaflets are treated as variety *sativa.*

Bloom Season: April–June.

Habitat/Range: Weedy roadsides, fields, lawns, and other disturbed sites. Throughout the region.

Comments: This non-native weed was introduced from Mediterranean Europe and is a common component of an extensive collection of roadside weeds that line many roads and highways in the southeastern United States. It is often found growing in conjunction with the red-flowered Crimson Clover *(Trifolium incarnatum).*

AMERICAN WISTERIA, SWAMP WISTERIA, OR ATLANTIC WISTERIA
Wisteria frutescens (Linnaeus) Poiret
Pea Family (Fabaceae or Leguminosae)

Description: This deciduous, high-climbing twining vine is our only native wisteria. Plants vary 6–45' long and typically clamber on shrubs and trees at the edges of wetland streams and depressions. The leaves are alternate, pinnately compound, and 4–12" long, with 1–2½" stalks and 9–15 leaflets. Leaflets are 1–3" long, ovate or lance shaped in outline, with entire margins. Flowers are purplish blue or blue and borne in a many-flowered 2–10" raceme. The fruit is a narrow, glabrous, oblong 1½–5½" legume.

Bloom Season: April–July.

Habitat/Range: Margins of swamps and wetland drains. Throughout the region.

Comments: Two non-native wisteria have been introduced to our region for horticultural purposes. Chinese Wisteria *(W. sinensis)* is probably the more common of the 2 and has been used in landscaping for many years but is very weedy and is now listed as an invasive pest plant in Florida. Japanese Wisteria *(W. floribunda)* is also commonly cultivated. The 2 may be distinguished from American Wisteria by their hairy legumes.

PINEBARREN GENTIAN

Gentiana autumnalis Linnaeus
Gentian Family (Gentianaceae)

Description: Exquisite indigo-blue funnel-shaped flowers with delicately spotted petals distinguish this species from all others within our region. Though it is easy to see when flowering, the thin, weakly erect stem of this 9–45" perennial herb makes spotting flowerless plants extremely difficult. Leaves are opposite and often narrowly linear in outline but may be wider on some plants. Leaves at mid-stem are up to about 2½" long but become shorter above. Blue is the more common flower color, but flower color may vary from nearly white to greenish white, lilac, or purple. Flowers are 1–1½" long.

Bloom Season: September–November (but this species responds well to fire and may bloom at other times of the year following controlled burns).

Habitat/Range: Sandhills, savannas, flatwoods, and moist to very dry pinelands. South Carolina, North Carolina, and Virginia.

Comments: The epithet *autumnalis* means "pertaining to autumn," in reference to Pinebarren Gentian's fall flowering period. Pinebarren Gentian ranges northward along the coastal plain to central New Jersey but is considered vulnerable or critically imperiled throughout its range. Its beauty and rarity make it a popular target species for fall wildflower excursions. Two other blue-flowered gentians occur in our area, including Coastal Plain Gentian (*G. catesbaei*) and Soapwort Gentian (*G. saponaria*), neither of which has spreading petals.

COASTAL PLAIN GENTIAN
Gentiana catesbaei Walter
Gentian Family (Gentianaceae)

Description: Distinguishing between the Coastal Plain Gentian and Soapwort Gentian *(G. saponaria)* in the field is a difficult task as they are similar in form, habit, and flowers. The leaves of Coastal Plain Gentian are mostly 1–3" long, widest near the base, and finely toothed along the margins. (The leaves of Soapwort Gentian tend to be widest toward the middle.) Plants average 12–32" tall and are topped by a cluster of blue to purple 5-parted flowers. Flowers often have the appearance of large, unopened buds. A few flowers in any population of Coastal Plain Gentian spread slightly at the apex, at least wide enough to allow entry by bumblebees and other pollinators. The sepals (calyx lobes) are usually longer than the calyx tube, which is another helpful field character for distinguishing between this species and Soapwort Gentian.

Bloom Season: September–November.

Habitat/Range: Moist pinelands and savannas, wet weather drainages through pinelands, and pocosins. Throughout the region.

Comments: This fairly common gentian is named in honor of Mark Catesby (1682–1749), a naturalist from Sudbury, England, and author of *A Natural History of Carolina*, a volume that is still often referenced by natural historians. The genus is named for Gentius, king of Illyria in about 500 B.C. King Gentius reportedly discovered the medicinal values of Bitterwort *(G. lutea)* and reportedly used it to ease the symptoms of malaria in his troops. A bitter or tonic made from the roots of Bitterwort is also said to stimulate digestion and ease stomach pain.

57

SKYFLOWER
Hydrolea corymbosa J. Macbride ex Elliott
Hydrolea Family (Hydroleaceae)

Description: The common name Skyflower for this attractive, showy herb is not difficult to understand. Few plants of the coastal plains produce flowers that come close to matching the intensity of its deep blue blossoms. The erect, slender stems are up to about 30" tall and topped with a branching corymb (hence the name *corymbosa*) of 5-petaled flowers that have an elongated pistil surrounded by 5 showy stamens. Individual petals are about ½" long. The leaves are alternate, entire, up to about 1½" long, and elliptic or lance shaped in outline. The leaf axils usually lack spines (although spines may be occasionally encountered), unlike the somewhat similar *H. ovata* that occurs mostly south and west of our region.

Bloom Season: July–September.

Habitat/Range: Wet roadside ditches, cypress savannas, wet meadows. Florida, Georgia, and South Carolina.

Comments: Only 2 species of *Hydrolea* are likely to be encountered in our region and are easily distinguished. The flowers of the closely related Waterpod *(H. quadrivalvis)* are borne from the leaf axils rather than in terminal corymbs and the axils of at least some leaves bear sharp spines. Spines are usually absent from the leaf axils of Skyflower or, if present, are very small and inconspicuous. The genus name *Hydrolea* comes from the Greek word *hydor,* "water," and the Latin suffix *olea* or Greek suffix *elaia,* both of which mean "olive." The name was given based on the supposed resemblance of the leaves of *H. spinosa* (a tropical species sometimes used horticulturally in Florida) to those of the olive.

SAVANNAH IRIS
Iris tridentata Pursh
Iris Family (Iridaceae)

Description: The petals of Savannah Iris are so small and inconspicuous that they are barely noticeable without close observation. They are about equal in length to the claw of the sepal (the narrowed, stalklike portion at the sepal base) and look more like a small erect appendage than a true petal. Three showy, yellow-spotted purple sepals arch from the center of the flower and droop at the tip. Most plants produce several alternate, narrow, swordlike 12–16" leaves, each of which forms a sheath around the stem. The fruit is a conspicuous, 3-angled, 1–1⅝" capsule with numerous seeds.

Bloom Season: May–June.

Habitat/Range: Flatwoods and wet savannas. Florida, Georgia, South Carolina, and North Carolina.

Comments: Savannah Iris is more abundant in the Carolinas than in Florida and Georgia. The short petals of Savannah Iris easily distinguish it from all of our other native wetland irises. Nevertheless, it is sometimes confused with Southern Blueflag *(I. virginica)*, a more robust plant with long, conspicuously erect petals.

DWARF IRIS
Iris verna Linnaeus
Iris Family (Iridaceae)

Description: Dwarf Iris is a low-growing herb with 4" stems that are completely hidden by the leaf sheaths. Five to 9 elongated leaves arise from the base of the plant, varying 6–24" in length and ⅛–⅜" in width. The 1–3" fragrant bluish to violet flowers bear yellow markings and seemingly arise directly from the ground. Dwarf Crested Iris *(I. cristata)* is similar but occurs mostly in the Piedmont and mountains. It is distinguished by habitat and by having an elevated ridge (or crest) along the upper surface of the sepals.

Bloom Season: March–May.

Habitat/Range: Sandy woods and hammocks. Georgia, South Carolina, North Carolina, and Virginia (also Florida, but west of our region).

Comments: Authorities recognize 2 varieties of this species. Variety *smalliana* occurs mostly in upland woods of the Piedmont and mountains, while variety *verna* is restricted mostly to the Atlantic Coastal Plain. The epithet *verna* means "of the spring," an allusion to the early spring flowering period. Most of our other irises begin flowering a month or two later.

SOUTHERN BLUEFLAG IRIS
Iris virginica Linnaeus
Iris Family (Iridaceae)

Description: This robust iris typically occurs in saturated soils, often in standing water. Typical plants are about 3' tall with large flexuous leaves that may be more than 30" long and up to about 1½" wide. Mature plants often produce several flowers, including a single flower at the base of the inflorescence and 2–3 flowers at the top. Three showy deep blue or purple sepals arch outward from the center of the flower, alternating with 3 conspicuously erect petals. The fruit is a 1¼–2½" capsule with numerous brown seeds.

Bloom Season: April–May.

Habitat/Range: Marshes, wet ditches, swamps, canals, and shaded lake edges. Throughout the region.

Comments: The leaflike bract that subtends the lowest flower of Southern Blueflag is usually not long enough to reach the top of the uppermost flower, which is helpful in distinguishing this species in the field. The morphology of iris flowers can be confusing. In most of our species, the showy arching segments that arise as the outermost whorl of parts are the sepals, while the next inner whorl of parts consists of petals. The inner side of each sepal is overlaid for at least part of its length by an expanded, somewhat petal-like style that typically turns upward at the tip. The typically jagged edge of this upturned tip is actually the stigmatic (pollen gathering) surface. To confuse matters further, some iris experts do not distinguish between sepals and petals, preferring instead to call them tepals, a botanical term used when the petals and sepals are not clearly differentiated.

GEORGIA CALAMINT
Calamintha georgiana (R. M. Harper) Shinners
Mint Family (Lamiaceae or Labiatae)

Description: Georgia Calamint is a low, leafy, very aromatic, slenderly branched deciduous shrub to about 2' tall. The branches are green when young but turn brown with age. Leaves are opposite, ⅜–1½" long, and mostly oval to lance shaped in outline. The flowers are predominately bluish purple to lavender outside, whitish within, and borne mostly in 3-flowered clusters from the leaf axils. Individual flowers are 2 lipped, with the lowermost lip deeply lobed at the apex. The fruit is a tiny, brown nutlet.

Bloom Season: August–September.

Habitat/Range: Dry, sandy woodlands, Longleaf Pine sandhills, roadsides, and wooded borders of rivers and streams. Georgia, South Carolina, and North Carolina (also Florida, but west of our region).

Comments: Georgia Calamint is still referred to by the scientific name *Satureja georgiana* by some botanists. It was originally given the name *Clinopodium georgianum* by Roland Harper, who first described it. Harper's name for the plant is preferred by some authorities. Species of *Calamintha* are closely related to the thymes and Catnip. Some species of calamint have been used as replacements for Pennyroyal oil for flavoring food. Dried leaves of some European species have been brewed as tea, both as a household drink and for medicinal use in the treatment of stomach distress. There is evidence, however, that the oils from some members of this genus are hepatotoxic, meaning that they are potentially damaging to the liver.

CAROLINA BIRDS-IN-A-NEST
Macbridea caroliniana (Walter) Blake
Mint Family (Lamiaceae or Labiatae)

Description: The overlapping, nestlike bracts that subtend the flowers give this species its common name. The erect 1–3' stem lacks hairs at maturity but may be vested with tiny glandular dots that require magnification to see clearly. Up to 4 ornate 1–1½" flowers arise from a congested head at the top of the plant. Corollas are mostly blue to lavender or pinkish (white forms are not uncommon) and striped with purple or white. The 2–5" stem leaves are opposite and mostly stalked on the lower part of the plant but become sessile below the flowers.

Bloom Season: July–November.

Habitat/Range: Forested seepage bogs, swamp forests, wet to moist ditches, margins of savannas. Georgia, South Carolina, and North Carolina.

Comments: This genus includes only 2 species, both of which are endemic to the Southeastern Coastal Plains. Both are also quite rare. White Birds-in-a-Nest *(M. alba),* listed as a threatened species by the U.S. Fish and Wildlife Service (USFWS), is found only in the Florida panhandle, at the western extent of our region. The present species is listed by USFWS as a species of special concern.

SAVANNA MOUNTAINMINT OR APPALACHIAN MOUNTAINMINT
Pycnanthemum flexuosum (Walter) Britton, Sterns, & Poggenberg
Mint Family (Lamiaceae or Labiatae)

Description: The relatively large, headlike flower clusters (technically cymules) that may be more than 1" wide help to distinguish this erect, aromatic 2–3' tall mountainmint from most other members of its genus. Tiny, tubular, lavender to white 2-lipped flowers protrude from a whitish, 5-parted calyx. Leaves are elliptic to lance shaped and are up to about 2" long and ¾" wide. All parts of the plant have a grayish cast.

Bloom Season: June–September.

Habitat/Range: Moist to wet pinelands, pocosin margins, savannas, and bogs. Throughout the region.

Comments: At least a dozen species of *Pycnanthemum* occur in our region, many of which are closely similar and difficult to distinguish from each other. Savanna Mountainmint is probably most similar to *P. setosum*. Both have calyx lobes with elongated, whitish, bristlelike tips. However, the main stem leaves of *P. setosum* are generally greater than ¾" wide whereas those of *P. flexuosum* are mostly narrower than ¾".

HELMET SKULLCAP
Scutellaria integrifolia Linnaeus
Mint Family (Lamiaceae or Labiatae)

Description: This clump-forming herb may produce several hairy 6–32" branched or unbranched stems. The lower leaves are triangular or egg-shaped in outline with toothed margins. The upper leaves are entire or bluntly toothed. Several 2–8" racemes of bluish purple flowers terminate the stem.

Bloom Season: May–July.

Habitat/Range: Moist pine flatwoods, edges of savannas, and moist roadsides. Throughout the region.

Comments: Helmet Skullcap is most similar to Hoary Skullcap *(S. incana)*. The 2 may be distinguished by their leaves. The leaves of Hoary Skullcap are uniformly toothed throughout the stem, whereas the uppermost leaves of Helmet Skullcap are usually entire or wavy (or only occasionally toothed). The tubular calyx of this and other species of *Scutellaria* is characterized by a small but conspicuous dishlike crest or "cap" (scutellum), which persists when the plant is in fruit, hence the common name Skullcap. *Scutella* is Latin for dish or saucer. In many species the saucer-shaped crest resembles the open seat of an old-time farm tractor.

SMALL'S SKULLCAP
Scutellaria multiglandulosa (Kearney) Small ex Harper
Mint Family (Lamiaceae or Labiatae)

Description: The flowers of Small's Skullcap are lighter blue than those of Helmet Skullcap *(S. integrifolia)*, its closest look-alike. The 4-angled stem is hairy, erect, and grows to about 15" tall. Leaves are opposite with glandular hairs, 1–2" long, and are often slightly rolled under along the margins. The 2-lipped flowers are borne in a conspicuous raceme at the top of the stem and vary in color from pale blue to nearly white.

Bloom Season: April–July.

Habitat/Range: Sandy pinelands and roadsides. Florida, Georgia, and South Carolina.

Comments: About a dozen species of *Scutellaria* occur in the southeastern United States. Small's Skullcap is most similar to Helmet Skullcap and Hoary Skullcap *(S. incana)* but may be distinguished by flower color and habitat. Helmet Skullcap occurs mostly in moist areas, whereas Hoary Skullcap typically occurs in mixed deciduous woodlands. The epithet *multiglandulosa* means "with many glands," in reference to this species' glandular leaf surfaces.

DWARF SKULLCAP

Scutellaria parvula Michaux
Mint Family (Lamiaceae or Labiatae)

Description: The erect flowering stems of this clump-forming diminutive mint arise from creamy yellow runners that contribute to the formation of large colonies in yards and along disturbed roadsides. Flowering stems are usually much less than 11" tall with short ⅜–⅝" leaves. Lower leaves have petioles that may be as long as the blade. Upper leaves are sessile or very short-stalked. The small blue flowers are about ¼" long and borne individually in the leaf axils along the upper 1–4" of the stem. All parts of the plant are hairy.

Bloom Season: March–June.

Habitat/Range: Roadsides and disturbed sites. Throughout the region.

Comments: Dwarf Skullcap can be mostly easily distinguished by combination of its small overall size, small axillary flowers, and short, sessile upper leaves. The epithet *parvula* means "small, little, or insignificant," an excellent moniker for this miniature species. Dwarf Skullcap displays weedy tendencies but is considered native to our region.

AMERICAN GERMANDER OR WOOD SAGE

Teucrium canadense Linnaeus
Mint Family (Lamiaceae or Labiatae)

Description: This is perhaps the most widespread native species in North America and has been reported from all 48 lower states and much of Canada. Its upright stature, conspicuous inflorescence, pale blue or pinkish flowers, and spreading leaves make it easy to identify. The stem is square in cross section, characteristic of the mints, and may be up to about 5' tall. Leaves are elliptic to lance shaped, 2–5" long, and coarsely toothed along the margins. Numerous 1-lipped flowers are borne in a somewhat crowded thyrse (a compound inflorescence with a central axis of branched cymes) that may be up to 1' long in robust plants. The stamens of the flowers protrude through the upper petals and arch over the flower.

Bloom Season: June–August.

Habitat/Range: Marshes, meadows, and wet roadsides, mostly near the coast. Throughout the region.

Comments: Some observers suggest that this species might be confused with species of *Stachys,* a related genus in the Mint Family. However, species of *Stachys* have 2-lipped flowers.

BLUE BUTTERWORT
Pinguicula caerulea Walter
Bladderwort Family (Lentibulariaceae)

Description: This is the only butterwort in our region with the combination of lavender-blue flowers (although white-flowered individuals are sometimes encountered) and an enlarged palate. The flowers are borne singly at the top of a 5–10" scape. The blue- and white-striped petals enclose a striking densely hairy palate that protrudes from the corolla tube. Yellowish green leaves are borne in a 2–4" rosette at the base of the flowering scape and are visible early in the year, long before flowering begins. It should be noted that the basal leaf clusters of several coastal plains butterworts are very similar in general appearance and are difficult to assign to species when flowers are absent.

Bloom Season: March–May.

Habitat/Range: Savannas, wet flatwoods, and the margins of roadside ditches. Florida, Georgia, South Carolina, and North Carolina.

Comments: The epithet *caerulea* means "dark blue." Although few plants with true dark blue flowers are encountered in any population of this insectivorous herb, Blue Butterwort's flower color remains an excellent field identification character. The flowers of Small Butterwort *(P. pumila)* are sometimes pale violet, but Blue Butterwort and Small Butterwort are easily distinguished by size and palate. Small Butterwort has a very small cluster of basal leaves, its scape averages only about 5" tall, and its hairy yellow palate is recessed within the floral tube.

FLORIDA BLUEHEARTS
Buchnera floridana Gandoger
Broomrape Family (Orobanchaceae)

Description: Florida Bluehearts is a common roadside herb in northern Florida and southeast Georgia, especially where highways pass through healthy pine flatwoods. The erect, herbaceous stem is 1–2½' tall and is normally terminated with a single flowering spike, although minor branching is sometimes evident. The bluish to purple or occasionally white flowers are tubular below but spread at the apex into 5 petals. The 1–3" leaves are mostly opposite and borne on the lower half of the stem.

Bloom Season: April–October.

Habitat/Range: Seepage bogs, savannas, flatwoods, and moist roadsides, typically in sandy sites. Florida, Georgia, South Carolina, and North Carolina.

Comments: Some authorities consider Florida Bluehearts and American Bluehearts *(B. americana)* to constitute the same species and use the scientific name *B. americana* for both. However, the 2 display several distinguishing morphological features, and it is more likely that the 2 are distinct species. The true *B. americana* has flower tubes longer than ⅜" and occurs primarily on rocky barrens in the Piedmont regions of Georgia, North Carolina, and Virginia, whereas *B. floridana* is mostly a coastal plains species and its flower tubes are usually less than ⅜" long. American Bluehearts is considered rare in Virginia and North Carolina and a species of special concern in Georgia. It should probably be more diligently searched for in limestone barrens in the Southeastern Coastal Plains.

ONE-FLOWERED BROOMRAPE OR ONE-FLOWERED CANCER ROOT
Orobanche uniflora Linnaeus
Broomrape Family (Orobanchaceae)

Description: One-Flowered Broomrape usually grows in small clusters of several, closely adjacent plants, but it is easily overlooked. The single stem is 3–6" tall, covered with gland-tipped hairs, and topped by a nodding, tubular ⅝–¾" flower that is typically pale blue or pale purple but may be nearly white. This species and several others of the Broomrape Family, notably Squaw Root *(Conopholis americana)* and Beech Drops *(Epifagus americana)*, are parasitic on the roots of oaks and other hardwood trees and are therefore normally associated with them. One-Flowered Broomrape is also apparently parasitic on Brazilian Cat's-Ear *(Hypochaeris brasiliensis* var. *tweedii)*, a non-native weed with which it is often associated.

Bloom Season: March–May.

Habitat/Range: Rich woods and close-cropped lawns closely adjacent to rich woods. Throughout the region, but perhaps mostly outside of the region in Virginia.

Comments: The common name Broomrape comes from Medieval Latin and means "broom knob" or "tuber," an apparent reference to the parasitic association between Great Broomrape *(O. major)* and the knoblike structures sometimes formed on the roots of broom *(Cytissus* sp.), a genus of easy-to-grow, European and Mediterranean shrubs that are used horticulturally in the United States. Related species have reportedly been used medicinally, both internally for bladder and kidney stones and externally as a treatment for sores and ulcers. Such sores and ulcers are sometimes referred to as cancers, which probably explains the species' common name. There seems to be no evidence that this species has been used or recommended as a cure for other cancers.

TRAILING PHLOX OR PINELAND PHLOX
Phlox nivalis Loddiges ex Sweet
Phlox Family (Polemoniaceae)

Description: The trailing habit, semi-woody or woody stem, and comparatively short (less than 1") leaves help distinguish Trailing Phlox. The other species of Phlox in our region have herbaceous stems and leaves longer than 1". The flowering shoots are erect, with numerous narrow opposite or clustered leaves and are topped by a showy arrangement of lavender to pink flowers with a darkened eye. Individual flowers consist of a narrow tube that spreads at the apex into 5 lobes. The stamens are shorter than the tube, which is a helpful field identification character.

Bloom Season: March–May.

Habitat/Range: Sandy roadsides, dry pinelands, and sandhills. Throughout the region.

Comments: The scientific epithet *nivalis* means "snow-white" or "growing near snow" and is in this instance somewhat misleading. White-flowered individuals of Trailing Phlox are only rarely encountered and the species occurs in largely snow-free regions of the Southeastern Coastal Plains, including peninsula Florida.

DRUMHEADS
Polygala cruciata Linnaeus
Milkwort Family (Polygalaceae)

Description: The comparatively large congested racemes help distinguish this perennial herb from similarly flowered milkworts. The stems are 4–20" tall, winged, 4-angled, and typically divided above into several branches, each topped by a densely flowered, headlike ½–2¾" raceme of purplish to pink flowers. The leaves are sessile, 3–4 per node, and are smallest near the base of the stem but increase progressively in size upwards.

Bloom Season: May–October.

Habitat/Range: Flatwoods, bogs, pocosins, wet roadsides, and savannas. Throughout the region.

Comments: The epithet *cruciata* means "in the form of a cross," an apt description of the 4-angled stem. The milkworts have unusual flowers, usually with 3 petals, 3 small sepals, and 2 larger sepals or wings. In most species the sepals and wings are petaloid and showier than the petals. The wings of Drumheads are triangular and easily seen. The flower stalks of the similarly flowered Shortleaf Milkwort *(P. brevifolia)* are usually over 1" long; those of Drumheads are typically shorter than ½".

HOOKER'S MILKWORT
Polygala hookeri Torrey & A. Gray
Milkwort Family (Polygalaceae)

Description: The whorled leaves and lavender
flowers of this upright herb make it at least
superficially similar to Drumheads *(P. cruciata)*.
However, the inflorescence of the present species
is not nearly so congested as the inflorescence of
Drumheads, clearly revealing the flower stalks,
even without magnification. The stems of
Hooker's Milkwort are typically unbranched and
tipped by a stalked, somewhat conical ½–2½"
raceme.

Bloom Season: June–September.

Habitat/Range: Wet prairies, flatwoods, and pine
savannas. Florida, South Carolina, and North
Carolina.

Comments: According to Bruce Sorrie and Alan
Weakley in their treatment of endemic species of
the Southeastern Coastal Plains, the distribution
of Hooker's Milkwort makes it one of about a
dozen species that are somewhat widespread on
the East Gulf Coastal Plain with disjunct
populations in North and South Carolina. This
group of species, which consists mostly of sedges
and grasses, also includes 2 species of Yellow-
Eyed Grass (*Xyris* sp.) and Goldencrest *(Lophiola
aurea)*.

RACEMED MILKWORT
Polygala polygama Walter
Milkwort Family (Polygalaceae)

Description: Racemed Milkwort typically
produces several leafy erect to leaning 12–20"
stems from a central taproot. The leaves are
alternate, mostly linear in outline, and ½–1½"
long. The central leaf vein extends beyond the
leaf tip as a tiny mucro. Flowers are borne in
2–10" terminal racemes at the ends of the stems
and branches. Most plants produce numerous
simultaneous racemes. Individual flowers are
small with a purplish corolla that is subtended by
green sepals with pinkish to whitish margins. The
fruit is a tiny black seed.

Bloom Season: May–July.

Habitat/Range: Dry pinelands and dry open
woods. Throughout the region.

Comments: Although the accompanying
photographs of Racemed Milkwort and Hooker's
Milkwort make these species appear somewhat
similar, they are unmistakable in the field by both
habit and habitat. Hooker's Milkwort never occurs
in dry uplands, nor does it produce numerous
leaning branches from a central crown. Hooker's
Milkwort is not nearly so leafy and its leaves are
whorled rather than alternate.

TINY BLUET
Houstonia pusilla Schoepf
(Syn: *Hedyotis crassifolia*)
Madder Family (Rubiaceae)

Description: The combination of solitary, red-throated flowers on an erect stalk that arises from a cluster of basal leaves distinguishes Tiny Bluet from all other species of *Houstonia* in this region. The slender, nearly threadlike stalks are about 4" tall and topped by a 4-petaled flower that is only about ¼" wide. The leaves are opposite, ¼–½" long, and mostly widest in the middle.

Bloom Season: February–April.

Habitat/Range: Woodlands and limestone glades, as well as roadsides, lawns, and other disturbed sites. Throughout the region.

Comments: The epithet *pusilla* means very small, an apt description. Quaker Ladies or Common Bluet *(H. caerulea)* is similar, but its flowers are about twice as wide and are pale blue to nearly white with a yellow throat. Most species of *Houstonia* were previously placed in the genus *Hedyotis,* a name derived from the Greek words for "sweet ear." The reason for this latter name is unclear.

EARLY BLUE VIOLET
Viola palmata Linnaeus
Violet Family (Violaceae)

Description: This extremely variable species has at least 36 synonymous scientific names (previous names by which it has been known). There is no stem; the 1–2½" leaves arise on 2–7" stalks directly from the rootstock. At least some leaves on any plant are deeply palmately lobed (originating from a single juncture, like the fingers of the human hand), hence the epithet *palmata.* The ⅝–1" flowers have 5 blue to violet petals that are splotched at the base and borne singly at the top of an upright scape that usually exceeds the length of the leaves.

Bloom Season: February–May.

Habitat/Range: Flatwoods, sandhills, wooded slopes, and alluvial bottoms. Throughout the region.

Comments: Of the 36 names for *V. palmata,* 2 are still regularly seen in guidebooks. If accepted as distinct species, *V. septemloba* is found in wet flatwoods and savannas whereas *V. esculenta,* the form pictured here, occurs in upland woods and rich southern mixed hardwood forests. *V. esculenta* is distinguished by having leaves with 3–5 lobes; the leaves of *V. septemloba* typically have 5–7 lobes.

PINK FLOWERS

This section includes flowers that vary in color from pale pink to deep rose. Since these colors grade into shades of blue and since some plants produce flowers that vary across the spectrum from blue to pink, you should check the section for blue and purple flowers if you don't find the flower you are looking for here.

PINEWOODS MILKWEED
Asclepias humistrata Walter
Dogbane Family (Apocynaceae)

Description: The stout, ascending to spreading 8–28" stem and large varicolored leaves of this sandhill herb are unique among our several species of milkweeds. The 2–4" leaves are 2–3" wide, broadest at the base, and taper to a dull-pointed tip. Leaf surfaces are dull green with a whitish cast and are decorated with conspicuous pink to lavender veins. The flowers appear whitish from above due to the pale color of the hoods but have ashy to pinkish gray strongly reflexed petals. The fruit is an elongated 3–5" follicle that splits at maturity to expose numerous dark brown ⅜" seeds, each with a conspicuous cottony appendage (technically a coma) that aids in dispersal.

Bloom Season: April–July.

Habitat/Range: Sandhills, dry pine-oak-hickory woods, and sandy roadsides. Florida, Georgia, South Carolina, and North Carolina.

Comments: The epithet *humistrata* means "low-growing or sprawling" in reference to the spreading stems that often lay nearly flat on the ground. The varicolored leaves immediately distinguish Pinewoods Milkweed from all of our other milkweeds.

PURPLE THISTLE OR BULL THISTLE
Cirsium horridulum Michaux
Aster Family (Asteraceae or Compositae)

Description: The 2–3" flower heads of Purple Thistle are protected by an intimidating cluster of narrow harshly spiny leaves at the top of a 1–5' stem, making this biennial herb our easiest thistle to recognize. The flowers are borne in erect pink to purplish or wholly yellow heads subtended by a 2" cluster of overlapping bracts (involucre). Numerous lobed 2–14" spiny leaves arm the stem and reduce in size gradually from the base of the stem to its apex.

Bloom Season: March–August.

Habitat/Range: Roadsides, coastal shell middens, flatwoods, and the borders of saltwater and freshwater marshes; often in somewhat sandy, disturbed areas. Throughout the region.

Comments: This is by far the most common of our native thistles. Entire populations of yellow-flowered plants are sometimes encountered. This has led to the alternate common name, Yellow Thistle. *Cirsium* derives from the Greek *kirsion*, meaning "thistle." The bristles (technically the pappus) on the seeds expand at maturity into fluffy thistledown and carry the seeds on the wind.

COASTAL TALL THISTLE

Cirsium nuttallii Augustin de Candolle
Aster Family (Asteraceae or Compositae)

Description: This robust thistle sometimes becomes so tall that it bends over nearly to the ground under its own weight. It is variable in stature, sometimes manifesting itself as plants less than 3' tall and at other times producing stems 10' tall or more. Large plants often have a distinctly grooved stem and produce a large, loosely branched inflorescence (technically a corymb) that may be up to about 4' tall and a 1½' wide. The flower heads are borne singly at the tips of the floral branches and consist of a conspicuous involucre subtending a mass of pale pink to nearly cream disk flowers. Involucres are less than 1" tall. There are no ray flowers. The 4–10" stem leaves are sessile and deeply divided into narrow lobes, each of which is terminated by a sharp spine that is piercing to the touch, making

the plant difficult to handle. The bases of the leaves, especially the lower leaves, extend down the stem (decurrent) as short, spiny wings.

Bloom Season: June–August.

Habitat/Range: Savannas, flatwoods, roadsides, and pastures. Throughout the region.

Comments: Coastal Tall Thistle is most similar to LeConte's Thistle, which occurs in similar habitats. However, the involucres of LeConte's Thistle are generally well over 1" tall and the inflorescence is usually unbranched or has only a few branches. The tips of the phyllaries on Coastal Tall Thistle are stiff, pointed, and curved outward and provide another good field identification character.

CAROLINA ELEPHANT'S-FOOT OR LEAFY ELEPHANT'S-FOOT

Elephantopus carolinianus Raeuschel
Aster Family (Asteraceae or Compositae)

Description: No other Elephant's-Foot in our region has the well-developed stems leaves of *E. carolinianus.* Most lower stem leaves on the present species are over 4" long, whereas those on other species are generally shorter than 2". This is an erect 1–3' perennial herb that is typically branched high on the stem rather than near the base. Flowers vary in color from pink to bluish purple and are borne in a congested head that is subtended by comparatively large conspicuous ⅜–⅞" triangular bracts.

Bloom Season: August–November.

Habitat/Range: Moist and dry forests, deciduous woodlands, and moist slopes. Throughout the region.

Comments: Four species of *Elephantopus* occur within our region, 3 of which have well-developed basal leaves but few or no stem leaves. The name *Elephantopus* means "resembling an elephant's foot" and references the supposed similarity of the well-developed basal leaf clusters in some species to the foot of an elephant. The common name obviously does not apply to the present species.

PINK THOROUGHWORT OR PINK EUPATORIUM

Fleischmannia incarnata (Walter) King & H. E. Robinson
(Syn: *Eupatorium incarnatum* Walter)
Aster Family (Asteraceae or Compositae)

Description: This erect, weak-stemmed herb typically produces numerous branches, each tipped with a small inflorescence of pink, purple, or pale blue flowers. The 1–3" leaves are opposite, stalked, and triangular in outline with coarsely toothed margins. Each leaf has 3 primary veins that arise at the base of the blade. The flat-topped inflorescence is composed of numerous ³⁄₁₆" heads, each with 18–24 tubular flowers. The fruit is a tiny achene with 5–8 vertical ridges.

Bloom Season: August–October.

Habitat/Range: Moist to somewhat dry hardwood forests; often in calcareous situations. Throughout the region.

Comments: The branches of Pink Thoroughwort sometimes climb on surrounding vegetation making large plants sometimes appear vinelike. Individual plants often flower profusely, with flower clusters terminating the tip of nearly every branch. This species was long included within the genus *Eupatorium,* which explains the alternate common name, Pink Eupatorium.

SANDHILLS BLAZING STAR

Liatris cokeri Pyne & Stucky
Aster Family (Asteraceae or Compositae)

Description: Sandhills Blazing Star is an upright or leaning 1–2½' perennial herb. Up to about 5 leafy stems are produced from a rounded cormlike root. The leaves are linear and 2–6" long with densely punctate surfaces. Tiny cilia often line the leaf margins near the base of the blade (punctations and cilia require magnification to see clearly). The pinkish tubular flowers are borne 4–10 per head in a crowded showy spikelike raceme. The fruit is a tiny achene.

Bloom Season: September–October.

Habitat/Range: Sandhills. South Carolina and North Carolina.

Comments: Sandhills Blazing Star is common in the Fall Line Hills region that cuts across the central Carolinas, although its natural range is very restricted. It was described as a new species in 1990 and is one of several Atlantic Coastal Plain endemics with similar distributions. Several species of *Liatris* occur in the Carolina Sandhills, some of which have overlapping morphological features. Sandhills Blazing Star is probably most similar to *L. secunda*. As plants of Sandhills Blazing Star mature, the flower heads tend to become increasingly secund in arrangement (appearing to grow on 1 side of the stem). This is a field identification feature that is normally associated with *L. secunda*. Individual flowers of *L. cokeri* are predominantly less than ¼" long, whereas those of *L. secunda* are predominantly greater than ¼" long.

DENSE BLAZING STAR OR DENSE GAYFEATHER
Liatris spicata (Linnaeus) Willd.
Aster Family (Asteraceae or Compositae)

Description: *Liatris spicata* arises from a subterranean cormlike base. The narrow, leafy, typically unbranched stems of this common Blazing Star may reach heights of 6' or more. The leaves are narrowly linear and about 16" long at the base of the plant but become shorter upwards. The flowers are borne in stalkless ¼–⅝" heads that are often densely crowded in an elongated spike along an extended portion of the upper stem. However, in some individuals the flowers may be more loosely arranged and well separated from one another. Individual flower heads typically contain 4–18 flowers.

Bloom Season: July–October.

Habitat/Range: Wet savannas, moist roadsides, flatwoods, and Longleaf Pinelands. Throughout the region.

Comments: The common and scientific names of this species come from its spikelike inflorescence. *Spicata* means "having a spike" or "growing in ears, like corn." Dense Blazing Star often occurs in large showy colonies, especially in recently burned wetlands. Plants are seldom strictly erect at maturity due to the weight of the flowering spike. Some authorities give the name *L spicata* var. *resinosa* to plants of this species that have short, purple involucres; the color of the involucre in variety *spicata* is green. Dense Blazing Star might be confused at a glance with *L. virgata*, *L. pilosa*, or *L. elegantula*. However, at least some of the flowering heads of these latter species display short stout stalks.

SCALY BLAZING STAR OR SCALY GAYFEATHER

Liatris squarrosa (Linnaeus) Michx.
Aster Family (Asteraceae or Compositae)

Description: Most blazing stars in our region are noted for a showy elongated inflorescence situated along an extended portion of the upper stem. Scaly Blazing Star differs by typically having 1 to few large flowering heads. Individual heads are 1–1½" long and are subtended by conspicuous stiff, sreading bracts. The stems are mostly 12–30" tall with linear leaves up to about 10" long.

Bloom Season: July–September.

Habitat/Range: Dry open ecotones, calcareous glades, and open pinelands. Throughout the region (but only at the extreme western edge of the region in Florida).

Comments: The epithet *squarrosa* means "spreading horizontally and curved at the tips," an obvious reference is to the spreading bracts that subtend the flowers; these bracts are an excellent field identification character. Scaly Blazing Star is a variable species with at least 5 varieties, 2 of which occur within our region. The stems of variety *hirsuta* display long spreading hairs whereas the stems of variety *squarrosa* have shorter, appressed or curved hairs. This species' Latin name is very similar to that of L. squarrulosa, Appalachian Gayfeather. The latter species also has relatively large heads, but occurs in our region only rarely. It is limited to only 4 counties in North Carolina, mostly in the Fall Line Hills. Although it is slightly more common in South Carolina, as its name suggests, it is more common to the west and northwest of our region.

SHORTLEAF BLAZING STAR OR SHORTLEAF GAYFEATHER
Liatris tenuifolia Nutt.
Aster Family (Asteraceae or Compositae)

Description: The erect stem of Shortleaf Blazing Star arises from a rounded corm and is thin, wandlike, and can be as much as 6' tall. Numerous narrow, linear leaves alternate on the stem, the lower ones to about 1' long and sometimes spreading or ascending. Upper leaves are abruptly and conspicuously shorter and often tightly appressed to the stem. The ¼–½" flower heads are borne on short stalks in a narrow elongated inflorescence.

Bloom Season: September–November.

Habitat/Range: Sandhill pinelands and dry, oak-dominated uplands. Florida, Georgia, and South Carolina.

Comments: The epithet *tenuifolia* means "thin, slender leaves," a good name for Shortleaf Blazing Star and one that highlights one of the species' more important field characters. No other species of *Liatris* has the combination of thin leaves (the uppermost of which are abruptly reduced in length and closely appressed to the stem), narrow inflorescence, and short-stalked flowers. Two varieties occur in our region: *tenuifolia* from South Carolina to Alabama and *quadriflora* in Florida.

ROSY CAMPHORWEED
Pluchea rosea R. K. Godfrey
Aster Family (Asteraceae or Compositae)

Description: Rosy Camphorweed has the general appearance of Stinking Camphorweed *(P. foetida)*, except the flowers are pinkish to purplish rather than dull white. The stem and leaves are often very hairy. The 2–4" leaves are sessile or clasping, lance shaped to elliptic in outline, typically toothed along the margins, and truncate at the base. The flowers are borne in compact 1–1½" clusters at the top of the stem. Plants may be up to about 3' tall.

Bloom Season: May–November.

Habitat/Range: Flatwoods, marshes, wet roadsides, and coastal swales. Florida, Georgia, South Carolina, and North Carolina.

Comments: The flower heads of Rosy Camphorweed are usually less than ¼" tall, whereas those of Stinking Camphorweed are usually greater than ¼" tall. The name Camphorweed comes from the pungent aroma of the crushed herbage that is characteristic of most species within the genus. Two purple-flowered *Pluchea* also occur in our region, both of which have stalked leaves by which they can easily be distinguished from Rosy Camphorweed.

CLIMBING ASTER

Symphyotrichum carolinianum (Walter) Wunderlin
& B. F. Hansen
(Syn: *Aster carolinianus* Walter)
Aster Family (Asteraceae or Compositae)

Description: Woody stems and a sprawling habit distinguish this species from all other blue-flowered asters in our region except, perhaps, Southern Swamp Aster *(S. elliottii),* which also occurs in wet habitats. The stems are slender, branching, hairy, climbing, and may be up to 16' long. The leaves are lance shaped, clasping at the base, 1½–4" long, and typically less than 1¼" wide. Flowering heads often terminate branches but may form a branched inflorescence. The central disk consists of small yellowish tubular disk flowers surrounded by 40–60, ¾" typically lavender to pinkish purple ray flowers.

Bloom Season: October–November.

Habitat/Range: Swamps, edges of salt marshes, border of springs and spring runs, coastal hammocks, riverbanks, and floodplains. Florida, Georgia, South Carolina, and North Carolina.

Comments: Climbing Aster is a popular native landscape plant throughout the region. It is tolerant of both sun and moderate shade and is especially useful in informal gardens, where its sprawling habit can be encouraged. Most gardeners prune it periodically to increase flower production.

GRASSLEAF ROSELING

Callisia graminea (Small) G. C. Tucker
(Syn: *Cuthbertia graminea* Small)
Spiderwort Family (Commelinaceae)

Description: Few sandhill plants can be confused with Grassleaf Roseling. The common name references the narrow, ascending dark green 1½–7" leaves; the epithet *graminea* means "grasslike." The leaves are less than ³⁄₁₆" in diameter and are much narrower than the opened sheath. Delicate pink 3-petaled flowers are borne in few-flowered cymes, usually not far above the ground (although some plants may be nearly 1½' tall). The flower petals are about ³⁄₈" long. The fruit is a tiny capsule.

Bloom Season: May–August. This species is responsive to fire. Spring burns may induce a flush of late summer flowers.

Habitat/Range: Sandhills, fields, sandy roadsides, and sandy woodlands, [chiefly in association with Longleaf Pine *(Pinus palustris)* and Turkey Oak *(Quercus laevis)*]. Throughout the region.

Comments: The genus name *Callisia* comes from the Greek word *kallos,* which means "beautiful" and is an apparent reference to the attractive leaves in some species. However, it applies equally well to the flowers of the present species.

TIEVINE OR COTTON MORNING GLORY
Ipomoea cordatotriloba Dennst.
Morning Glory Family (Convolvulaceae)

Description: The scientific name for this species may seem difficult to pronounce, but it provides an excellent description of the 1–3" leaves of this twining perennial. *Corda* means "heart shaped," in reference to the typically heart-shaped leaf bases, and *triloba* references the mostly 3-lobed blades. The flowers are funnel shaped, less than 2" long, vary in color from pink to rose-purple, and typically have a somewhat darkened center.

Bloom Season: May–October.

Habitat/Range: Roadsides, waste places, disturbed sites, bottomland woods, pond edges, and stream banks. Florida, Georgia, South Carolina, and North Carolina.

Comments: The wiry stems of this morning glory often produce dense entanglements on supporting vegetation, hence the common name Tievine. Though a native species throughout our region, Tievine often behaves like a weed on roadside fences and vegetation, making it a conspicuous roadside wildflower during summer and early fall.

SALTMARSH MORNING GLORY
Ipomoea sagittata Poir.
Morning Glory Family (Convolvulaceae)

Description: Saltmarsh Morning Glory is a low-growing twining vine found mostly in coastal habitats. It is confined entirely to the maritime zone throughout most of our region, although it becomes more widely distributed within the Florida peninsula. The leaves are alternate, 1½–4" long, well spaced along the stem, and borne on ½–1½" stalks. The blades are narrowly 3-lobed with the 2 basal lobes projecting in sharp opposition to the terminal lobe. All 3 lobes are nearly equal in size and shape. The funnel-shaped flowers are 2½–4" long and pink to rose-purple with a darkened center and a flaring apex.

Bloom Season: May–August.

Habitat/Range: Coastal fresh and saltwater marshes, interdune swales, and roadside ditches. Florida, Georgia, South Carolina, and North Carolina.

Comments: The name *sagittata* means "arrow shaped" in reference to the outline of the leaves. The combination of deeply sagittate leaves and rose-purple flowers is an excellent field identification character.

PINK SUNDEW
Drosera capillaris Poiret
Sundew Family (Droseraceae)

Description: Of the 3 species of sundew that occur primarily within the Southeastern Coastal Plains, Pink Sundew is the more widespread and commonly encountered. Its basal leaf clusters are usually less than 3" wide but may be up to 5" in robust plants, and the leafstalks have at least a few long hairs. Flowers are about ½" across and are borne near the top of a threadlike 1½–9" scape that lacks gland-tipped hairs. Although called Pink Sundew, flower color varies from pink to white and cannot be used as a reliable field identification character.

Bloom Season: May–August.

Habitat/Range: Savannas, wet flatwoods, and moist sandy openings in pinelands, including stump holes and the ruts of abandoned woods roads. Throughout the region.

Comments: Pink Sundew might be confused with either Dwarf Sundew *(D. brevifolia)* or Water Sundew *(D. intermedia)*. Dwarf Sundew is typically smaller and is easily distinguished by the gland-tipped hairs that adorn its flowering scape. The much longer leafstalks of Water Sundew lack hairs and the leaf cluster is raised above the ground on a short stalk.

HAIRY WICKY
Kalmia hirsuta Walter
Heath Family (Ericaceae)

Description: The tiny alternate leaves and hairy stems distinguish this small low-growing evergreen shrub from most other species of *Kalmia* in our region. Plants average less than 2' tall and are bushy and more or less rounded in form. The alternate light green leaves are variable in size and shape but are typically less than ⅝" long. Flowers petals are joined to form a ½–¾" cup-shaped pink or sometimes white corolla with maroon internal markings, including a ring of reddish spots near the base. The 10 stamens are curved backwards and the anthers are lodged in pockets in the petals. The fruit is a hardened capsule.

Bloom Season: June–July.

Habitat/Range: Flatwoods and pine savannas. Florida, Georgia, and South Carolina.

Comments: Although the specific epithet *hirsuta* means "hairy," the amount of hairiness varies significantly from plant to plant. White-flowered plants may be confused with White Wicky *(K. cuneata)*, a rare species of the Carolina Sandhills. The leaves of White Wicky are wider than ⅝"; those of Hairy Wicky are less than ⅝" wide.

MOUNTAIN LAUREL, MOUNTAIN IVY, OR CALICO-BUSH

Kalmia latifolia Linnaeus
Heath Family (Ericaceae)

Description: Mountain Laurel is widespread across the eastern United States but is far more common in the mountains than in the Piedmont and coastal plains. Its occurrences range in elevation from nearly sea level to about 5,000 feet. Mountain Laurel is a large sprawling evergreen shrub with thick, alternate, dark green 4" leaves. The 1" flowers are typical of the genus, with a cup-shaped corolla that contains 10 pockets that lodge the anthers. Typical plants bear pinkish flowers, although flower color varies widely and plants with mostly white flowers are not uncommon. The fruit is a hardened ⅜" 5-lobed capsule.

Bloom Season: March–June.

Habitat/Range: Bluffs and stream edges in rich deciduous forests. Throughout the region. but marginal to and mostly west of our region in Florida.

Comments: Honey produced from the flowers of Mountain Laurel contains grayanotoxins, which can cause "honey poisoning" similar to the poisoning from *Rhododendron* honey. This condition can produce dizziness, weakness, excessive perspiration, nausea, and vomiting.

SANDHILLS MILKVETCH

Astragalus michauxii (Kuntze) F. J. Hermann
Pea Family (Fabaceae or Leguminosae)

Description: This Southeastern Coastal Plains endemic is the tallest *Astragalus* in our region. Mature plants are ascending or erect perennial herbs 1–3' tall. Leaves are compound with 21–31, ⅜–1" leaflets and 1–6" stalks. Leaflets may be both alternate and opposite but are often un-paired along the main leaf axis. Several pink or rose-pink ½–¾" flowers are borne in a conspic-uous raceme. The fruit is a curving ¾–1¼" legume.

Bloom Season: April–June.

Habitat/Range: Sandhills. Florida, Georgia, South Carolina, and North Carolina.

Comments: *Astragalus* is the Greek word for another group of legumes but fits this genus as well. The genus includes 2,000 species worldwide, 500 of which occur in North America. Some species produce toxins and have been implicated in livestock poisoning. At least 1 western species is known as Locoweed due its deleterious effect on cattle. Livestock that ingest Locoweed suffer staggering, trembling, and paralysis. Sandhills Milkvetch is considered vulnerable in North Carolina and imperiled in Georgia.

PINK TASSELS
Dalea carnea (Michx.) Poir. var. *carnea*
Pea Family (Fabaceae or Leguminosae)

Description: Pink Tassels is a good name for this species. The flowers are borne in small, compact tassel-like ½–1⅝" spikes at the tips of mostly ascending branches on a diffusely branched stem. Each inflorescence consists of numerous small pinkish (to sometimes whitish) flowers less than ¼" long. The compound leaves are alternate, well spaced along the branch and divided into 7–11 narrow, oblong leaflets, each of which is usually less than ½" long.

Bloom Season: June–October.

Habitat/Range: Dry to slightly moist sandy pinelands and flatwoods. Florida and Georgia (where listed as critically imperiled).

Comments: *Dalea carnea* is considered by some authorities to consist of 3 varieties, including variety *albida* and *gracilis,* both of which have white flowers and also occur in our region only in Florida and Georgia. Other authorities treat all 3 as distinct species. The primary stem leaves of *D. albida* have only 5 leaflets and *D. gracilis* is a spreading to decumbent, vinelike herb confined mostly to the East Gulf Coastal Plain from southwest Georgia to Louisiana. *C. carnea* is considered critically imperiled in Georgia. All 3 of these species are only questionably secure throughout their ranges.

NAKED TICK TREFOIL

Desmodium nudiflorum (Linnaeus) DC.
Pea Family (Fabaceae or Leguminosae)

Description: The slender leafless flowering and fruiting (fertile) stem of this perennial herb seems out of proportion with its shorter leafy sterile stem. The 3-parted leaves have 2–4" stalks, appear to be clustered near the ground, and are well separated from the flowers. Fertile stems are up to about 30" tall and often arise from near the base of the plant. They are typically erect at first but droop or lean with age, often at an angle of less than 45°. Numerous pink to sometimes white long-stalked ⅜" pealike flowers adorn the upper ⅕ of the flowering stem. The fruit is a dry, flattened, mostly 1" 2–3 chambered legume (loment) that is straight across one edge and scalloped along the other and has a rough, sticky surface that aids in seed dispersal.

Bloom Season: July–August.

Habitat/Range: Rich, deciduous woods, hammocks, southern mixed hardwood forests, and bluffs. Throughout the region.

Comments: The genus *Desmodium* is a large group of closely related and sometimes difficult-to-identify species. The present species is immediately recognizable by its separate leaf-bearing sterile stem and leafless flowering stem (*nudiflorum* means "naked flower," an allusion to this condition). The genus name *Desmodium* is from the Greek for "band" or "chain" and is a reference to the deeply scalloped loment. The common name "tick" derives from the fruit, which attaches itself to passersby, reminiscent of a tick. Trefoil is from the Middle French word *trefeuil,* which was derived from the Latin word meaning "3-parted leaf."

SENSITIVE BRIER
Mimosa quadrivalvis Linnaeus
(Syn: *M. microphylla* Dryander; *Schrankia microphylla* [Dryander] Macbride)
Pea Family (Fabaceae or Leguminosae)

Description: No other trailing vine in our region has the combination of prickly stem, featherlike leaves, and rounded heads of bright pink flowers. Stems may be up to about 6' long but are usually shorter and lined with attractive, divided featherlike leaves, each of which has 4–11 pairs of leaflets. Flowers are typically bright pink but may be almost white and are borne in a globular ½–1" cluster from the leaf axils. The fruit is a linear to oblong 1–5" legume.

Bloom Season: June–September.

Habitat/Range: Sandhills, flatwoods, dry margins of savannas, disturbed areas. Throughout the region.

Comments: The common name Sensitive Brier derives from the habit of the leaf segments folding upward along the axis when touched. The genus name *Mimosa* comes from the Greek word *mimos,* or "a mimic," and is also reported to be a reference to the "sensitive" leaves. The thorns are typically small and only mildly irritating. The correct nomenclature for this species is controversial. It may be seen listed by several scientific names.

DWARF BRISTLY LOCUST
Robinia nana Elliott
(Syn: *Robinia hispida* var. *nana*)
Pea Family (Fabaceae or Leguminosae)

Description: It is not difficult to discern why some authorities consider this species to be a variety of Bristly Locust *(R. hispida)*. On first inspection flowering individuals have the appearance of poorly situated plants attempting to survive under xeric sandhill conditions. However, whereas Bristly Locust is a shrub or small tree, Dwarf Bristly Locust is a low, sparingly branched or unbranched shrub or subshrub to about 2½' tall. The stem is typically zigzag in appearance and often produces obvious nodal spines. The fruit is an oblong 1¼–2½" legume. However, plants seldom produce fruit, spreading instead by extensive clonal suckering.

Bloom Season: April–June.

Habitat/Range: Sandhills and dry forests. Georgia, South Carolina, and North Carolina.

Comments: Dwarf Bristly Locust is part of a confusing complex of clonally reproducing plants. About 15 species have been described, most of which are today considered varieties of Bristly Locust. The epithet *nana* means "dwarf," an apt appellation.

GOAT'S RUE
Tephrosia virginiana (Linnaeus) Persoon
Pea Family (Fabaceae or Leguminosae)

Description: The flower color of Goat's Rue qualifies it for at least 2 sections of this guide. The upright standard petal is green in bud but yellowish to cream at maturity; the wing petals are pink; and the keel petal is often striped pink and yellow. Goat's Rue is an erect 1½–3' perennial herb that may be an abundant ground cover component in healthy Longleaf Pinelands. The leaves are pinnately compound but have a single terminal leaflet (technically imparipinnate). Leaflets are entire and ½–1" long, and may number 25 or more, although leaves with fewer leaflets are more common. The fruit is a narrow, flattened 1–2" legume.

Bloom Season: May–June.

Habitat/Range: Sandhills, Longleaf Pinelands, and rocky woods. Throughout the region.

Comments: The genus name *Tephrosia* means "ash-colored," in reference to the grayish pubescence on the leaves of some species. Goat's Rue is easily distinguished from other members of its genus by its upright, single-stemmed shrubby appearance in conjunction with its densely flowered racemes of 2-colored flowers.

BITTER-BLOOM, COMMON MARSHPINK, OR ROSEPINK
Sabatia angularis (Linnaeus) Pursh
Gentian Family (Gentianaceae)

Description: Common Marshpink is considered by some authorities to be the most common and frequently encountered member of its genus. Its 8–32" stem is freely branched and conspicuously quadrangular or tetragonal in cross section, often with distinct (but tiny) wings at the stem angles. The leaves are opposite, lance shaped or ovate, and ¾–2" long. The 5-petaled flowers are pink (rarely nearly white) and borne in a conspicuous, panicle-like inflorescence. Flower petals are about ¾" long.

Bloom Season: July–August.

Habitat/Range: Upland forests, forest edges, glades, and meadows. Throughout the region.

Comments: The epithet *angularis* means "angular," an allusion to the sharply angled stems that provide an excellent field identification character. Unlike many of our Marshpinks, Common Marshpink is a mostly upland species, although it sometimes occurs along the edges of upland streams.

SLENDER MARSHPINK OR SLENDER ROSEGENTIAN
Sabatia campanulata (Linnaeus) Torrey
Gentian Family (Gentianaceae)

Description: Slender Marshpink is a perennial 1–2' herb that often produces several stems from a branched, knotlike, woody base. The leaves are ½–1¼" long, spreading or ascending in habit, and narrowly lance-shaped in outline. The 5-petaled flowers are rose-pink and borne at the tips of the branches. Petals are up to ¾" long and subtended by a narrow sepal that usually equals or exceeds the petal in length. The center of the flower bears a yellow spot outlined in maroon.

Bloom Season: June–August.

Habitat/Range: Savannas, bogs, and flatwoods. Throughout the region.

Comments: Slender Marshpink is very similar to Rose-of-Plymouth *(S. stellaris).* The two may be separated by the length of the sepals. Those of Slender Marshpink are equal to or occasionally longer than the petals, as shown in the photo. Those of Rose-of-Plymouth typically do not exceed about ¾ the length of the petals.

PINEWOODS ROSEPINK
Sabatia gentianoides Ell.
Gentian Family (Gentianaceae)

Description: Pinewoods Rosepink is the only pink-flowered *Sabatia* in our region that produces a headlike cluster of sessile flowers at the top of the stem. The flowers of all others are solitary. Each flower cluster is subtended by narrow 1–2" bracts that extend well beyond the petals and serve as conspicuous field marks. The petals are ¾–1" long. The stems are 12–18" tall, which is somewhat shorter than our other many-petaled Rosepinks. The basal leaves typically resemble a spatula in outline; those along the stem are narrowly linear.

Bloom Season: June–August.

Habitat/Range: Wet pine savannas, wet flatwoods, wet ditches, and seepage areas above drainages and depressions. Florida, Georgia, South Carolina, and North Carolina.

Comments: The epithet *gentianoides* means "like a gentian" and references the clustered flowers. Numerous species in the Gentian Family, especially of the genus *Gentiana,* bear multiple flowers closely set at the top of the stem.

ROSE-OF-PLYMOUTH
Sabatia stellaris Pursh
Gentian Family (Gentianaceae)

Description: Rose-of-Plymouth is an erect annual herb to about 20" tall with opposite ascending leaves. Upper leaves are narrow and up to about 1½" long; lower leaves are slightly shorter, thicker, and broader. Pink, 5-petaled flowers are borne on straight, slender 2–4" stalks. The petals are slightly over ½" long and subtended by narrow sepals that usually do not exceed ¾ the length of the petal.

Bloom Season: July–September.

Habitat/Range: Prairies, wet roadside, salt and brackish marshes, and coastal swales. Throughout the region.

Comments: Rose-of-Plymouth is likely to be confused only with *S. campanulata,* a perennial that typically has several stems from a single base and sepals that nearly equal the length of the petals. *S. stellaris* is an annual that is normally single stemmed, and its sepals do not exceed about ¾ the length of the petals. However, sepal length is variable in both species, making them sometimes difficult to identify.

HENBIT OR HENBIT DEADNETTLE
Lamium amplexicaule Linnaeus
Mint Family (Lamiaceae or Labiatae)

Description: Henbit is a non-native weed introduced from Eurasia. It has become well established in North America and has been reported from all of the lower 48 states. This is an erect or more often reclining annual herb that produces several 6–12" branches from the base. The leaves vary from triangular to nearly round in outline and are typically less than 1¼" long. Several tiny ¼–½" flowers are borne in a headlike arrangement near the top of the stem. The inflorescence is subtended by conspicuous leaflike bracts.

Bloom Season: Year around, but more prolifically in early spring from about February to April.

Habitat/Range: Lawns, roadsides, mowed fields, and similar disturbed areas. Throughout the region.

Comments: Henbit is 1 of several weeds that are common in lawns and roadsides and is often found growing in association with such non-native species as Common Chickweed *(Stellaria media),* Corn Speedwell *(Veronica arvensis),* and several species of clover (*Trifolium* spp.), as well as our native Wild Geranium *(Geranium carolinianum).* Large colonies are very showy.

SPOTTED BEEBALM OR DOTTED HORSEMINT
Monarda punctata Linnaeus
Mint Family (Lamiaceae or Labiatae)

Description: Spotted Beebalm is a showy perennial herb with a hairy 1½–3' stem. All parts of the plant are pleasantly aromatic. Handling the leaves and stem often imparts a fragrant scent to the skin. The leaves are lance shaped to elliptic, 1–4" long, and up to about ⅝" wide. The flowers are 2 lipped with a long upper lip and lobed lower lip. The petals are actually pale yellow to nearly white with dark purple spots but are nearly overshadowed by the large, showy, pink to lavender leaflike subtending bracts.

Bloom Season: July–October.

Habitat/Range: Fields, sandy woods, roadsides, and floodplains. Throughout the region.

Comments: The epithet *punctata* means "spotted," in reference to the flowers. American Indians used a leaf tea of Dotted Horsemint to treat flu, colds, fevers, and coughs; and medical doctors once prescribed it to treat digestive disorders. The more northern *M. punctata* var. *vilicaulis* occurs sparingly in the Coastal Plain of North Carolina but was probably introduced to the state.

EASTERN FALSE DRAGONHEAD OR SAVANNA OBEDIENT-PLANT
Physostegia purpurea (Walter) Blake
Mint Family (Lamiaceae or Labiatae)

Description: The stem of Obedient-Plant tends to hold its position if bent, hence its "obedience" to manipulation. Eastern False Dragonhead is an erect, square-stemmed perennial herb more than 3' tall. The leaves are opposite, lance shaped, 2–6" long, and up to 2½" wide but are reduced in size markedly below the inflorescence. The tubular corolla is very showy and averages about 1" long. The fruit is a tiny nutlet.

Bloom Season: Predominately May–August, sometimes later.

Habitat/Range: Savannas, marshes, and wet ditches. Florida, Georgia, South Carolina, and North Carolina.

Comments: Several species of *Physostegia* occur in our region. The blades of the uppermost pair of leaves below the inflorescence are usually about the same size as the floral bracts in Eastern False Dragonhead, which provides an excellent field identification character for distinguishing it from Tidal Marsh Obedient-Plant *(P. leptophylla)* and Southern Obedient-Plant *(P. virginiana),* both of which overlap in flowering time with Eastern False Dragonhead and also occur in wetland habitats.

FLORIDA BETONY, FLORIDA HEDGENETTLE, OR RATTLESNAKE-WEED

Stachys floridana Shuttleworth ex. Bentham
Mint Family (Lamiaceae or Labiatae)

Description: Florida Betony often forms large colonies in weedy lawns and roadsides. Stems are erect, 4–20" tall, and topped with a conical inflorescence of white to pale pinkish flowers with pink to purplish spots. The leaves are ovate, 1¾–2¾" long, coarsely toothed along the margins, and truncate at the base. The stalks of the lower and basal leaves are at least ⅓ as long as the blade. The belowground portion of the plant consists of a snakelike rhizome that gives the species one of its common names.

Bloom Season: April–July.

Habitat/Range: Roadsides, weedy fields, and moist lawns and gardens. Presumably native only to Florida, but widespread throughout our region.

Comments: The name *Stachys* is common to many plant names and is Greek for "ear of corn." Florida Betony is very weedy and can be difficult to eradicate once established. The combination of comparatively long leafstalks that can be as long as the leaf blades, conspicuous rhizomes, and flowers exceeding ⅜" long help distinguish Florida Betony from similar members of the genus.

SMALL BUTTERWORT

Pinguicula pumila Michx.
Bladderwort Family (Lentibulariaceae)

Description: This is our smallest butterwort, averaging less than 5" tall with a basal leaf cluster not usually exceeding about 1¾" wide. The leaves are pale green with conspicuously in-rolled margins and down-turned apices. The upper surfaces of the leaves and all sides of the flowering stem are covered with sticky glandular hairs that are adapted to the plant's insectivorous habit. The flowers are about ½–¾" wide when fully open and range in color from pale violet to almost white. The hairy, pale yellow palate does not protrude from the floral tube.

Bloom Season: January–May.

Habitat/Range: Moist to wet roadsides, savannas, bogs, and boggy flatwoods depressions. Florida, Georgia, South Carolina, and extreme southeastern North Carolina.

Comments: Small Butterwort often grows in extensive colonies populated by a few dozen to several hundred plants. The combination of its small size, pale flowers, and short palate easily distinguishes it from all of our other butterworts. The butterworts constitute one of our several groups of insectivorous species.

PURPLE BLADDERWORT
Utricularia purpurea Walt.
Bladderwort Family (Lentibulariaceae)

Description: Purple Bladderwort is a free-floating, carnivorous aquatic with pink to purplish flowers borne near the tops of 2–4" stems. Flower stalks may have up to 5 flowers, though only 1 is typically open at time. Each flower is less than ½" long. Most of the plant's vegetative structure is submerged and consists of whorls of brownish to tan branches adorned with tiny traplike bladders that are adapted to capture insects. Each bladder is equipped with a tiny orifice covered by a thin membrane. When stimulated, the membrane snaps open. The lower pressure within the bladder forces passing insects inside before the membrane recloses

Bloom Season: All year, but predominately May–September.

Habitat/Range: Swamp edges, ditches, roadside pools, acid ponds, manmade impoundments, and beaver ponds. Throughout the region.

Comments: Purple Bladderwort is a food source for ducks and geese and is probably spread by waterfowl. Though considered a protected species in Mississippi, it is widespread across the eastern United States and can be somewhat weedy once established. Robust colonies can cover the entire surface of small ponds and roadside pools. When in full flower, such massed populations cast an attractive purplish to pinkish haze over the water surface.

HALBERDLEAF ROSEMALLOW OR SMOOTH MARSHMALLOW

Hibiscus laevis Allioni
Mallow Family (Malvaceae)

Description: Halberdleaf Rosemallow takes its common name from its distinctive leaves, which are shaped like an arrowhead with a sharp-pointed tip and have basal lobes that diverge at nearly right angles from the midrib. The 3–7" leaves are alternate, toothed along the margins, and borne on medium to long stalks that may equal the blade in length. Stems normally do not exceed about 6' tall but may reach 8'. The flowers have 5 pink or pale pink 2–2½" petals with a deep pink base. The 1½" capsules are essentially without hairs on the outside but split at maturity to produce densely hairy reddish brown seeds.

Bloom Season: May–September.

Habitat/Range: Wet roadside ditches, marshes, floodplains, and swamps. Throughout the region.

Comments: The epithet *laevis* means "smooth," in reference to the general lack of hairs on all parts of the plant surface. The combination of Halberdleaf Rosemallow's pink flowers and distinctive leaves help identify it.

SEASHORE MARSHMALLOW OR VIRGINIA SALTMARSH MALLOW

Kosteletzkya virginica (Linnaeus) C. Presl ex A. Gray
Mallow Family (Malvaceae)

Description: The showy hibiscus-like flowers make this species immediately recognizable as a member of the Mallow Family. Several branching stems are produced from the base and sometimes reach 8' tall, although somewhat shorter plants are more common. The leaves are alternate, toothed, 2½–7" long, and mostly triangular in outline with a heart-shaped or flared base. However, leaf shape can be quite variable from plant to plant or even on a given plant. Numerous pinkish flowers with 1–1½" petals are borne in a branching inflorescence at the top of the stem. The fruit is a hairy 5-chambered capsule containing numerous smooth dark brown seeds.

Bloom Season: June–August.

Habitat/Range: Margins of fresh and saltwater marshes, ditches, and coastal clearings. Throughout the region.

Comments: This species is sometimes called the Polish Hibiscus due to its scientific name but is actually named in honor of Vincenz Franz Kosteletzky, a Czechoslovakian writer on topics of medical botany. The genus name should be pronounced Kos-te-letz'-kya.

SAVANNA MEADOW BEAUTY

Rhexia alifanus Walter
Melastome Family (Melastomataceae)

Description: Savanna Meadow Beauty is perhaps our showiest meadow beauty and is easily identified by combination of its tall glabrous stem, opposite lance-shaped leaves, and comparatively large rose-pink flowers. The erect stems are wandlike, up to about 3' tall, and seldom branched. Leaves are bluish green with 3 distinctive longitudinal veins. Four mostly 1" flower petals are subtended by a conspicuous urn-shaped ⅜–½" floral tube that remains on the plant long after the petals have fallen. Eight conspicuous stamens are terminated by bright yellow anthers that give the stamens a hooklike appearance.

Bloom Season: June–August.

Habitat/Range: Bogs, flatwoods, savannas, roadsides, and the margins of ditches. Florida, Georgia, South Carolina, and North Carolina.

Comments: The epithet *alifanus* is used for no other plant. Allifae (now Alife) is a town north of Naples, Italy, where large drinking mugs called *Allifani* were once made. The Roman poet Horace writes of a feast during which wine was consumed from such mugs. Hence, *alifanus* may well be an allusion to the large, muglike floral tube (fruit) subtending the flower petals. Urn-shaped floral tubes are consistent features among our *Rhexia* and constitute a very helpful field identification character. The tall glabrous stem and opposite glabrous leaves help make this species one of our easier meadow beauties to identify.

WEST INDIES MEADOW BEAUTY

Rhexia cubensis Grisebach
Melastome Family (Melastomataceae)

Description: This colony forming herb sometimes spreads by underground rhizomes. Most plants are 1–2' tall with glandular-hairy stems. The stem is slightly angled in cross section but with uneven sides. Two sides of the stem are mostly narrow and concave whereas the other 2 are wider and convex. Flowers are borne in several-flowered cymes at the tips of the branches. Petals are up to about ⅞" long and lack glandular hairs but are subtended by a hairy floral tube that is typically ½" or longer. Leaves are opposite, linear, and ¾–1½" long.

Bloom Season: June–September.

Habitat/Range: Limesinks, saltmarshes, flatwoods, and pond margins. Florida, Georgia, South Carolina, and North Carolina; more common in the Florida peninsula, south of our region.

Comments: The specific epithet *cubensis* refers to this species' Caribbean distribution. In the northern parts of our region, it is found mostly nearer the coast but is widespread in Florida. The combination of uneven stem sides, long floral tubes, and mostly glabrous flower petals help distinguish it.

NUTTALL'S MEADOW BEAUTY

Rhexia nuttallii James
Melastome Family (Melastomataceae)

Description: Nuttall's Meadow Beauty and Fringed Meadow Beauty *(R. petiolata)* are very similar in habitat, form, and habit. They may be easily distinguished from one another by their floral tubes (hypanthia). Those of Nuttall's Meadow Beauty have conspicuous glandular hairs; those of Fringed Meadow Beauty are smooth. Plants of Nuttall's Meadow Beauty are erect herbs, usually less than 1' tall. The opposite, ovate ½–¾" leaves are conspicuously hairy along the margins. Up to about 8 rose-colored flowers with ½" petals are borne near the top of the stem.

Bloom Season: June–August.

Habitat/Range: Flatwoods, savannas, and bogs. Florida and Georgia; much more common and widespread in Florida.

Comments: The more widespread Fringed Meadow Beauty is typically taller and leafier than Nuttall's Meadow Beauty. Nuttall's Meadow Beauty is named in honor of Thomas Nuttall (1786–1839), an English botanist who traveled extensively throughout the southeastern United States during the early 1800s. Several species from our region are named for or by him.

FRINGED MEADOW BEAUTY
Rhexia petiolata Walt.
Melastome Family (Melastomataceae)

Description: The 1 to several stems of Fringed Meadow Beauty are 6–30" tall and arise from a hardened base. The leaves are less than 1" long, opposite, sessile, and often angle sharply upwards. The margins of the leaves are lined with short conspicuous hairs. The flowers are borne singly or more often in small, compact, few-flowered clusters at the tip of the stem. The petals are pink and usually less than ¾" long; the anthers are showy and hooklike. The ⅜" urn-shaped floral tube below the petals lacks hairs.

Bloom Season: June–September.

Habitat/Range: Savannas, flatwoods, and bogs. Throughout the region.

Comments: Fringed Meadow Beauty is often so low growing that it escapes notice below taller savanna grasses and flatwoods shrubs. It is most similar in habit, foliage, and flower color to *R. nuttallii*. The floral tube of *R. nutallii* is conspicuously covered with glandular hairs, whereas the flora tube of *R. petiolata* lacks hairs.

HANDSOME HARRY
Rhexia virginica Linnaeus
Melastome Family (Melastomataceae)

Description: Handsome Harry produces an erect, somewhat rigid, often robust stem that divides into several flowering branches at or near its apex. The mid portion of the stem is angled or squared in cross section with all 4 sides equal in width. The opposite, mostly lance-shaped leaves bear 3–5 conspicuous parallel veins and are up to about 3" long, finely toothed along the margins, and spreading to moderately ascending in habit. The flowers are an attractive pink or rose-purple with 4, ¾" petals and bright yellow hooklike anthers. The urn-shaped ⅜" floral tube below the petals may be hairy or smooth.

Bloom Season: July–October.

Habitat/Range: Wet ditches, savannas, flatwoods, and pond margins, sometimes in standing water. Throughout the region.

Comments: The common name for this showy Meadow Beauty isn't difficult to understand. A colony of these plants in full flower is a spectacular sight.

95

BEARDED GRASS-PINK
Calopogon barbatus (Walt.) Ames
Orchid Family (Orchidaceae)

Description: The slender, rigid, erect 9–27" stem of Bearded Grass-Pink is greenish below and often purplish or tinged with purple above. Only 1 or 2 narrow "grasslike" leaves are usually present, although these may disappear by flowering time leaving only a wiry stem terminated by a showy inflorescence. Up to 7 bright pink or magenta mostly 1" wide flowers may be open at once. The lateral sepals and petals are overtopped by an upright lip petal that produces a showy beard of yellow clublike hairs, giving this species its common name.

Bloom Season: March–June.

Habitat/Range: Moist to wet pinelands, savannas, moist roadside ditches, and the edges of bays and swamps. Florida, Georgia, South Carolina, and North Carolina.

Comments: Several species of *Calopogon* occur in our region. Common Grass-Pink *(C. tuberosus)* is closest in color to the present species but has larger flowers that open 1 or 2 at a time in delayed succession. Pale Grass-Pink, which is sometimes pale pink and at other times almost white, is similar in flower and stem size. The flowers of Pale Grass-Pink also open a few at a time in gradual succession up the stem but the lateral sepals are reflexed and often strongly curving, unlike those of Bearded Grass-Pink. The pollination mechanism is similar for all of the Grass-Pinks. Visiting insects are drawn to the upright arching lip, which bends under the insect's weight, causing the visitor's back to come into contact with the fertile portions of the flower.

PALE GRASS-PINK
Calopogon pallidus Chapman
Orchid Family (Orchidaceae)

Description: Pale Grass-Pink is a 6–18" terrestrial orchid with a slender erect stem that is often zigzag near the apex. It has 1–2 narrow "grasslike" basal leaves. Flower color is extremely variable and varies from pink to white. The flowers typically open 1 at a time sequentially up the stem. The ½–1" lateral sepals are distinctively reflexed backwards with their apices behind the flower. The ascending lip petal is adorned with a conspicuous deep purple splotch and yellowish orange hairs.

Bloom Season: April–June.

Habitat/Range: Savannas, bogs, wet to moist pinelands and flatwoods, moist roadside ditches, and sphagnum bogs. Throughout the region.

Comments: This genus includes only 5 species worldwide, all of which occur in the United States mostly in the Southeastern Coastal Plains. Only the large-flowered Common Grass-Pink *(C. tuberosus)* occurs outside of the continental U. S. The epithet *pallidus* means "pale," referring to the supposition that the flowers are much less colorful than those of *C. barbatus* or *C. tuberosus,* 2 of the closest look-alikes. The common and scientific names notwithstanding, some individuals may have strikingly deep pink to almost magenta flowers. The strongly reflexed lateral petals are an excellent field identification character. Hybrids between *C. pallidus* and the Many Flowered Grass-Pink *(C. multiflorus)* have been reported but are not common.

COMMON GRASS-PINK

Calopogon tuberosus (Linnaeus) BSP
Orchid Family (Orchidaceae)

Description: The slender erect stem of this Common Grass-Pink may be nearly 3' tall, although heights less than 2' are more typical. One or 2 (occasionally more) slender leaves arise from near the base of the stem. Fifteen or more bright rose-pink, mostly 1½" flowers often adorn the upper third of the stem and open progressively from the base of the inflorescence to its apex; fewer than 4 are usually open at any one time. The comparatively large conspicuous capsules that follow flowering make the plant identifiable even after all of the flowers have fallen.

Bloom Season: March–August, although mostly May–June.

Habitat/Range: Savannas, moist to wet pinelands, sphagnum bogs, marshes, and the edges of cypress ponds. Throughout the region.

Comments: Common Grass-Pink is the tallest, largest-flowered *Calopogon* in our region and is widespread across the eastern United States. It was long known by the scientific name *C. pulchellus*, the epithet of which means "beautiful or pretty," a fitting appellation. The genus name derives from the Greek *kalos*, meaning "beautiful," and *pogon*, meaning "a beard," in reference to the showy hairs that adorn the lip of most of this genus's North American species. Common Grass-Pink occurs in situations similar to Bearded Grass-Pink but typically flowers somewhat later. Plants with pale pink or even white flowers are sometimes encountered but are easily distinguished from Pale Grass-Pink *(C. pallidus)* by the larger flower size.

LARGE SPREADING POGONIA OR ROSEBUD ORCHID

Pogonia divaricata (Linnaeus) R. Br .
(Syn: *Cleistes divaricata* [Linnaeus] Ames)
Orchid Family (Orchidaceae)

Description: Two species of Spreading Pogonia occur in our region; the other is *P. bifaria*. As its common name suggests, Large Spreading Pogonia is a more robust plant than its counterpart, with taller stems (up to about 28") and larger flowers. The lip and wing petals of Large Spreading Pogonia usually exceed 1¼" in length and the sepals normally exceed 1⅝"; longer in all cases than the corresponding flower parts of *P. bifaria*. Flower color in Large Spreading Pogonia is generally pink in contrast to the mostly white-flowered *P. bifaria*. Both species are characterized by the attractive spreading sepals that give them their common names.

Bloom Season: May–June.

Habitat/Range: Open pinelands and pine flatwoods. Throughout the region.

Comments: There is disagreement about the correct scientific name for the 2 species of Spreading Pogonia. Some authorities classify them within the genus *Cleistes,* a Greek word meaning "closed" in reference to the narrow corolla. The epithet *divaricata* means spreading, an excellent description of the ornate recurved sepals.

ROSE POGONIA OR SNAKEMOUTH ORCHID

Pogonia ophioglossoides (Linnaeus) Ker Gawl.
Orchid Family (Orchidaceae)

Description: The name *Pogonia* is Greek for "bearded," in reference to the conspicuously fringed lip petal, which is adorned along the central veins with short, fleshy, yellowish to whitish beardlike bristles. Most species of orchids in this genus have a fringed and bearded lip. The ⅝–1¼" flowers of Rose Pogonia vary from rosy pink to lavender or almost white and are borne singly or in clusters of 2–3 at the tip of the stem. Individual flowers consist of 3 petals and 3 often spreading sepals. Stems are slender and erect. Typical plants are less than 16" tall but may reach 2'. Most plants have a single leaf about halfway up the stem and a leaflike bract subtending the flowers, although plants with 2 stem leaves are occasionally encountered. The fruit is a capsule.

Bloom Season: March–May.

Habitat/Range: Savannas, bogs, flatwoods, and wet roadside ditches. Throughout the region.

Comments: This delicate somewhat low-growing orchid is distributed throughout the eastern United States but is considered vulnerable in our region in all states but South Carolina.

SCALELEAF FALSE FOXGLOVE OR SCALELEAF AGALINIS

Agalinis aphylla (Benth.) Pennell
Broomrape Family (Orobanchaceae)

Description: This 1–3' herb is 1 of 2 species of False Foxglove in our region that have scalelike leaves. The stem is stiff, erect, and wiry, and tends to be taller than the surrounding ground cover. The leaves are opposite, whitish, and well spaced along the stem, and reduced to obscure ⅛" triangular bracts (the epithet *aphylla* means "without leaves"). Flowers are purple to pink, to about ¾" long, and decorated within the throat with yellow lines and purple spots.

Bloom Season: September–November.

Habitat/Range: Moist pinelands and wet pine savannas. Florida, Georgia, South Carolina, and North Carolina.

Comments: Scaleleaf False Foxglove is similar in many respects to *A. filicaulis*, another species that has scalelike leaves but occurs mostly west of our region. The two may ordinarily be distinguished by their flower stalks. Those of *A. filicaulis* are slender and more than ³⁄₁₆" long while those of *A. aphylla* are shorter than ³⁄₁₆". In addition, *A. filicaulis* typically produces 1–2 flowers per branch; *A. aphylla* usually produces several.

TENLOBE FALSE FOXGLOVE

Agalinis obtusifolia Rafinesque.
Broomrape Family (Orobanchaceae)

Description: This small-flowered annual *Agalinis* occurs in habitats that are somewhat similar to those of the previous species, but it has short, linear, well-developed ¼–¾" stem leaves. The stems are greenish, wiry, and typically moderately to profusely branched above. Flowers are less than ⅝" long, pink to pale purplish, and borne on conspicuous ⅜–1" stalks.

Bloom Season: August–October.

Habitat/Range: Sandhills, flatwoods, savannas, and bog margins. Throughout the region.

Comments: This is a large and complicated genus. More than 15 species occur in our region, many of which are difficult to distinguish. The present species is probably most easily confused with Pineland False Foxglove *(A. divaricata)*. The length of the leaves and the flower stalks overlap between these 2 species, but longer leafstalks and flower stalks predominate in *A. divaricata*. Also, the calyx that subtends the flowers in *A. obtusifolia* is tapering more or less like an inverted pyramid, whereas the calyx of *A. divaricata* is more or less rounded and cup shaped.

HAIRY PHLOX OR CHALICE PHLOX
Phlox amoena Sims
Phlox Family (Polemoniaceae)

Description: The conspicuous floral bracts and glabrous flowers of this mostly unbranched perennial herb are helpful field identification characters. The pink to lavender flowers are borne in a congested cluster at the top of the stem. The corolla is ½–1" long and subtended by stiff, hairy ⅜" sepals that are nearly obscured by the large floral bracts. Leaves are linear to narrowly elliptic and spreading, making them similar in general appearance to those of *P. pilosa*.

Bloom Season: April–June.

Habitat/Range: Pinelands, dry hammocks, sandhills, and sandy roadsides. Throughout the region.

Comments: The genus *Phlox* is a complex group with many overlapping morphological features and numerous difficult-to-identify species. Some authorities list at least 20 taxa (species, varieties, and subspecies) for our region, though this number varies widely. The present species is most easily confused with Downy Phlox (*P. pilosa*) but differs from it by lacking hairs on the corolla. *P. floridana*, which occurs in the southern part of our region, also has hairy flowers.

SMOOTH PHLOX
Phlox glaberrima Linnaeus
(Syn: *P. carolina* Linnaeus)
Phlox Family (Polemoniaceae)

Description: With few exceptions our species of *Phlox* are confusing and difficult to identify. Even the experts disagree about the taxonomy of the genus and synonymous scientific names abound in the botanical literature. Smooth Phlox, for example, is considered by some authorities to constitute 2 species, each with several varieties. It is included here as an erect perennial herb with a 12–60" stem and opposite 2–6" lance-shaped leaves. Plants are mostly glabrous but may display scattered pubescence. The flowers consist of a narrow, glabrous ⅝–1" tube with spreading petals and protruding stamens.

Bloom Season: April–July.

Habitat/Range: Upland woods and wet bottomlands. Throughout the region.

Comments: The combination of field characters that is most useful for distinguishing Smooth Phlox include its lance-shaped leaves, the larger of which are borne above mid-stem, its glabrous flower tube, and its exerted stamens. The specific epithet *glaberrima* means "completely without hairs," in reference to the smooth flower tubes.

SHOWY MILKWORT
Polygala grandiflora Walter
Milkwort Family (Polygalaceae)

Description: The epithet *grandiflora* is a relative term and is applied to this species only in comparison to other members of its genus. The flowers are only slightly more than ½" wide when fully open, hardly large enough to be called large flowered. What appear to be latterly spreading petals are actually rounded petaloid sepals, or wings. The leaves are ½–2" long, to about ⅛–⅝" wide, alternate, and elliptic or more often oblanceolate (reverse lance shaped) in outline.

Bloom Season: May–August.

Habitat/Range: Sandhills, flatwoods, roadsides, and fields; most often in sandy soils. Florida, Georgia, South Carolina, and North Carolina.

Comments: Some species of milkworts, including Seneca Snakeroot *(P. senega)*, a widespread species across the eastern U. S. and Canada, have been used medicinally. American Indians used a tea from the roots of *P. senega* and perhaps other species as an emetic and expectorant, and in the treatment of a variety of ailments and discomforts.

CAROLINA ROSE
Rosa carolina Linnaeus
Rose Family (Rosaceae)

Description: Carolina Rose is a sparingly branched, upright shrub with an herbaceous or vinelike appearance. Stems arise from belowground runners and may by up to about 5' long. Both the stem and branches are armed with sharp, mostly straight prickles that diverge at right angles from the axis. The 1–4" leaves are compound with 3–9 toothed ½–1¼" leaflets. Flowers are borne singly in the axils of the upper leaves and consist of 5 pink ¾–1" petals subtending a showy congested mass of stamens and pistils. The fruit is a rounded red hip that often bears the remains of the sepals at its apex.

Bloom Season: April–June.

Habitat/Range: Upland woods. Throughout the region.

Comments: Carolina Rose is very similar in general form to Swamp Rose *(R. palustris)*. The genus *Rosa* constitutes a large worldwide group of showy, well-loved plants. At least 20 species are found in the southeastern United States, only 2 of which are native to the region. Several are garden specialties that have escaped cultivation to become established in the wild.

SWAMP ROSE
Rosa palustris Marshall
Rose Family (Rosaceae)

Description: Swamp Rose and Carolina Rose have almost identical flowers. Plants of these species are very similar in form, habit, and general appearance. However, the 2 species can be easily and reliably distinguished by habitat and by the shape of the prickles that line their stems. As its name suggests, Swamp Rose is found along streams and the edges of ponds and swamps—always in wet places—whereas Carolina Rose is an upland species of dry sites. The prickles of Swamp Rose are stout, curved, and hooked; those of Carolina Rose are predominantly narrow and straight.

Bloom Season: May–July.

Habitat/Range: Streams, ponds, and swamp margins. Throughout the region.

Comments: The epithet *palustris* means "marsh loving," an appropriate name for this attractive rose. The banks of small rivers and clear water streams sometimes support large tangles of Swamp Rose that produce numerous showy blooms in early summer. The genus name *Rosa* is the ancient Latin name for this group.

CAROLINA VERVAIN OR CAROLINA FALSE VERVAIN
Stylodon carneum (Medikus) Moldenke
(Syn: *Verbena carnea* Medicus)
Vervain Family (Verbenaceae)

Description: This 3' perennial herb has pale pink flowers, and its wandlike spikes of 5-lobed flowers are reminiscent of our species of *Verbena*, a genus within which Carolina Vervain was once included. The stems are hairy, square in cross section, and often ascending or leaning. The leaves are opposite, sessile, lance-shaped, 1½–3½" long, and reduce in length up the stem. The 1–5 flowering spikes are stiffly erect and up to about 16" long. Only a few flowers are typically open at any one time.

Bloom Season: April–July.

Habitat/Range: Sandhills, Longleaf Pinelands, and sandy woodlands. Throughout the region.

Comments: Carolina Vervain is not uncommon but is not included in many wildflower guides. It is somewhat similar to several species of *Verbena*, a genus whose species some observers find difficult to identify. Carolina Vervain is responsive to fire and is a common component of healthy ground cover in Longleaf Pinelands.

SOUTHERN BEARDTONGUE OR SANDHILL BEARDTONGUE
Penstemon australis Small
Speedwell Family (Veronicaceae)

Description: The genus *Penstemon* includes about 250 perennial herbs and shrubs, almost all of which are confined to North America (a single species is known from Asia). Species within this genus are notoriously difficult to distinguish from one another. Southern Beardtongue is an erect 8–28" herb with opposite 2–5" leaves and a terminal inflorescence. Flowers are ½–¾" long and rose, reddish purple, or sometimes mostly white, with reddish purple guidelines inside that serve to direct insects to the nectar. The hairy inflorescence and typically deeply colored flowers help distinguish this species within our region

Bloom Season: May–July.

Habitat/Range: Sandhills, dry pinelands, and sandy roadsides. Throughout the region.

Comments: The genus name *Penstemon* comes from the Greek words *pente*, or "five," and

stemon, "stamen." Plants of the genus have 5 stamens, 4 of which are fertile. The sterile stamens (staminodes) are more prominent than the fertile ones and are hairy. This explains the common name Beardtongue for many plants in this genus. The epithet *australis* means "southern," a reference to Southern Beardtongue's southern distribution; it occurs in only 7 southeastern states. The family placement of the genus *Penstemon* is confusing. The genus was long included with the figworts (Schrophulariaceae), a family that has been significantly reduced in size due to recent genetic discoveries and taxonomic realignments. Some authorities include *Penstemon* in the Speedwell Family, as has been done here, while others include it within the Plantain Family (Plantaginaceae).

WHITE FLOWERS

This section includes flowers that vary from creamy white to bright white. Some of these plants also produce flowers that tend toward pale yellow or pale green. Check the sections for yellow and green flowers if you don't find your flower here.

SPANISH DAGGER OR SPANISH BAYONET
Yucca aloifolia Linnaeus
Agave Family (Agavaceae)

Description: The long very sharp-pointed lance-shaped leaves give this species its common names. Typical plants are erect and 5–10' tall with a densely leafy stem. The stiff, rigid, dark green leaves are 1–2' long and 1–2" wide with a grayish tip. Lower leaves often spread at nearly right angles from the stem but become strongly ascending upwards. A conspicuous panicle of bright white flowers is produced at the top of the stem. The inflorescence may be up to about 2' tall and 1' wide and is nestled in the upper leaves. Individual flowers are borne on stout ¾" stalks and consist of 6, 1½–2" tepals (undifferentiated petals and sepals). The fruit is a leathery berry that may be up to about 4" long but is often shorter.

Bloom Season: June–July.

Habitat/Range: Dunes and coastal islands. Florida, Georgia, South Carolina, and North Carolina.

Comments: Spanish Dagger is best known as a hardy landscape plant with a long history of use in the southeastern United States, especially in poor, sandy soils within 50 miles of the coast. Despite its widespread occurrence, it is probably native only to sandy dunes along the narrow coastal fringe. The specific epithet *aloifolia* means "with leaves like aloe," but the leaves of *Yucca* are not as succulent as are many of the aloes. The genus name *Yucca* is from the Carib name for Manihot, a genus in the Spurge Family *(Euphorbiaceae)*. The Caribs are a group of American Indians from South America, the Lesser Antilles, and the eastern coast of Central America. The Agave and Spurge families are not at all closely related.

BEARGRASS OR ADAM'S NEEDLE

Yucca filamentosa Linnaeus
Agave Family (Agavaceae)

Description: Beargrass is an evergreen woody shrub characterized by a mounded basal rosette of grayish 1–3' leaves. Leaf margins are often decorated with curly, brownish, threadlike filaments, hence the epithet *filamentosa*. Flowers are borne in a large, conspicuous, showy inflorescence at the top of a 3–9' stem. The flowering stem arises from the center of the leaf cluster, reminiscent of the agaves. The fruit is an erect 1½" capsule with black seeds.

Bloom Season: April–June.

Habitat/Range: Sandy Longleaf Pinelands, coastal dunes, and thin, dry, relatively open mixed pine and hardwood forests. Throughout the region.

Comments: Beargrass is frequently seen listed under 2 scientific names: *Y. filamentosa* and *Y.*
flaccida. Plants of *Y. filamentosa* display significant morphological variation from region to region, and there continues to be disagreement about whether this variation constitutes more than 1 species. Some authorities lump all plants under the name *Y. filamentosa*, whereas others distinguish the two species based on tepal length, leaf width, and several less obvious morphological features. Since resolution of this taxonomic dilemma is beyond the scope of this book, Beargrass is treated here as a single species. Beargrass has a history of medicinal, cultural, and culinary uses. American Indians used the plant to treat sores and skin abrasions and the filaments as a source of fiber. The roots of most species of Yucca contain saponins and have been used in making soap.

GRASSY ARROWHEAD
Sagittaria graminea Michaux
Water Plantain Family (Alismataceae)

Description: The common name Arrowhead is a misnomer for this species. Whereas several species of *Sagittaria* have large expanded leaf blades that are shaped like an arrowhead, the leaves of Grassy Arrowhead are narrowly linear and often "grasslike." Grassy Arrowhead is an aquatic herb that arises from a coarse rhizome. Some leaves are phyllodial, meaning that they are actually composed of a flattened, bladeless petiole that functions as a leaf. Other leaves are bladed and stalked. Leaves and phyllodes may be up to 18" long. The inflorescence contains whorls of 2–12 flowers, each with 3 white petals and thick filaments. The fruiting head is about ⅜" wide and borne on a stout, ascending, or spreading stalk.

Bloom Season: May–November.

Habitat/Range: Ponds, swamps, and wet ditches. Throughout the region.

Comments: At least a dozen species of *Sagittaria* occur in our region, all of which are wetland species with similarly constructed flowers. The epithet *graminea* means "resembling grass," in allusion to this species' narrow leaves.

WILD ONION
Allium canadense Linnaeus var. *mobilense* (Regel) Ownbey
Onion Family (Alliaceae)

Description: Wild Onion often produces extensive colonies that are very showy when flowering. The leaves are flat, shiny, very narrow, and up to about 12" long. Flowers are produced in a conspicuous umbel at the top of a 6–24" stem and vary in color from white to pinkish lavender. The fruit is a capsule with tiny black seeds. Bruised leaves and stems of this species give off an onion-like aroma.

Bloom Season: April–May.

Habitat/Range: Dry woodlands and glades. Florida, Georgia, and South Carolina.

Comments: Two varieties occur in our region. The inflorescence of variety *canadense* is composed partly or entirely of bulblets, whereas the inflorescence of variety *mobilense* is composed of normal flowers, all of which arise from a central point, producing an umbel. Plants of variety *canadense* often divide into several branches from the umbel, each branch of which terminates with a smaller umbel. Wild Onion is one of several native onions that occur in the southeastern United States, several of which occur mostly in the Piedmont and mountains.

STRING-LILY, SWAMP-LILY, OR SEVEN-SISTERS
Crinum americanum Linnaeus
Amaryllis Family (Amaryllidaceae)

Description: This showy perennial herb arises from a succulent, squared-off bulb that produces several 2–5' dark green straplike leaves that are overlapping and stalklike at the base. Elegant white flowers (sometimes tinted pinkish) are borne in a 2- to 7-flowered umbel at the apex of an erect scape that equals the length of the leaves. Individual flowers are divided into 6 narrow 3–6" segments, each of which gives rise to a conspicuous stamen with a purplish pink filament and yellowish anther. The fruit is a fleshy capsule that is often heavy enough to bend the scape to the ground before releasing its seeds.

Bloom Season: June–October.

Habitat/Range: Swamps, marshes, and stream margins. Florida, Georgia, South Carolina, and North Carolina (uncommon in South Carolina and confined mostly to the southeastern portion of the state).

Comments: String-Lily is sometimes erroneously called Spider-Lily. The flowers of true spider-lilies (genus *Hymenocallis*) produce a staminal cup from which the anthers arise. The genus *Crinum* includes about 130 species, many of which are widely used as garden plants. The non-native Milk-and-Wine-Lily *(C. bulbispermum)* is one of these and has escaped cultivation and become naturalized in parts of our area. Its flower petals bear a deep magenta or reddish linear marking. The genus name derives from the Greek word for lily, although species of this genus are not true lilies. Both the leaves and bulbs are reportedly poisonous to humans.

109

RAIN-LILY OR TREAT'S ZEPHYRLILY
Zephyranthes treatiae S. Watson
Amaryllis Family (Amaryllidaceae)

Description: Rain-Lily arises from a bulbous root and often occurs in large colonies along moist to wet roadside ditches. The mostly linear leaves are shiny green, 6–18" long, less than ³⁄₁₆" wide, and borne a few at the time at the base of the plant. The 4–12" flowering scape is terminated by a showy, white (sometimes with blushes of pink), tubular or funnel-shaped 2–4" flower with 6 spreading or reflexed segments (undifferentiated petals and sepals). Six stamens with pale orange anthers arise from the throat of the flower and surround a somewhat longer pistil that has a 3-parted stigma. The fruit is a 3-lobed capsule.

Bloom Season: January–April.

Habitat/Range: Wet savannas, moist roadsides, and the edges of wet roadside ditches. Florida and Georgia.

Comments: Four species of *Zephyranthes* occur in our region, 3 of which are native. The present species is treated by some authorities as a variety of Atamasco-Lily *(Z. atamasca)*. The leaves of Atamasco-Lily are generally wider than ¼" whereas those of Rain-Lily are generally less than ¼" wide.

HAIRY ANGELICA
Angelica venenosa (Greenway) Fernald
Carrot Family (Apiaceae or Umbelliferae)

Description: Members of the Carrot Family are noted for showy umbels of tiny flowers, hence the older family name Umbelliferae. In Hairy Angelica the flowers are white and borne in 2–5" umbels, mostly well above the leaves at the top of an erect 1½–3' stem. The stem leaves are dark green, thick, and compound. Leaflets are toothed along the margins and may be a little over 2" long and up to about 1" wide. The tiny fruit is flattened but adorned with conspicuous wings and vertical ridges.

Bloom Season: June–August.

Habitat/Range: Mesic hammocks, moist to dry woodlands, clay roadsides, and sandhills. Throughout the region.

Comments: This fairly common species is more representative in our area of mesic woodlands than sandy uplands. Its occurrence with Longleaf Pine is restricted mostly to the Fall Line Hills where, according to Weakley (2004), leaflets are smaller and more coarsely toothed and basal leaves are appressed to the ground. He suggests that these plants may represent an unnamed variety or species.

SOUTHERN CHERVIL OR HAIRYFRUIT CHERVIL

Chaerophyllum tainturieri Hooker
Carrot Family (Apiaceae or Umbelliferae)

Description: The finely divided, parsleylike 1–4"
leaves of this erect annual herb are reminiscent
of many members of the Carrot Family. Most
plants average about 1½' tall, but some plants
may be nearly twice this height. Smaller
individuals are typically unbranched whereas
larger plants are often divided into several
branches near the top of a short hairy stem.
Numerous tiny white flowers are borne in several
small 3–10 flowered ½–1" umbels.

Bloom Season: March–April.

Habitat/Range: Roadsides, fields, disturbed sites,
and sunny openings in southern mixed hardwood
forests. Throughout the region.

Comments: This native species has distinctly
weedy tendencies. It is occasionally found in
mixed hardwood forests but is more often seen
along weedy roadsides in association with other
native weeds, including Wild Geranium *(Geranium
carolinianum)* and Cornsalad *(Valerianella radiata)*.
The genus name derives from the Greek word
chairo meaning "to please or rejoice," and *phyllon*,
or "leaf." The leaves of many species in the genus
are pleasantly fragrant.

QUEEN-ANNE'S-LACE OR WILD CARROT

Daucus carota Linnaeus
Carrot Family (Apiaceae or Umbelliferae)

Description: Few roadside wildflowers are as
conspicuous as Queen-Anne's-Lace. Flowering
stems may be up to about 6' tall and usually
produce several branches, each of which is
terminated by a flat-topped 2–5" umbel of tiny
white flowers. The flowers are eventually
replaced by bristly ⅛" egg-shaped fruit. The finely
divided, multiply compound leaves are 2–8" long.

Bloom Season: May–October.

Habitat/Range: Roadside, fields, and other
disturbed sites. Throughout the region, but more
common in the coastal plains in the Carolinas and
Virginia than farther south.

Comments: This non-native weed is of European
origin, but it has been recorded in all of the lower
48 states. It is probably more common in the
eastern United States in the Piedmont and
mountains but is frequent in the Atlantic Coastal
Plain, especially in North Carolina and Virginia. It
is often the dominant roadside wildflower during
its predominantly late summer and fall flowering
period. Though not native to our region, it has
been included here due to its conspicuous
presence.

SOUTHERN RATTLESNAKE-MASTER
Eryngium yuccifolium Michaux
Carrot Family (Apiaceae or Umbelliferae)

Description: Few species in our region can be mistaken for Southern Rattlesnake-Master. Although the lower leaves are very distinctive, unlike most of our other herbaceous plants, when flowers are absent, they may go unnoticed in the dense savanna vegetation. At flowering time, however, this species is anything but inconspicuous. The 2–3' stems of this perennial herb are stiffly erect and often occur in colonies of numerous plants, all of which flower at about the same time. Flowers are borne in dense, globular ½–¾" heads subtended by 4–10 lance-shaped involucral bracts. Individual flowers are small, white, and seemingly embedded in the ball-like cluster. Each flower is subtended by a small bractlet with a long-pointed tip that, especially when combined with the long pistils,

gives a bristly appearance to the head. The leaves are borne mostly at the base of the plant and may be up to about 40" long and 1½" wide. The lower leaves have branched marginal bristles and bear a superficial resemblance to the leaves of *Yucca*, hence the specific epithet *yuccifolium* ("with foliage like *Yucca*").

Bloom Season: June–August.

Habitat/Range: Savannas and moist pinelands. Throughout the region.

Comments: Rattlesnake-Master *(E. aquaticum)* is similar in form and stature, but its flowers are blue, and its leaves lack marginal bristles. Blueflower Eryngo *(E. integrifolium)* is also similar, but it, too, has blue flowers, and its lower leaves are typically less than 4" long.

SWAMP MILKWEED
Asclepias perennis Walter
Dogbane Family (Apocynaceae)

Description: The bright white to sometimes pinkish flowers of this showy wetland perennial contrast sharply with its dark green leaves. The 12–24" stems are mostly solitary from a thickened base and conspicuously leafy. The 2–6" leaves are short stalked, opposite, and typically lance shaped in outline. Flowers are borne in 2–6 axillary umbels, each of which is 1–2" wide. Hoods have a prominent protruding horn. The fruit is a 2½" follicle that splits to release smooth seeds that lack the cottony appendage common to many milkweeds.

Bloom Season: May–September.

Habitat/Range: Floodplain forests, swamps, wet roadsides, ditches, marshes, and cypress wetlands. Florida, Georgia, and South Carolina.

Comments: *A. perennis* is likely to be the only white-flowered milkweed encountered in swamps, floodplains, and cypress wetlands. The inflorescence begins as a compact, buttonlike cluster at the top of the stem and may be yellowish when it first appears. The epithet *perennis* refers to Swamp Milkweed's perennial life cycle.

WHITE MILKWEED
Asclepias variegata Linnaeus
Dogbane Family (Apocynaceae)

Description: The stem of this erect, unbranched, leafy perennial is 1–3' tall. The medium to dark green leaves are opposite, up to about 6" long and 3" wide, and borne on short but conspicuous stalks. Flowers are borne in 1–4 stalked rounded 1–2½" umbels at the tip of the branch or from the axils of the upper leaves. Individual flowers are white (often with pinkish markings below) and typical of the milkweeds. The horns are exposed but are shorter than the hoods and turn inward at the tip. The 4–5" follicles are borne on short stalks. Leaves, stems, and flower stalks exude a milky sap when bruised.

Bloom Season: April–June.

Habitat/Range: Rich upland forests and moist hardwood hammocks. Throughout the region (but mostly west of our region in Florida).

Comments: This is our only upland milkweed with the combination of erect stature, white flowers, and large, opposite leaves. The specific epithet means "irregularly colored" and probably alludes to the leaves but applies equally well to the pinkish "waist" that gives many flowers a 2-toned appearance.

113

WHORLED MILKWEED
Asclepias verticillata Linnaeus
Dogbane Family (Apocynaceae)

Description: Whorled Milkweed takes its common name and specific epithet from the numerous whorls of linear leaves that decorate its slender stalk; *verticillata* means "having whorls" or "forming a ring around an axis." The stems are very slender and weakly erect; when in flower, they sway and bend at the slightest breeze. The flowers are borne in 2–8 compact ¾–1¼" umbels in the axils of the upper leaves. The greenish white flower petals are turned downward and are often purplish tipped. The upright hoods are topped by protruding horns. The fruit is a 2–3½" follicle that splits at maturity to release cottony seeds.

Bloom Season: April–September.

Habitat/Range: Sandhills, Longleaf Pinelands, roadsides, and flatwoods. Throughout the region.

Comments: The conspicuous whorls of linear leaves on a slender stem make this an easy milkweed to recognize, even before the flowers open. When flowering, it is a showy component of sandhill pinelands. Milkweeds are noted for the white milky sap that exudes from their leaves and stems when bruised or broken. Though typically harmless, the sap of these plants can cause irritation to some people, and is toxic if ingested. Whorled Milkweed is widespread across the eastern ⅔ of the United States and Canada and is considered imperiled only in those states and provinces at the northern and western edges of its expansive range.

SAW PALMETTO
Serenoa repens (Bartram) Small
Palm Family (Arecaceae or Palmae)

Description: Saw Palmetto is the signature shrub of the flatwoods ecosystem. The thickened trunk may be up to about 10' long but is typically prostrate and often partially buried. A cluster of yellowish green fan-shaped 1–4' leaves arises from the tip of the stem. Leaves are borne on stiff erect petioles that are lined along 2 edges with sharp, sawlike teeth, hence the common name. Numerous showy 3–6" spikes of tiny, creamy white or greenish white flowers arise from within the clustered leaves. The ¾–1" ellipsoid, drupelike fruit is more or less rusty orange at first but turns dark blue or bluish black at maturity.

Bloom Season: May–July, but at other times following a fire.

Habitat/Range: Flatwoods and coastal hammocks. Florida, Georgia, and South Carolina.

Comments: Saw Palmetto is very common in the southern parts of the Atlantic Coastal Plain but reaches the northern limit of its range in extreme southern South Carolina. It is a slow-growing, long-lived species (some authorities suggest that plants may reach ages of 700 years or more) and has been touted for various medicinal and culinary uses. Recent research suggests that it is useful in reducing the symptoms of benign prostatic hyperplasia, a suggestion that has led to the development of several over-the-counter herbal remedies and preventive treatments. In parts of the Far East the fruit of Saw Palmetto is believed to be a powerful aphrodisiac.

OVATELEAF INDIAN PLANTAIN OR OVATELEAF CACALIA

Arnoglossum ovatum (Walt.) H. E. Robins.
Aster Family (Asteraceae or Compositae)

Description: Indian Plantain is an erect perennial herb to about 6' tall. The stem is round in cross section and marked lengthwise with conspicuous grooves. Leaf blades are up to 12" long and 6" wide, typically ovate or egg shaped in outline with entire to bluntly toothed margins and conspicuous parallel veins that converge near their tips. Leaf surfaces commonly have a whitish cast. Flowers are borne in numerous upright ⅜–⅝" heads within a flat-topped inflorescence. Each head is narrowly cylindrical and contains 5 creamy white tubular flowers. The fruit is a tiny nutlet.

Bloom Season: August–October.

Habitat/Range: Flatwoods, bogs, wet roadside ditches, marshes, acid swamps, and seepage slopes. Florida, Georgia, South Carolina, and North Carolina (where uncommon).

Comments: The parallel-veined leaves and round stem help distinguish this species from other Indian plantains in our region. Two varieties occur in the Atlantic Coastal Plain, variety *lanceolatum* with narrow, lance-shaped stem leaves and variety *ovatum* with ovate stems leaves.

SOUTHERN WHITETOP OR POCOSIN FLAT-TOPPED ASTER

Doellingeria sericocarpoides Small
Aster Family (Asteraceae or Compositae)

Description: Southern Whitetop is a robust upright herb that is 3–6' tall. Leaves are entire, 1–4½" long, and up to about 2" wide. Flower heads are borne in a conspicuous branched inflorescence at the top of the stem. Individual flower heads are composed of up to about 14 tubular disk flowers surrounded by 2–7 creamy white ray flowers.

Bloom Season: July–October.

Habitat/Range: Pocosin margins, edges of wet openings in power-line easements, bogs, margins of sandhill drainages, and sandhill seepages. Florida, Georgia, South Carolina, and North Carolina.

Comments: Southern Whitetop is very similar to Tall Whitetop Aster *(D. umbellata)*, which is more common in the Piedmont and mountains. The flower heads of Tall Whitetop Aster generally have more than 7 ray flowers. Tall Whitetop Aster and Southern Whitetop were recently included within the genus *Aster*, which partially explains their common names. The specific epithet *sericocarpoides* means "resembling *Sericocarpus*," another genus in the Aster family.

WHITE THOROUGHWORT OR WHITE-BRACTED THOROUGHWORT
Eupatorium album Linnaeus
Aster Family (Asteraceae or Compositae)

Description: Leaf width and flower size help to distinguish this species from its closest look-alike, Justiceweed *(E. leucolepis)*. The leaves of White Thoroughwort are typically at least ¾" wide whereas those of Justiceweed are typically less than ½" wide. Plants of White Thoroughwort are often up to 3' tall, although the height of flowering specimens on freshly burned sandhills often does not exceed about 18". Leaves are sessile, opposite, coarsely toothed, 1½–5" long, and mostly elliptical in outline. Numerous creamy white flower heads are borne in a branched, flat-topped inflorescence at the top of the stem. Individual heads are typically more than ⅜" tall and contain 5 flowers. The flower heads of Justiceweed also contain 5 flowers but are usually less than ⅜" tall.

Bloom Season: June–October.

Habitat/Range: Sandhills and dry flatwoods. Throughout the region.

Comments: The specific epithet *album* means "white," in reference to the flowers. However, several white-flowered *Eupatorium* occur in our region, making field identification difficult.

SPOONSHAPE BARBARA'S BUTTONS
Marshallia obovata (Walter) Beadle & F. W. Boynton
Aster Family (Asteraceae or Compositae)

Description: Flowering stems of this perennial herb may be up to 16" tall and are topped by a congested ½–1½" head of creamy white disk flowers. Leaves are 1–6" long and are typically widest near the tip but may be narrowly elliptic in outline; the epithet *obovata* means "reverse or inverted egg-shaped." The leaves of typical plants are borne in basal clusters. However, up to 5 leaves may be present a little ways up the stem.

Bloom Season: April–May (or later following a fire).

Habitat/Range: Pine savannas and margins of flatwoods. Georgia, South Carolina, and North Carolina.

Comments: Some authorities recognize 2 varieties of this species. Variety *scaposa* is restricted to the Atlantic Coastal Plain and has mostly basal leaves or only a few stem leaves (usually less than 5). Variety *obovata*, which occurs mostly in the Piedmont with a disjunct population in the central panhandle of Florida, has up to 10 stem leaves and may be up to 2½' tall. Several species of *Marshallia* occur in our region, most of which have pink rather than whitish flowers.

117

WHITETOP ASTER OR PINEBARREN ASTER

Oclemena reticulata (Pursh) G. L. Nesom
(Syn: *Aster reticulatus* Pursh)
Aster Family (Asteraceae or Compositae)

Description: The scientific epithet for this species refers to its conspicuous netted (reticulate) leaf venation. The common name alludes to the flat-topped inflorescence of creamy white flowers. This species produces numerous closely clustered 16–36" stems from a single knotlike root. The 1–4" soft green leaves are alternate, mostly elliptic in outline, entire to remotely dull-toothed, and distinctively and attractively veined, especially when viewed from below. Numerous flower heads are borne at the tips of the branches, each with a yellow central disk and 8–30 creamy white ray flowers.

Bloom Season: March–May.

Habitat/Range: Savannas, flatwoods, bogs, and pond margins. Florida, Georgia, and South Carolina.

Comments: Whitetop Aster is normally associated with the spring but is responsive to fire. Fresh burns may trigger a vigorous flush of new growth in late summer and fall. Young plants may appear only days after the flames die and new flowers within only a few weeks.

COMMON WILD QUININE

Parthenium integrifolium Linnaeus
Aster Family (Asteraceae or Compositae)

Description: Common Wild Quinine is native to our region but occurs most frequently in dry disturbed habitats, often in conjunction with common non-native weeds. Plants are upright and 1½–5' tall with 1 to several stems originating from a thickened root. Leaves are alternate, toothed, lance shaped or elliptical in outline, and 4–10" long, with the smallest leaves nearer the top of the stem. Both basal and stem leaves are present. Numerous small, congested heads of tiny white flowers are borne in a 3–6" flat-topped inflorescence (corymb).

Bloom Season: May–August.

Habitat/Range: Sandy roadsides, dry open woods, and clearings. South Carolina, North Carolina, and Virginia.

Comments: Common Wild Quinine has been used in the treatment of malaria and other fevers, hence the common name "quinine." It is also known as American Fevertree but is not a woody plant and does not grow to treelike proportions. Although it has been used medicinally for a variety of purposes, it is also reported to produce skin irritations in some individuals.

STINKING CAMPHORWEED, MARSH FLEABANE, OR STINKING FLEABANE

Pluchea foetida (Linnaeus) DC.
Aster Family (Asteraceae or Compositae)

Description: The foul-smelling herbage of this 1½–3' perennial explains its common and scientific names: *foetida* means "stinking." Plants typically have a single purplish, often somewhat sticky stem, although individuals with multiple stems are not uncommon. The alternate stalkless leaves are 1–5" long, up to about 1½" wide, typically clasp the stem, and display conspicuous venation, especially on the lower surfaces. Flower heads consist only of disk flowers and are borne in clusters at the tips of lateral branches.

Bloom Season: July–October.

Habitat/Range: Swamps and shrub bays, margins of marshes, wet flatwoods, pineland depressions, and ditches. Throughout the region.

Comments: This is the only white-flowered *Pluchea* likely to be encountered throughout most of our region, although the range of *P. longifolia,* a Florida endemic, is marginal to our area in north-central counties of the Florida peninsula. Rosy Camphorweed *(P. rosea)* is vegetatively very similar but has rose-pink flowers.

CAROLINA WAREA OR CAROLINA PINELAND-CRESS

Warea cuneifolia (Muhl. ex Nutt.) Nutt.
Mustard Family (Brassicaceae or Cruciferae)

Description: Carolina Warea sometimes occurs in large colonies that can be spectacular during its late summer and early fall flowering period. The erect wiry stem of this annual herb may be 2–3' tall with ascending branches that are topped by a 1–1½" cluster of delicate, white 4-petaled flowers. The fruit is a dry, stalked, very narrow 1–2" beanlike structure (technically a silique).

Bloom Season: July–September.

Habitat/Range: Sandhills, usually on very dry white sand. Georgia, South Carolina, North Carolina, and Florida.

Comments: Four species of *Warea* occur in the United States, all of which are confined to portions of the Southeastern Coastal Plains and all of which are considered critically imperiled, imperiled, or vulnerable in at least part of their ranges. Carolina Warea is the most widespread of these species but is rare in the northern part of our region and considered critically imperiled in North Carolina.

CAROLINA SANDWORT
Minuartia caroliniana (Walter) Mattfeld
(Syn: *Arenaria caroliniana* Walter)
Pink Family (Caryophyllaceae)

Description: Dense clumps of Carolina Sandwort are particularly showy and attractive during this species' late spring and early summer flowering period. Numerous flowering stems arise from a central taproot, each one seemingly terminated by a small white 5-petaled ½" flower. The leaves are opposite, narrow, less than ½" long, and about 1/16" wide, and overlap each other at the base of the stem. The fruit is a tiny ¼" triangular capsule.

Bloom Season: April–June.

Habitat/Range: Sandhills, especially in deep sands. Georgia, South Carolina, North Carolina, and Virginia (also Florida, but west of our region).

Comments: Few plants of dry sandy habitats can be confused with Carolina Sandwort. Large clumps of this species can be 1' or more in diameter and often occur in sizable populations, the individual plants of which are typically well separated from each other. The old genus name for this group was once *Arenaria,* from the Latin word *arena,* or "sand." Many species of this genus occur in sandy habitats, hence the name Sandwort. Wort is an old English word that means "plant."

GODFREY'S SANDWORT
Minuartia godfreyi (Shinners) McNeill
Pink Family (Caryophyllaceae)

Description: This is a low-growing, mostly prostrate or weak-stemmed 4–16" perennial herb with opposite, linear ½–1½" by 1/16" leaves. Flowers arise on comparatively long, thin stalks from the leaf axils and consist of 5 white to very pale pink ⅜" petals. The fruit is a ⅛" egg-shaped capsule.

Bloom Season: April–June.

Habitat/Range: Moist roadside ditches, spring banks, and edges of tidal freshwater marshes, mostly in full sun and often in association with limestone. Florida, South Carolina, and North Carolina.

Comments: This is a peculiarly distributed species, known from only 1 or 2 counties in each of the 6 southeastern states where it has been reported. It is listed as critically imperiled globally as well as by most states in which it occurs. It is not common and has disappeared over much of its range. It is included here to encourage the discovery of more populations. In weedy locations it sometimes grows with the somewhat similar Carolina Cranesbill *(Geranium carolinianum)* but is easily distinguished by its narrow, opposite leaves.

COMMON CHICKWEED
Stellaria media (Linnaeus) Villars
Pink Family (Caryophyllaceae)

Description: Common Chickweed is an annual herb with reclining to weakly erect stems and opposite ⅜–½" leaves. Close examination with at least 10X magnification reveals distinct lines of hairs along the stem. The tiny ¼" flowers have 3 stigmas, bright red anthers, and 5 white petals. However, the petals are deeply divided almost to the base into 2 equal lobes, which gives the appearance of a 10-petaled flower.

Bloom Season: All year, but mostly January–April.

Habitat/Range: Lawns, gardens, and other disturbed sites. Throughout the region.

Comments: Common Chickweed was introduced to the United States from Europe and is not native to our region. Flowers of species in the related genus *Cerastium,* especially those of the aptly named Mouse-Ear Chickweed *(C. glomeratum),* are similar but may be distinguished by having 5 stigmas. Many species of the Pink Family are weedy herbs that occur in our region mostly in lawns and along regularly mowed roadsides.

GOPHER-APPLE OR GROUND-OAK
Licania michauxii Prance
Coco-Plum Family (Chrysobalanaceae)

Description: This low-growing evergreen plant is typically described as a woody shrub, but it has the aspect of an herb. Stems can be up to about 2' tall and have alternate, simple 4" leaves that are elliptic or oblanceolate in outline. Flowers are tiny, white, and borne in a conspicuous branched ½–2½" cluster, typically well above the leaves. The fruit is an elliptical 1" drupe that is brownish or coppery at maturity.

Bloom Season: April–August.

Habitat/Range: Sandhills, pine ridges, old dunes, and sandy roadsides. Florida and Georgia.

Comments: The Coco-Plum Family is a mostly tropical family that includes about 17 genera and more than 400 species worldwide, only 2 species of which occur in the United States. Gopher-Apple takes its common name from the combination of its fruit and habitat. It often forms large colonies that share their sandhill habitat with the Gopher Tortoise *(Gopherus polyphemus),* an endangered species that is North America's only land tortoise. The Gopher Tortoise occurs in Florida and southwest Georgia and feeds at least partly on the fruit of Gopher-Apple.

COASTAL SWEET PEPPERBUSH
Clethra alnifolia Linnaeus
White Alder Family (Clethraceae)

Description: Sweet Pepperbush is a deciduous, much branched, profusely flowering woody shrub. Some plants may reach 9' tall, but heights of 3–5' are typical. The leaves are simple, alternate, and 1½–4" long, with sharply toothed margins and parallel lateral veins. Individual flowers are small but are bright white and borne in showy terminal 2–6" racemes beyond the uppermost leaves. The fruit is a small, hairy, 3-valved capsule.

Bloom Season: June–July.

Habitat/Range: Flatwoods, pocosins, and swamp edges. Throughout the region.

Comments: Sweet Pepperbush is a popular native landscape shrub across much of its range. It typically occurs in moist acid soils in nature but adapts to slightly drier and somewhat less acidic conditions in the garden. The flowers are sweetly aromatic and are attractive to bees and butterflies. It is sometimes confused with Virginia Sweetspire *(Itea virginica)* but is easily distinguished at any time of year by its leaf margins, which are toothed only on the upper ½ of the blade. The leaf margins of Sweetspire are toothed throughout.

CAROLINA PONYFOOT
Dichondra caroliniensis Michaux
Morning Glory Family (Convolvulaceae)

Description: You may have to get down on your hands and knees for a clear view of the tiny 5-petaled flowers of this native herb. The leaves average about 1" long and are often produced in conspicuous mats that are visible much of the year. Fully developed flowers are densely hairy, less than ¼" wide, borne singly in the leaf axils, and look like whitish specks among the leaves. The fruit is a tiny 2-lobed capsule, each lobe of which typically contains a single seed.

Bloom Season: March–May.

Habitat/Range: Lawns, roadsides, glades, moist pinelands, and regularly mowed areas. Throughout the region.

Comments: Although Carolina Ponyfoot is native to our region, it is most easily and often seen in close-cropped lawns and often occurs in conjunction with non-native lawn weeds. The common name derives from the shape of the leaves; with imagination they resemble the hooves of a horse. The genus name *Dichondra* is Greek for "two lumps" in reference to the 2-lobed fruit. Most observers find little to suggest that this species is a member of the Morning Glory Family.

COMMON DAWNFLOWER
Stylisma patens (Desrousseaux) Myint
Morning Glory Family (Convolvulaceae)

Description: Common Dawnflower is 1 of 3 white-flowered dawnflowers that occur in our region. All are prostrate, mat-forming vines. The larger leaves of Common Dawnflower are narrowly elliptic to linear and normally do not exceed about ½" in width. The flowers are white, long-stalked, bell shaped, ½–1" wide and borne singly from the leaf axils. The sepals are hairy on the back, a feature that requires magnification to see clearly.

Bloom Season: May–August.

Habitat/Range: Sandhills and dry sandy woods. Florida, Georgia, South Carolina, and North Carolina.

Comments: Southern Dawnflower *(S. humistrata)* is very similar in appearance, distribution, habit,

and habitat. Its flowers are borne mostly in clusters of 2–3 from the leaf axils and its sepals lack hairs on the back. Pickering's Dawnflower *(S. pickeringii)* has hairy sepals, but its flowers are subtended by conspicuous ½–1" leaflike bracts, and it produces arching and trailing stems from a central point. Pickering's Dawnflower is considered imperiled or critically imperiled across much of its range. The common name Dawnflower derives from these species' daily flowering cycles. All 3 species tend to flower very early in the day and are at their best before 10:00 A.M. The epithet *patens* means "spreading," which is an accurate description of the Common Dawnflower's growth form but is not particularly helpful as an identifying feature since at least 2 of our species have spreading habits.

SOUTHERN SWAMP DOGWOOD
Cornus foemina P. Miller
Dogwood Family (Cornaceae)

Description: Many people associate the name Dogwood with Flowering Dogwood *(Cornus florida)*, a well-known native tree that is often used to decorate southern lawns and city streets. Southern Swamp Dogwood is an upright shrub or small tree to about 25' tall with opposite 1½–4" leaves. The inflorescence of Southern Swamp Dogwood lacks the distinctive creamy white bracts of its better-known cousin. Instead, its flowers are borne in a flat 1–2½" cluster. The globular ⅛–¼" fruit is grayish at first but becomes blue with age.

Bloom Season: April–May.

Habitat/Range: Swamps, marshy edges, floodplains, and other wetlands with standing water. Throughout the region.

Comments: This is 1 of 2 species of dogwood with similar leaves, habit, and flowers. Southern Swamp Dogwood is most easily confused with Eastern Roughleaf Dogwood *(C. asperifolia)*. Roughleaf Dogwood is much less common in our area and is generally confined to moist uplands, especially where limestone is present near the ground surface. The upper surfaces of the leaves of Eastern Roughleaf Dogwood are rough to the touch whereas those of Southern Swamp Dogwood are smooth. Silky Dogwood *(C. amomum)* occurs sparingly in our region and is found mostly in wet edges of marshes, swamps, and alluvial woods. Some authorities include the genus *Cornus* within the Sour Gum Family (Nyssaceae). However, the 2 families are better treated as only closely related.

NARROWLEAF WHITETOP SEDGE
Rhynchospora colorata (Linnaeus) H. Pfeiffer
(Syn: *Dichromena colorata* [L.] Hitchcock)
Sedge Family (Cyperaceae)

Description: Narrowleaf Whitetop Sedge is similar in general form and appearance to the somewhat more common and widespread Whitetop Sedge *(R. latifolia)*; these are our only sedges with showy white bracts subtending the inflorescence. The 2 species can be distinguished by size and by the number of subtending bracts. Narrowleaf Whitetop Sedge is an erect, herbaceous perennial to about 2' tall. The solitary stem is triangular in cross section and topped by a congested inflorescence of 10–20, ¼" spikelets. The inflorescence is subtended by 4–6 narrowly linear long-tapering 1½–3" bracts. The leaves are also narrowly linear and long tapering and are shorter than the stem.

Bloom Season: May–September.

Habitat/Range: Savannas, ditches, and moist roadsides (more common near the coast). Throughout the region, but rare in Virginia.

Comments: The similar Whitetop Sedge typically has 7–10 bracts subtending the inflorescence, most of which are well over ¼" wide. Both of species of Whitetop Sedge have long been included in the genus *Dichromena* and are still treated as such in many popular wildflower guides. The genus *Rhynchospora* is a very large and complex genus with many similar and difficult-to-distinguish species, none of which bear a field resemblance to the 2 Whitetop Sedges. The genus name means "beaked seeds" and references the tiny terminal appendage that is found on the achenes of many species in the genus.

TITI OR SWAMP CYRILLA
Cyrilla racemiflora Linnaeus
Titi Family (Cyrillaceae)

Description: Bumblebees are highly attracted to Titi's elongated racemes of tiny white flowers. The edges of wet pineland depressions can be alive with the sound of insects during Titi's early summer flowering period. This is a woody shrub or small tree to a little more than 30' tall. The leaves and inflorescences are variable in size from population to population or sometimes even from plant to plant. On some plants the leaves are mostly less than 2" long and the inflorescences less than 3½" long, whereas on other plants the leaves are mostly 2–4" long and the inflorescences over 4" long. The fruit is a tiny conspicuous capsule. Although this species flowers in early summer, the remains of its inflorescences are present nearly all year, a field character that aids in identification.

Bloom Season: May–July.

Habitat/Range: Flatwoods, bay swamps, pocosins, and margins of pineland depressions. Throughout the region.

Comments: The Titi Family is represented by 2 genera and perhaps 3 species in our region. The closely related and somewhat similar Black Titi *(Cliftonia monophylla)* is easily distinguished by its shorter, upright inflorescence, and earlier flowering period and by the lower surfaces of its leaves lacking a distinct ridge along the central vein. Some authorities distinguish Littleleaf Titi *(C. parviflora)* as a distinct species. However, there is much intergradation between the large-leaved and small-leaved forms, leading other authorities to suggest that there is but a single, albeit quite variable species. Titi is an indicator of swamp habitat and often grows in dense, almost impenetrable populations.

VENUS FLYTRAP, MEADOW CLAM, OR TIPPITIWITCHET
Dionaea muscipula Ellis
Sundew Family (Droseraceae)

Description: Charles Darwin called this species "one of the world's most wonderful plants." Darwin's reference was to the plant's unique ½–1" leaves, which augment the plant's nutritional intake by capturing and absorbing insects. These highly modified leaves are borne in a conspicuous 4–6" cluster at the base of the plant and are composed of a clamshell-like blade attached to a relatively long winged stalk. The blade is "hinged" in the middle to produce 2 halves, each lined along the outer edges with conspicuous long stiff bristles that are also called guard hairs. Three inconspicuous trigger hairs are borne inside near the bottom of each blade half. When stimulated, the trigger hairs prompt the halves to clamp together rapidly, enclosing whatever happens to be inside. Flowers are 5 petaled, about ⅝" wide, and are borne on 1–12" scapes.

Bloom Season: May–June.

Habitat/Range: Wet savannas, sandhill seepages, wet sandy ditches, and the margins of open bogs. South Carolina and North Carolina, generally within about 100 miles of Wilmington, North Carolina. The popularity of this plant has resulted in it now being naturalized in other locations, most notably the central part of the Florida panhandle.

Comments: Carnivorous plants employ 2 mechanisms for trapping prey. Species such as pitcher plants *(Sarracenia)* utilize passive traps that allow insects to enter but not retreat, whereas sundews *(Drosera)* and most notably the Venus Fly Trap use active traps in which parts of the plants actually grasp visiting prey. After the initial rapid closure, the margins of the leaf seal shut until the insect is digested. The epithet *muscipula* means "mousetrap."

TARFLOWER OR FLYCATCHER
Bejaria racemosa Ventenat
Heath Family (Ericaceae)

Description: Tarflower takes both of its common names from the sticky fluid that exudes from the upper stem and flowers. This is a slender, sparsely branched, evergreen, 3–7' shrub with hairy twigs and stiff, erect branches. The simple 1–2" leaves are alternate, entire, elliptic to ovate, and leathery, and are typically angled upward along the stem and twisted on the stalk. Flowers are sticky, fragrant, and bright white (often tinged with pink and sometimes entirely pink toward the apex) with conspicuous stamens and 7 narrow ¾–1¼" petals. The fruit is a sticky capsule. The sticky fluid on the flowers and upper branches often captures insects, especially ants. However, captured insects are not consumed as in the true carnivorous or insectivorous plants and do not contribute to nutrient intake.

Bloom Season: June–July.

Habitat/Range: Moist to dry flatwoods. Florida and Georgia.

Comments: This species was long known by the genus name *Befaria*, a name that was originally proposed to commemorate Donald Bejar. However, Linnaeus, who described the first species within the genus, misread the handwritten spelling of Bejar's name, interpreting the Old English "j" as an "f." The official name of the genus was recently changed to the correct spelling and is now considered a "conserved" name according to the rules of botanical nomenclature, which means its validity has been accepted even though it was not the first validly published name for the genus.

STAGGERBUSH
Lyonia mariana (Linnaeus) D. Don
Heath Family (Ericaceae)

Description: Flower size alone is enough to distinguish this 3–6' deciduous shrub from other species of *Lyonia*, as well as species of *Leucothoe*, a closely related genus with plants at least somewhat similar to Staggerbush. The urn-shaped corolla is white, ⅜–⅝" long, and subtended by conspicuous purplish red ¼–⅜" sepals that make the flowers attractive even before opening. The elliptic leaves are short stalked, 1½–4" long, to about 2" wide, and smooth above but short hairy beneath. Numerous tiny seeds are borne in a hard ¼" capsule.

Bloom Season: April–May.

Habitat/Range: Flatwoods, savannas, hillside bogs, and pocosin-sandhill interfaces. Throughout the region.

Comments: The common name Staggerbush for this and other species in the genera *Lyonia* and

Leucothoe derives from the presence of grayanotoxins or andromedotoxins present in the leaves. Ingestion of the foliage can cause staggering in livestock. The leaves of some species in the genus are also toxic to humans and are reported to cause nausea, vomiting, abdominal pain, weakness, and a variety of other deleterious symptoms. Plants of *Lyonia mariana* have contrasting forms in their northern and southern locations. In the sandhills of North Carolina it is not unusual to find large populations of low-growing plants. In Florida the plant is less common, populations are smaller, and the leaves tend to have a somewhat paler appearance. Although *L. mariana* is not readily available in the landscape trade, its attractive flowers make it a worthy candidate for home landscaping.

INDIAN PIPE
Monotropa uniflora Linnaeus
Heath Family (Ericaceae)

Description: At first glance it is difficult to believe that this species is a member of the blueberry and rhododendron (heath) family. The stems are herbaceous, lack chlorophyll, and have a texture more reminiscent of fungi than flowering plants. Stem color ranges from almost wholly red to reddish tinged, lavender, yellow, or white. The leaves are less than ¾" long and clasp the stem. A single, nodding, urn-shaped ¾–1¼" flower tops the stem, an excellent field character for distinguishing this species from the closely related and somewhat similar Pinesap *(M. hypopithys)*, which has several flowers per stem. Individual flowers have 5 petals and 10 stamens. The fruit is a 5-chambered capsule that splits at maturity to expose tiny brown seeds.

Bloom Season: Mostly August–October, but potentially at any time of year.

Habitat/Range: Moist to dry evergreen and deciduous forests. Throughout the region.

Comments: Species of *Monotropa* are often described as saprophytic herbs, meaning that they extract food from dead or decaying organic matter rather than producing food through the process of photosynthesis. In reality they may actually be parasitic on mycorrhizal fungi, a group of beneficial fungi that develop symbiotic relationships with the roots of many plants by extracting minerals and water from the soil for the host plant in return for access to the host plant's natural sugars. The stems of Indian Pipe turn black on drying, a character that is readily evident in aging plants.

VINE-WICKY OR CLIMBING FETTERBUSH
Pieris phillyreifolia (Hooker) Augustin de Candolle
Heath Family (Ericaceae)

Description: Two species of *Pieris* occur naturally in the southeastern United States, one in the mountains and Piedmont and the other in the Southeastern Coastal Plains. Vine-Wicky is a weakly erect woody shrub that takes its common name from it curious habit of growing just under the bark of cypress, titi, Atlantic white cedar, and other loose-barked wetland trees. Some individuals will grow far up the trunk of supporting trees. The tips of the stems often protrude from the tree's bark several meters above the ground, giving the appearance of adventitious branches from the trunk. The leaves are ¾–3" long, dark green, oblong, and leathery. Leaf margins are often smooth but may be minutely toothed from about the middle of the leaf to its tip. The ⅜" flowers are white, urn shaped, typical of the blueberry family, and borne in multiflowered racemes at the tips of the branches. The fruit is a hardened 5-valved woodlike capsule.

Bloom Season: February–March.

Habitat/Range: Wet flatwoods and bay swamps. Florida, Georgia, and South Carolina.

Comments: The tongue-twisting epithet *phillyreifolia* literally means "with foliage like *Phillyrea*," or Mock Privet, a genus of the Olive Family that occurs naturally in the Mediterranean region and the Middle East. The genus contains 4 species of evergreen shrubs and trees that are used horticulturally. At least some species of *Phillyrea* have leathery, toothed leaves. Vine-Wicky is not widespread but generally occurs in large populations in the few places where it is found. Despite its growth habit, it is not parasitic and uses its host only for support.

131

SWAMP AZALEA OR CLAMMY AZALEA

Rhododendron viscosum (Linnaeus) Torrey
Heath Family (Ericaceae)

Description: The tubular white flowers of this deciduous, summer-flowering shrub are more reminiscent of honeysuckles than azaleas, leading some observers to give it the common name Swamp Honeysuckle. The attractive, scaly flower buds appear in late spring, well after the new leaves have formed, and give way in late May to a showy collection of bright white ¾–1¾" flowers. Typical plants are 5–15' tall with ascending branches and alternate ½–3" leaves. The leaves are green above but often whitish below. The fruit is a hairy ⅜–⅝" capsule.

Bloom Season: May–August.

Habitat/Range: Swamps, bogs, pocosins, and wet flatwoods. Throughout the region.

Comments: Swamp Azalea is similar in many ways to Dwarf Azalea *(R. atlanticum)*. However, Dwarf Azalea typically flowers before or with the development of the new leaves, about a month earlier than Swamp Azalea. Swamp Azalea is included in some wildflower guides as *R. serrulatum,* a name that is considered by most modern taxonomists to be synonymous with *R. viscosum.*

HONEY-CUPS OR DUSTY ZENOBIA

Zenobia pulverulenta (Bartram ex Willdenow) Pollard
Heath Family (Ericaceae)

Description: Honey-Cups is an excellent name for this attractive woody shrub. The white cuplike ¼–½" flowers occur en masse in congested corymbs and are attractive to bees and other insects. The leaves are deciduous, alternate, up to about 2" long, and variable in color. On some plants, especially those of the Inner Coastal Plain, the leaves are conspicuously glaucous with a bluish white cast. Other plants, especially those nearer the coast, have dark green leaves (those with green leaves have been named forma *nitida* by some authorities). However, both forms often occur together. The fruit is a ¼" capsule.

Bloom Season: April–June.

Habitat/Range: Margins of pineland ponds and depressions, pocosins, and shrubby wetland edges. Georgia, South Carolina, North Carolina, and Virginia.

Comments: The genus name *Zenobia* is apparently in honor of Queen Zenobia, the Queen of Palmyra in the 3rd century AD. The epithet *pulverulenta* means "powdered as with dust," a reference to the bluish white coloring of the foliage.

FLATTENED PIPEWORT OR HAT PIN
Eriocaulon compressum Lamarck
Pipewort Family (Eriocaulaceae)

Description: Several species of pipewort occur in the Atlantic Coastal Plain, only 2 of which are widespread and common. Both produce erect 1–3' flowering scapes topped by a dense hemispherical head of small grayish white flowers. Both also produce a basal cluster of mostly narrow, long-tapering "grasslike" leaves. The ½–¾" heads of Flattened Pipewort are soft and easily flattened or compressed between the fingers, a field identification character that explains both the common name and scientific epithet. The heads of the closely related *E. decangulare*, which is also called Pipewort or Hat Pin, are hard and knotlike. The sheath that surrounds the lower portion of the scape is typically longer than the leaves on plants of Flattened Pipewort, whereas the sheath is usually shorter than the leaves on plants of *E. decangulare*. The flowers are composed of 2 hairy

sepals and 2 at least partly fused petals. Sepals and petals are individually very small and require magnification to see clearly. The fruit is a minute, bumpy seed.

Bloom Season: February–October, but not continuously during this period; some plants flower mostly in early spring and others mostly in late summer or fall.

Habitat/Range: Margins of ponds and lakes, wet flatwoods, wet savannas. Throughout the region.

Comments: The several species of *Eriocaulon* as well the related Bog-Buttons of the genus *Lachnocaulon* hold their shape after drying and have been used extensively in dried plant arrangements. Unfortunately, indiscriminate collecting of mature plants can reduce the seed source in natural areas and lead to reduced populations.

AMERICAN HOG-PEANUT
Amphicarpaea bracteata (Linnaeus) Fernald
Pea Family (Fabaceae or Leguminosae)

Description: Clusters of white to pale lavender flowers are borne mainly from the leaf axils of this trailing or climbing herbaceous vine. The stem is minutely hairy and may be up to about 6' long. The leaves are long stalked and compound. The 3 stalked 1–4" leaflets have entire margins. Individual flowers are up to about ¾" long and appear somewhat tubular but are typical of the Pea Family, with an upper standard above the lateral and keel petals. The fruit is a flattened 2- to 4-seeded ¾–1¼" legume.

Bloom Season: July–September.

Habitat/Range: Moist hammocks to dry woodlands. Throughout the region.

Comments: American Hog-Peanut actually produces 2 types of flowers and fruit. The aboveground flowers described above are chasmogamous, meaning that they have exposed anthers and stigmas that are intended for cross-pollination. Belowground flowers are self-fertile, or cleistogamous. These subterranean flowers do not cross-pollinate and produce rounded, mostly 1-seeded subterranean legumes that give the plant its common name. The genus name *Amphicarpaea* derives from the Greek words *amphi*, meaning "both" and *carpus*, or "fruit," in reference to the 2 types of legumes. The epithet *bracteata* alludes to the leaflike bracts subtending the flowers.

THICK-POD WHITE WILD INDIGO

Baptisia alba (Linnaeus) Ventenat
Pea Family (Fabaceae or Leguminosae)

Description: This bushy upright herb looks more like a woody shrub that an herbaceous perennial. Typical plants grow to about 3' tall from an erect 4–8" stem. Leaves are 3 parted. Leaflets are up to about 3" long and often have a milky bloom on the upper surface. Flowers are slightly more than ¾" long, creamy white, and borne in a conspicuous showy raceme. The fruit is a spreading or hanging ¾–1¾" legume that becomes black with age.

Bloom Season: April–July.

Habitat/Range: Woodlands and dry roadsides. Florida, Georgia, South Carolina, and North Carolina.

Comments: The black fruit and slightly larger flowers help distinguish this species from *B. albescens,* its closest look-alike. The fruit of *B. albescens* is yellow-brown and the length of the flowers usually does not exceed about ¾". The names of these 2 species have been previously confused. Both have been referred to as *B. lactea,* and what we now know as *B. albescens* was once even called *B. alba.* Older wildflower guides sometimes have them reversed.

SUMMER FAREWELL OR EASTERN PRAIRIE-CLOVER

Dalea pinnata (J. F. Gmelin) Barneby
Pea Family (Fabaceae or Leguminosae)

Description: The leafy stems of this 2–3' perennial herb are sometimes rigid and erect in habit but are more often strongly leaning or ascending. The leaves are pinnately divided into 3–15 short, threadlike ¼" leaflets. Individual flowers are small with bright white petals and are borne in dense, conspicuous, headlike clusters.

Bloom Season: September–October.

Habitat/Range: Sandhills, sandy ridges, and dry roadsides. Florida, Georgia, and South Carolina, North Carolina.

Comments: Summer Farewell is a well-named species. Its showy heads of bright white flowers appear in early fall at the close of the summer flowering period. The genus name *Dalea* is in honor of English botanist and physician Dr. Samuel Dale (1659–1739). The specific epithet *pinnata* refers to the pinnately divided or featherlike leaves. This species is endemic to the southeastern United States and has been known by several previous scientific names, the most recent being *Petalostemon pinnatum.*

WHITE SCREWSTEM
Bartonia verna (Mich.) Raf. ex Barton
Gentian Family (Gentianaceae)

Description: The tiny white 4-petaled flowers of this diminutive gentian arise at the top of a purplish, threadlike 2–8" stem. Petals are white, ¼–⅜" long, and widest above the middle. The inconspicuous scalelike leaves are less than ¼" long and are typically arranged oppositely or suboppositely along the stem but may be few in number and remotely alternate. The fruit is a tiny ovoid capsule with numerous minute seeds.

Bloom Season: January–March.

Habitat/Range: Wet meadows, savannas, bogs, seepages in pinelands, moist to wet roadsides, and shallow ditches. Throughout the region.

Comments: Three species of *Bartonia* occur in our region, all of which are inconspicuous herbs with tiny leaves and threadlike stems. Twining Screwstem *(B. paniculata)* and Yellow Screwstem *(B. virginica)* typically flower in late summer and fall, and their inflorescences have several spreading or erect flowering branches. The epithet *verna* means "of the spring" and distinguishes White Screwstem by flowering time, although the flowering periods of Yellow Screwstem and White Screwstem may overlap with it in late winter. The common name alludes to the twisted flowering scape, which is common to the genus. White Screwstem is often very low growing and may be hidden below the accompanying grasses and forbs. Though somewhat common across its range, its relatively small size and low-growing habit make it easy to overlook.

VIRGINIA BARTONIA OR YELLOW SCREWSTEM

Bartonia virginica (Linnaeus) Britton, Sterns, & Poggenberg
Gentian Family (Gentianaceae)

Description: This fall-flowering herb has an erect, wiry 4–16" stem that is purplish below and yellowish above. The inconspicuous scalelike leaves are opposite just below the inflorescence, but alternate or subopposite leaves may be present on the lower stem. Several tiny greenish white flowers are borne at the top of an ascending raceme or narrow panicle. The lobes of the corolla are erect or ascending.

Bloom Season: July–January, sometimes into February in its Florida locations.

Habitat/Range: Savannas, wet flatwoods, bogs, swamps, and pocosins; often hidden by surrounding vegetation. Throughout the region.

Comments: Virginia Bartonia is often reported as uncommon in our region, which may have more to do with size and camouflage than with abundance. It is most similar to Twining Screwstem *(B. paniculata),* which flowers mostly in late summer and early fall and has alternate leaves just below the inflorescence. The leaves of Virginia Bartonia are opposite below the inflorescence and appear in late fall or early winter.

LANCE-LEAF ROSE-GENTIAN

Sabatia difformis (Linnaeus) Druce
Gentian Family (Gentianaceae)

Description: The 5 bright white flower petals of this robust herb are much longer than ⅜", a field identification character that easily distinguishes it from the somewhat similar Large-Leaf Rose-Gentian *(Sabatia macrophylla).* The oppositely branched inflorescence is 1½–6" wide and borne at the top of a stiffly erect 1–3' stem. Upper stem leaves are ¾–1½" long, opposite, strongly ascending, and sessile or strongly clasping. The lowest leaves are often submersed or subterranean.

Bloom Season: May–September.

Habitat/Range: Bogs, pocosins, pine savannas, and moist flatwoods. Throughout the region.

Comments: Several white-flowered Sabatia occur in our region, most of which are much smaller in stature than the 2 mentioned here. The closely related *S. macrophylla* has larger leaves, smaller flowers, and occurs in our region only in southwest Georgia and northeast Florida. The specific epithet *difformis* implies that the present species has an unusual form that is not typical of the genus.

REDROOT

Lachnanthes caroliana (Lam.) Dandy
Bloodwort Family (Haemodoraceae)

Description: The blood-red roots and rhizomes of this perennial herb easily justify its common name. The erect 1–2' flowering stem is topped by a solitary, terminal, branching inflorescence of small woolly ½" flowers. Leaves are alternate, linear, less than ¼" wide, and form a sheath around the stem. Basal leaves overlap one another at the base, reminiscent of the leaves of an iris, and are much longer and more closely spaced than those above. The fruit is a rounded ⅛" capsule with flat brown seeds.

Bloom Season: May–October.

Habitat/Range: Wet ditches and roadsides, wet flatwoods, bogs, swamp margins, and savannas, especially in disturbed areas. Throughout the region.

Comments: The genus name *Lachnanthes* derives from the Greek words *lachne,* meaning "wool or down," and *anthos,* meaning "flower," an allusion to the hairy flowers. The family name comes from the Greek word *haima,* which means "blood," in recognition of the red color of the roots, rhizomes, and internal fluids. The epithet is seen spelled two ways: *caroliniana* and *caroliana.* The original description of the plant used the latter name, which some authorities accept as the oldest valid name for the species. Other authorities consider this name to have been the result of a typographical error that is permitted to be corrected under the rules of botanical nomenclature.

DWARF WITCHALDER
Fothergilla gardenii Linnaeus
Witch Hazel Family (Hamamelidaceae)

Description: The leaves of Dwarf Witchalder are reminiscent of those of the closely related small tree, Witch Hazel *(Hamamelis virginiana)*. Witchalder is an erect, compact, slow-growing 2–4' branching deciduous shrub. The 1–4" leaves are colorful in the fall. Numerous flowers are borne on densely crowded 1–1¾" spikes at the tips of naked branches mostly prior to the emergence of the new leaves. Flowers lack petals. The fruit is a ¼–⅜" capsule.

Bloom Season: April–May.

Habitat/Range: Longleaf Pinelands, margins of swamps and seepages, savannas, pocosins. Georgia, South Carolina, North Carolina, and perhaps Virginia (also Florida, but west of our region).

Comments: This is an uncommon shrub in our region and is considered imperiled in Georgia. Though rare in nature, it has found great favor as a garden plant. It is widely used throughout the southeastern United States for its showy flowers and colorful leaves, which are bronze in early spring, dark green in summer, and varying shades of yellow, orange, pink, violet, and scarlet in autumn.

WHITE SUNNYBELL
Schoenolirion albiflorum (Rafinesque) R. R. Gates
Hyacinth Family (Hyacinthaceae; included within the Agavaceae by some authorities)

Description: White Sunnybell has elongated, closely set basal leaves and an erect flowering stem. Flowers are small (about ⅜" wide), white, and 6-parted with conspicuous yellow anthers and a yellowish green ovary. They are borne singly at the tips of slender branches.

Bloom Season: May–July.

Habitat/Range: Wet pinelands, savannas, bogs, and edges of cypress depressions. Florida and Georgia.

Comments: The branched inflorescence and long-stalked flowers help distinguish White Sunnybell from the similar and closely related false asphodels of the genus *Tofieldia*. All 3 of these species are similar in habitat, form, and morphology and were formerly included within the Lily Family. White Sunnybell is sparsely distributed in our region. Although it is widespread in northern Florida, it occurs in only a handful of counties in southeast Georgia and is considered critically imperiled in that state. It is distinguished from Bog False Asphodel *(T. racemosa),* the only False Asphodel with which it overlaps in range, by its flowers being borne 1 to the node.

CLIMBING HYDRANGEA OR WOODVAMP
Decumaria barbara Linnaeus
Hydrangea Family (Hydrangeaceae)

Description: Observing the flowers of this common wetland vine is not easy. Woodvamp normally climbs high into the trees and often flowers only near the top of the stem. Some of the best places in our region to see it flowering include the extensive boardwalk systems at Francis Beidler Forest and Congaree National Park, both of which are located in South Carolina. Plants at these locations often take advantage of the filtered light coursing though gaps in the forest canopy and sometimes flower even at eye level. The tiny flowers are borne in showy 1–4" clusters at the tips of new lateral branches. Leaves are opposite, ovate, 2–6" long, and bluntly toothed along the margins. The fruit is a small-ribbed ¼" capsule that has the superficial appearance of a king's crown (when viewed with magnification).

Bloom Season: May–June.

Habitat/Range: Bottomlands, swamp forests, and seepage heads. Throughout the region.

Comments: Climbing Hydrangea is easy to identify by its leaves alone. Though numerous vines with opposite leaves occur in association with it, including Trumpet Creeper *(Campsis radicans)*, Cross Vine *(Bignonia capreolata)*, and several species of *Clematis*, none has the large, fleshy leaves with bluntly toothed margins of Climbing Hydrangea. The rare and somewhat hard to find Bay Star Vine *(Schisandra glabra)* occupies similar habitats and is similar in general appearance but has alternate leaves with smooth margins.

VIRGINIA WILLOW, VIRGINIA SWEETSPIRE, OR TASSEL-WHITE
Itea virginica Linnaeus
Sweetspire Family (Iteaceae)

Description: Virginia Sweetspire is a somewhat viny deciduous shrub with arching stems that may be up to about 6' tall. The alternate leaves are 2–4" long and mostly elliptical in outline. The margins of the leaves are finely toothed throughout, a field character that helps distinguish it from the somewhat similar Sweet Pepperbush *(Clethra alnifolia)*. Tiny white flowers are borne in a conspicuous showy 1–4" raceme at the tips of the branches. The fruit is a hardened capsule.

Bloom Season: May–June.

Habitat/Range: Swamps and swampy edges, wet shaded ditches, moist woodlands, and narrow forested drainages. Throughout the region.

Comments: In the absence of flowers, Virginia Willow may also be confused with Swamp Doghobble *(Leucothoe racemosa)*, another woody wetland shrub. The leaves of Virginia Willow are mostly over 2" long whereas the leaves of Swamp Doghobble are generally less than 2" long. The genus *Itea* has been included within several botanical families, including the Saxifragaceae, Grossulariaceae, and Escalloniaceae, a testament to its uniqueness. About 20 other species occur in the genus, all of which are restricted to eastern Asia and western Malaysia. Virginia Willow, or Virginia Sweetspire as many gardeners prefer to call it, has become a popular native landscape plant that is regularly used in naturalistic landscapes as well as to conceal the borders of decks and patios. Several horticultural cultivars have been developed, some with larger, brighter flowers.

SWAMP ROSEMALLOW
Hibiscus moscheutos Linnaeus
Mallow Family (Malvaceae)

Description: This robust mallow is a 6' tall herbaceous perennial of freshwater and brackish-water marshes. The leaves are narrowly to broadly lance-shaped and variable in size. Typical leaves are 3–6" long and 1–2" wide, but larger leaves may reach lengths of 8" and widths of 5". The lower surfaces of the leaves are grayish from a dense feltlike covering of matted hairs. The flowers are large and showy with 5, 3–4" white or sometimes pinkish petals that have red or purple bases. The fruit is a conspicuous 1–1½" capsule.

Bloom Season: June–September.

Habitat/Range: Tidal fresh and brackish marshes, swamps, and wetland depressions; especially common and showy in ditches along interstate highways. Throughout the region.

Comments: Some authorities recognize 3 subspecies of *H. moscheutos* for our region, distinguishing between them by flower color, type and amount of pubescence, and characteristics of the flower stalks. Swamp Rosemallow may be distinguished from Pineland Hibiscus *(H. aculeatus)* by the shape of its leaves.

FLY POISON
Amianthium muscitoxicum (Walter) A. Gray
(Syn: *A. muscaetoxicum* (Walter) A. Gray)
Melanthium Family (Melanthiaceae)

Description: Fly Poison is an erect perennial herb that grows to 3' tall. The stem arises from a subterranean bulb and is terminated by a showy, cone-shaped 2–4" many-flowered inflorescence. The stalked flowers are less than ½" wide with 6 bright white petals and 6 green sepals. Stem leaves are small, lance-shaped, and reduced in size upwards. Basal leaves are narrow, strap shaped, and up to 2' long but typically less than 1" wide. The fruit is a thin-walled capsule with shiny, brownish black ³⁄₁₆" seeds.

Bloom Season: April–July.

Habitat/Range: Sandhills, rich woods, southern mixed hardwood forests, drier flatwoods, and moist slopes. Throughout the region.

Comments: Fly Poison contains poisonous alkaloids that are toxic to livestock. A concoction of crushed bulbs and sugar has been used to kill flies. The specific epithet derives from the Latin words *muscae,* meaning "flies," and *toxicum,* meaning "poison." This is the only species in this genus.

CROW POISON OR OSCEOLA'S PLUME
Stenanthium densum (Desr.) Zomlefer & Judd
(Syn: *Zigadenus densus* (Desr.) Fernald)
Melanthium Family (Melanthiaceae)

Description: The ground cover of recently burned flatwoods and pine savannas can be filled with the showy plumes of Crow Poison. The nearly leafless stem grows to about 5' tall and is topped by a conspicuous 3–5" cone-shaped inflorescence of densely crowded flowers. The flowers have 6 petals that are white when fresh but usually turn an attractive rose-purple as they mature. The fruit is a 3-lobed purplish to brownish ½" capsule. Most of the leaves are borne at the base of the plant and are narrowly linear in outline but may reach lengths nearly equaling the height of the stem.

Bloom Season: March–June.

Habitat/Range: Flatwoods, bogs, savannas, and moist pinelands. Throughout the region.

Comments: Species of *Stenanthium* and *Zigadenus* are often referred to as Death Camas due to the presence of several toxic alkaloids in their tissues. Crow Poison is considered to be among the 5 most poisonous members of this group and has reportedly been implicated in the deaths of grazing livestock. The bulbs resemble onions. If eaten, they are said to cause headache, dizziness, dry mouth, salivating, burning sensations and numbness to the lips, vomiting, nausea, difficulty breathing, muscle weakness, low blood pressure, and irregular heartbeat. In severe cases coma or death may result. *Stenanthium densum* is often seen listed under the name *Zigadenus densus,* by which it was long known. Recent evidence suggests that the genus *Zigadenus* contains only a single species, *Z. glaberrimus.*

143

VIRGINIA BUNCHFLOWER
Veratrum virginicum (Linnaeus) Aiton f.
Melanthium Family (Melanthiaceae)

Description: Virginia Bunchflower is a coarse perennial herb from a stout bulblike root. The stems are up to 6' tall and are branched at the top into a showy, many-flowered inflorescence. The leaves are linear in outline, usually less than 1" wide, and up to about 2' long. The lower leaves are closely spaced and sheath the stem but reduce in both size and sheathing upward and become more widely spaced. The stalks of the inflorescence are up to about 3' tall with numerous, greenish white flowers that turn purplish as they mature. Individual flowers consist of 6 flat, spreading ¼–⅜" tepals (undifferentiated petals and sepals). The seeds are borne in a 3-chambered capsule that changes from brownish to reddish with age.

Bloom Season: June–September.

Habitat/Range: Swamps, bogs, wet pinelands, savannas, seepages, and alluvial bottomlands. Throughout the region (but in Florida mostly south and west of the region).

Comments: Virginia Bunchflower is listed as an obligate wetland herb, meaning that it is unlikely to be found far from saturated habitats. It is most similar to Death Camas (*Zigadenus glaberrimus*) and, like it, is poisonous if ingested. The two may be distinguished by their flower stalks. The stalks of Virginia Bunchflower are hairy, while those of Death Camas are glabrous. Virginia Bunchflower has recently been transferred to the genus *Veratrum* on the strength of similarities between it and other plants in the genus but is still referred to as *Melanthium virginicum* in many texts and plant lists.

SANDBOG DEATH CAMAS
Zigadenus glaberrimus Michx.
Melanthium Family (Melanthiaceae)

Description: This is an erect, coarse, clump-forming perennial from a thickened rhizome. The stems are up to 5' tall. The pyramidal inflorescence is relatively open and up to about 16" tall. Individual flowers have 6 creamy white ⅜–½" tepals, each of which is vested at the base with 2 conspicuous golden glandular dots. The fruit is a more or less conical capsule a little less than ½" long.

Bloom Season: July–September.

Habitat/Range: Flatwoods, bogs, wet roadside ditches, and pine savannas. Throughout the region, but only at the western edge of the region in Florida and uncommon in Georgia.

Comments: Sandbog Death Camas is more similar to *Veratrum virginicum* than it is to other species of death camas. Until somewhat recently the genus *Zigadenus* included several species but is now considered monotypic, meaning that it consists of only a single species. The tissues of Sandbog Death Camas contain poisonous alkaloids similar to those of Crow Poison.

LITTLE FLOATING HEART
Nymphoides cordata (Elliott) Fernald
Buckbean Family (Menyanthaceae)

Description: The shallow margins of sandhill and pineland lakes can be nearly covered with the tiny heart-shaped leaves of Little Floating Heart. The leaves are variegated purple and green above and typically less than 2" long (sometimes longer). The small white 5-petaled flowers are about ½" wide and appear to float on the water's surface but are borne on slender 1¼" stalks. The submerged stems are slender and filiform.

Bloom Season: April–August.

Habitat/Range: Pineland ponds, slow-moving streams, and beaver ponds. Georgia, South Carolina, and North Carolina (also Florida, but west of our region).

Comments: Little Floating Heart occurs in our region mostly in the Fall Line Hills. In Florida it occurs in sandhill ponds of the western panhandle, similar to those of its Carolina locations. It is superficially similar to the more widespread Big Floating Heart *(N. aquatica)*. However, the leaves of Big Floating Heart are normally well over 2½" long and are purple beneath whereas the leaves of Little Floating Heart are typically much less than 3" long.

MEALY COLICROOT OR NORTHERN WHITE COLICROOT

Aletris farinosa Linnaeus
Bog Asphodel Family (Nartheciaceae)

Description: The common and scientific names of this perennial herb come from the mealy appearance of the flowers (*farinosa* means "mealy or powdery"). Unlike the similar Southern Colicroot, the flowers of Mealy Colicroot exceed ¼" in length, are longer than broad, and are in general form reminiscent of a white-flowered form of Yellow Colicroot *(A. lutea)*. Flowering stems are 1–3' tall and subtended by a close-set cluster of yellowish green lance-shaped 2–5" basal leaves. Flowers are borne in a narrow raceme at the top of the flowering stem.

Bloom Season: May–August.

Habitat/Range: Dry uplands, bogs, and moist pinelands. Georgia, South Carolina, North Carolina, and Virginia (also Florida, but west of our region).

Comments: Decoctions from the roots of this species have been used to stimulate appetite, relieve indigestion, and treat diarrhea. This is the only Colicroot that occurs outside of the Southeastern Coastal Plains and is very common along roadsides in South Carolina and North Carolina. Flower shape distinguishes it from Southern Colicroot.

SOUTHERN COLICROOT

Aletris obovata Nash
Bog Asphodel Family (Nartheciaceae)

Description: The creamy white or white flowers of Southern Colicroot are borne along the uppermost portion of a 2–3' flowering scape. Individual flowers are urn shaped, about ¼" long, and curve inward at the tip, thus being ellipsoid in outline. The yellowish green leaves are about 4" long and borne in a tufted rosette at the base of the plant.

Bloom Season: April–June.

Habitat/Range: Moist to wet pinelands and savannas. Florida, Georgia, and South Carolina.

Comments: Concoctions from the roots of the genus *Aletris* were used by American Indians and European immigrants to relieve colic and other stomach ailments. Southern Colicroot is similar in many respects to White Colicroot *(A. farinosa).* The two may be distinguished by the length-to-width ratio of their flowers. Flowers of Southern Colicroot are typically about as broad as long at maturity while those of White Colicroot are typically longer than broad at maturity and are slightly spreading or opened at the apex.

AMERICAN WHITE WATER-LILY, FRAGRANT WHITE WATER-LILY, OR POND-LILY
Nymphaea odorata W. T. Aiton
Water Lily Family (Nymphaeaceae)

Description: White Water-Lily takes its common name from its floating habit and showy white blossoms, which are actually quite different from the flowers of the true lilies. The families Nymphaeaceae and Liliaceae are not closely related. White Water-Lily is characterized by large 5–12" rounded floating leaves that are green above and often purplish below. The many petaled flowers are white (sometimes tinged with pink), floating, and very fragrant. The conspicuous rounded 1–2" fruit contains numerous tiny seeds.

Bloom Season: April–September.

Habitat/Range: Ponds, lakes, and slow-moving backwaters of rivers and streams. Throughout the region.

Comments: White Water-Lily is an extremely variable species. Some authorities recognize several varieties, including variety *gigantea,* which has larger flowers, and variety *minor,* which has smaller flowers. The family and genus names derive from the Greek word for "water nymph." The epithet *odorata* means fragrant. Yellow Water-Lily *(N. mexicana)* also occurs in parts of our region but has yellow flowers.

FRINGE-TREE OR OLD MAN'S BEARD
Chionanthus virginicus Linnaeus
Olive Family (Oleaceae)

Description: This nondescript shrub or small deciduous tree is easily overlooked for much of the year. However, in early spring numerous individuals seem to burst into blossom all at the same time, often appearing to dominate the woodlands and leaving little doubt about its relative abundance. Flowering specimens vary 3–10' tall and have opposite, pale green, mostly 2–7" leaves. The flowers have 4 creamy white strap-shaped ¾–1¼" petals that are unmistakable. The fruit is a ½–¾" olivelike drupe that is borne in a dangling cluster from the previous year's twigs.

Bloom Season: April–May.

Habitat/Range: Wet pinelands, dry upland forests, southern mixed hardwood forests, and swamp margins. Throughout the region.

Comments: Fringe-Tree's showy flowers, slow growth, and attractive form have made it a sought after southern landscape plant. It produces flowers when very young, making it a nice addition to the garden. The genus name *Chionanthus* means "having snow-white flowers," a description that doesn't fit the flowers of the present species.

147

LONG-HORNED REINORCHID OR MICHAUX'S ORCHID
Habenaria quinqueseta (Michx.) Eaton
Orchid Family (Orchidaceae)

Description: The reason for the common and scientific names for this terrestrial orchid is not difficult to discern: *quinqueseta* is a Latin adjective meaning "five-bristled," referring to the conspicuous hornlike lobes of the lip and lateral petals. The lip is deeply divided into 2 narrow outer lobes and 1 slightly wider inner lobe. The ½–1" lateral petals are 2-parted with one part being elongated and narrowly filiform. A long, clublike spur droops below the flower, sometimes measuring 6" in length. Spurs turn brown with age and sometimes look like fallen twigs or other debris that have become entangled in the flowers. As many as 14 greenish white flowers are borne along the upper portion of an erect leafy stem that may be more than 18" tall. Broad parallel-veined 1–4" leaves sheath the lower stem but decrease in size upwards.

Bloom Season: August–September.

Habitat/Range: Moist to wet pinelands, flatwoods, hammocks, and swamps. Florida, Georgia, and South Carolina.

Comments: Individuals with exceptionally long spurs are considered by some authorities to represent a distinct variety and by other authorities to represent a distinct species. This and other species of *Habenaria* are sometimes called reinorchids. *Habenaria* comes from the Latin *habena*, which means "strap or rein," in reference to the strap-shaped spur common to some species within the genus. This reference might apply equally well to the middle lobe of the lip in the present species.

WHITE FRINGED ORCHID
Platanthera blephariglottis (Willd.) Lindl.
Orchid Family (Orchidaceae)

Description: The stout, strongly ribbed leafy stem of White Fringed Orchid may be 3' tall or more. Leaves are broadly lance-shaped below but become slightly more linear above. Larger leaves may be up to about 32" long and 2" wide. As many as 60 creamy white 1–2" flowers are borne in a conspicuous terminal 3–6" conical inflorescence. Flowering begins on the lower part of the raceme and progresses upwards. Unopened flowers are clublike. Fully opened flowers have spreading lateral sepals, an upright hood, a long-fringed, tonguelike lip, and an exceptionally long spur. The fruit is a 1½–2" capsule.

Bloom Season: July–September.

Habitat/Range: Moist pinelands, meadows, bogs, flatwoods, pineland depressions, roadside ditches, and transition zones between ridges and bay swamps. Throughout the region.

Comments: Two varieties occur in our region. Variety *conspicua* is a large-flowered, luxuriant southern form whereas the northern variety, *blephariglottis,* is smaller and prefers cooler soil temperatures. Snowy Orchid *(P. nivea)* is white flowered but smaller in stature.

SNOWY ORCHID OR BOG SPIKE
Platanthera nivea (Nuttall) Luer
(Syn: *Habenaria nivea* (Nuttall) Spreng.
Orchid Family (Orchidaceae)

Description: No other terrestrial orchid in our region has flowers as bright white as those of Snowy Orchid. At peak flower it is unmistakable. Stems are slender, rigidly erect, and topped by a cylindrical, congested, many-flowered raceme that may be up to about 5" long and 1¼" wide. Flowers are about ½" long overall, with a curving spur petal. The fruit is a darkened capsule.

Bloom Season: May–September, but flowering is irregular; given populations may not flower every year.

Habitat/Range: Savannas and bogs. Throughout the region.

Comments: The flowers of Large White Fringed Orchid (*P. blephariglottis* var. *conspicua*) are also white, but the raceme and individual flowers are much larger; the inflorescence, cone shaped; and the flower color, more nearly creamy white than bright white. Snowy Orchid is a Southeastern Coastal Plains endemic that was once much more common and abundant. It is currently considered vulnerable in Florida, imperiled in Georgia, and critically imperiled in North Carolina.

SHADOW WITCH
Ponthieva racemosa (Walt.) Mohr
Orchid Family (Orchidaceae)

Description: This upright terrestrial orchid is normally about 1' tall at flowering time. Flowering stems are greenish and lack stem leaves but are subtended at ground level by a basal rosette that may be visible for several months prior to and following flowering. The leaves are medium to light green and vary in size to about 2" wide and 6" long. The flowers are ¾–1" long, greenish white, and borne in a well-spaced raceme along the upper stem. The fruit is a capsule.

Bloom Season: September–November.

Habitat/Range: Typically found in shaded calcareous areas where limestone is near the ground surface. Throughout the region.

Comments: Shadow Witch is not common but sometimes occurs in large colonies. Though not always easily identified by leaves alone, it may be distinguished from other fall-blooming orchids by combination of its greenish white long-stalked flowers, greenish stalk, and basal leaf rosette. It is considered rare across much of the Atlantic Coastal Plain and is found in the Carolinas and Virginia mostly in the coastal counties.

GRASS-LEAVED LADIES'-TRESSES OR GIANT LADIES'-TRESSES
Spiranthes praecox (Walter) S. Watson.
Orchid Family (Orchidaceae)

Description: Numerous species of ladies'-tresses occur in the Atlantic Coastal Plain. Most are erect, terrestrial herbs with narrow stems and an elongated, often spiraling inflorescence of white or creamy white to sometimes greenish flowers. In Grass-Leaved Ladies'-Tresses the stems are 10–30" tall with 2–5 narrow basal leaves that are reminiscent of grass leaves. The 10–40 flowers are ¼–⅜" long, white with distinctive green veins inside, and subtended by appressed sepals, a combination of features that is helpful with field identification.

Bloom Season: February–July.

Habitat/Range: Savannas, bogs, moist roadsides, and upland meadows. Throughout the region.

Comments: More than a dozen species of *Spiranthes* occur in our region, many of which are difficult to distinguish from one another. The genus name *Spiranthes* comes from the Greek words *speira,* meaning "spiral" or "twisted object," and *anthos,* "flower." The epithet *praecox* means "early," an allusion to the early spring flowering period, especially in its more southern locations.

BLOODROOT OR RED PUCCOON
Sanguinaria canadensis Linnaeus
Poppy Family (Papaveraceae)

Description: *Sanguinaria* is a monotypic genus, meaning that the present species is its only member. Bloodroot is a low-growing perennial herb that grows from a thickened rhizome that exudes copious amounts of red sap when bruised or broken (hence, the common name). The 1½–5" leaves are more or less rounded in outline with shallowly lobed margins and are green above but distinctly silvery white below. Striking white flowers with 8–16, ¾–1" petals and up to about 24 stamens are borne singly on a leafless stem that eventually produces a distinctive, ellipsoid 1½–2½" capsule. The leaves continue to grow after the fruit has fallen and may reach 6–10" in width.

Bloom Season: February–April.

Habitat/Range: Rich deciduous woods. Throughout the region.

Comments: Two forms of this species have been reported for eastern North America. More northern plants (sometimes referred to as variety *canadensis*) have more deeply lobed leaves. The form most common in our area (referred to as variety *rotundifolia*) has rounded leaves with shallow lobbing. However, single populations often exhibit a variety of leaf shapes from plant to plant. This species is probably poisonous to humans if eaten in quantity, although its roots are sold as an herb. The red sap is a skin irritant to some and overdoses of the plant for medicinal purposes have reportedly caused burning of the mouth, nausea, vomiting, and respiratory distress. The genus name derives from the Latin *sanguis*, or "blood," in reference to the color of the sap.

CAROLINA GRASS-OF-PARNASSUS
Parnassia caroliniana Michaux
Parnassia Family (Parnassiaceae)

Description: Nothing about *Parnassia* resembles grass. Its simple flowering stalk arises from the center of a cluster of stalked fleshy leaves and is topped by a striking flower with white ⅝–¾" petals and a creamy white ovary that turns brownish with age. The flower petals are further adorned with an intricate network of parallel veins that arise as branchlets from the lowermost lateral veins. The 1–3½" leaves are medium to dark green, heart to egg shaped in outline, and borne from the base of the plant and along the lower portion of the flowering stem. Though the flowering period is somewhat short, the leaves are visible for an extended period before and after flowering.

Bloom Season: October–November.

Habitat/Range: Seepages, bogs, savannas, and the edges of drainages, streams, and depressions in pinelands. Florida, South Carolina, and North Carolina (near the western edge of our region in Florida).

Comments: Large-Leaved Grass-of-Parnassus *(P. grandifolia)* is similar but is easily recognized at flowering time by its dark green ovary and the dark green veins on its flower petals. Carolina Grass-of-Parnassus and Large-Leaved Grass-of-Parnassus are very similar vegetatively but may be tentatively distinguished when not flowering by habitat. Large-Leaved Grass-of-Parnassus tends to occupy wetter sites than Carolina Grass-of-Parnassus, though the habitat preferences for both are similar. Large-Leaved Grass-of-Parnassus is sparingly distributed in the coastal plain of North Carolina and in 2 counties in north-central Florida but also occurs in the Appalachian Mountains.

COASTAL PLAIN MILKWORT
Polygala setacea Michaux
Milkwort Family (Polygalaceae)

Description: This diminutive milkwort has an extremely slender and wiry 4–14" stem that is often branched at the apex. The leaves are alternate but are reduced to scalelike appendages that require close observation and 10X magnification to see clearly. Individual flowers are tiny, creamy white (sometimes tinged with pink), and borne in a congested ¼–⅝" raceme. Individual flowers are less than ⅛" long.

Bloom Season: June–August.

Habitat/Range: Savannas and flatwoods. Florida, Georgia, and perhaps the Carolinas.

Comments: This is the only one of our numerous milkworts that has creamy white flowers and alternate, scalelike leaves. Though small in stature with an imperceptibly slender stem, flowering specimens are not particularly difficult to spot in the sometimes sparse ground cover of flatwoods pinelands. However, it may first appear to be a tiny cocoon or other insect manufacture. The epithet *setacea* means "bristled," apparently in reference to the hairy seeds.

SANDHILL WILD-BUCKWHEAT, SOUTHERN WILD-BUCKWHEAT, OR DOG-TONGUE
Eriogonum tomentosum Michaux
Buckwheat Family (Polygonaceae)

Description: Whorled stem leaves and a large conspicuous inflorescence of creamy white flowers distinguish this species from most other sandhill herbs. Stem leaves are sessile, elliptical in outline, 1–2½" long, and borne 3–4 at the node. Basal leaves are stalked, to about 6" long, and are usually somewhat larger than those along the stem but may wither by flowering time. Lower leaf surfaces are densely covered with whitish to tan hairs. Flower heads are sessile or short stalked with 10–20 white to pinkish flowers. The pinkish tan fruit contains brown, flattened 3-ribbed nutlets.

Bloom Season: July–September.

Habitat/Range: Sandhills. Florida, Georgia, South Carolina, and North Carolina (rare in North Carolina and not recently seen).

Comments: The genus name *Eriogonum* means "woolly knee," an allusion to the hairy leaf nodes. The epithet *tomentosum* means "woolly" or "very hairy with matted hairs," in reference to the dense covering of hairs on the lower surfaces of the leaves. The common name Dog-Tongue alludes to the shape of the basal leaves.

DENSE-FLOWER SMARTWEED
Polygonum densiflorum Meisn.
Buckwheat Family (Polygonaceae)

Description: Dense-Flower Smartweed takes its common name and scientific epithet from the crowded racemes of tiny white flowers, a character that is not particularly helpful in field identification. This is a wetland perennial herb with spreading underground rhizomes and decumbent stems that root at the nodes. The narrow leaves are lance shaped and up to about 7" long and 2" wide. The flowers are creamy to greenish white with 5 very small petals that are about ⅛" long. The sepals bear glandular dots. The fruit is a hard 3-angled achene, reminiscent of the fruit of the sedges.

Bloom Season: June–October.

Habitat/Range: Marshes, swamps, pond and lake margins, and bottomland forests; commonly in standing water. Throughout the region (rare in Virginia).

Comments: About 15 species of *Polygonum* occur in this region, many of which are difficult to identify. The genus name *Polygonum* derives either from the Greek words for "many seeds" or "many knee-joints." Most smartweeds have swollen stem joints. Spreading rhizomes and gland-dotted sepals help distinguish Dense-Flower Smartweed.

COMMON NEW JERSEY TEA OR REDROOT
Ceanothus americanus Linnaeus
Buckthorn Family (Rhamnaceae)

Description: This is a low, rounded, deciduous woody shrub to about 3' tall, but it often has the aspect of a bushy herb. Stems are typically multibranched and covered with short, curly hairs interspersed with long, shaggy hairs. The ¾–3½" leaves are simple, alternate, and mostly lance shaped in outline. Small white flowers are borne in rounded clusters in the leaf axils and at the branch tips. The fruit is a brown 3-chambered ¼" drupe.

Bloom Season: May–June.

Habitat/Range: Dry woods, woodland borders, sandy roadsides, and dry forest ridges. Throughout the region.

Comments: The foliage, flowers, and roots of New Jersey Tea were dried, brewed, and used as a substitute for tea during the American Revolution, a technique that was probably learned form the American Indians. Root tea, in particular, has been used medicinally for coughs, asthma, and other chest ailments. The flower clusters are often fluffy and have led to the common name Snowball in some locales. The name *Ceanothus* is from the Greek name for a European plant of the same genus.

RED CHOKEBERRY
Photinia pyrifolia (Lamarck) K. R. Robertson & J. B. Phipps
(Syn: *Aronia arbutifolia* (Linnaeus) Persoon)
Rose Family (Rosaceae)

Description: The compact clusters of small ornate flowers make it easy to see why this 3–9' deciduous shrub is a member of the Rose Family. The flowers start out pinkish in bud but become white at maturity and are composed of 5 rounded to obovate petals with crinkly margins. The petals subtend a mass of 5 pistils and 15–25 attractive stamens that are tipped with pinkish red anthers. The 1–4" leaves are simple, alternate, green above, paler below, and finely toothed along the margins. The marginal teeth are tipped with purplish red glands that are a distinctive field character but require magnification to see clearly. The fruit is a bright red ⅜" pome that often remains on the plant well into winter, long after the leaves have fallen.

Bloom Season: March–May.

Habitat/Range: Bogs, wet flatwoods, pocosins, swamp edges, wet savannas, and creek margins. Throughout the region.

Comments: Red Chokeberry is one of several shrubby members of the Rose Family that occurs in our region. It is easily distinguished from the others by the combination of its alternate leaves with gland-tipped marginal teeth and terminal clusters of 25 or more flowers. In late fall it might be confused with one of our deciduous hollies due to its bright red fruit; the hollies typically have smaller fruit with a hard central stone. Red Chokeberry has many scientific synonyms and has been placed in a variety of genera, including *Aronia* (the Chokeberries), *Pyrus* (the Pears), *Sorbus* (Mountain Ash), and *Crataegus* (the Haws). Some authorities still recognize it as *Aronia arbutifolia*. The scientific epithet *pyrifolia* means "with leaves like a pear."

155

CHEROKEE ROSE
Rosa laevigata Michaux
Rose Family (Rosaceae)

Description: This high climbing thorny vine is a common sight along rural southern roadsides. The dark green leaves are divided into 3 lance-shaped ¾–3" leaflets with toothed margins. The large white flowers are borne singly in the axils of the upper leaves and have 5 broad 1–1½" petals that subtend a mass of golden yellow anthers. The fruit is a reddish 1" hip.

Bloom Season: March–May.

Habitat/Range: Roadsides, fence lines, and the disturbed margins of upland woodlands. Florida (where mostly marginal to our region), Georgia, South Carolina, and North Carolina.

Comments: Cherokee Rose became Georgia's "floral emblem" on August 18, 1916, by a resolution of the Georgia General Assembly, which erroneously suggested that the species had "its origin among the aborigines of the northern portion of the state of Georgia, is indigenous to its soil, and grows with equal luxuriance in every county of the State." The species is actually native to China and was probably introduced to the United States in the middle 1700s for horticulture and cultivation. Some authorities suggest that the common name results from early distribution of the plant by the Cherokee Indians. Other legends associate it with the famous Trail of Tears when the Cherokee Nation was forced from its historical land. One of these legends holds that the rose grew in answer to a prayer to give strength to the mothers to care for their children during their forced migration, and that the flower's yellow center represents the gold stolen from the Cherokee Nation.

BUTTONBUSH

Cephalanthus occidentalis Linnaeus
Madder Family (Rubiaceae)

Description: Buttonbush is a large, coarse, wetland shrub that takes its common name from the rounded buttonlike fruiting heads that remain on the plant long after the flowers have fallen. It is probably best known for its tiny creamy white flowers, which are borne in pendulous 1–1½" pincushion-like clusters. The leaves are opposite or whorled 3–4 to the node and up to about 7" long and 4" wide. Typical plants are 8–10' tall but may be much taller.

Bloom Season: June–July.

Habitat/Range: Wetland depression, margins of shallow ponds, stream- and riverbanks, most often in standing water. Throughout the region.

Comments: This large woody shrub is common and widespread across the eastern United States. It occurs most often in relatively large colonies, especially along the edges of shallow lakes and ponds. Although it is a wetland plant under natural conditions, it adapts well to landscape use and is widely planted by native plant enthusiasts. It is vegetatively similar to the pink-flowered Fevertree *(Pinckneya bracteata)* but is easily distinguished by its flowers.

INNOCENCE, ROUNDLEAF BLUET, TRAILING BLUET, OR CREEPING BLUET

Houstonia procumbens (Walter ex J. F. Gmelin) Standley
(Madder Family (Rubiaceae)

Description: The common name Bluet is not a good fit for this species. Whereas the flowers of many plants in the genus are at least blushed with a bluish tint, those of Roundleaf Bluet are bright white. This is a creeping, often mat-forming perennial herb with decumbent stems and ovate to nearly rounded ¼–½" leaves that are often hidden by other ground-cover vegetation, especially in lawns and roadsides. On dunes and in sparsely vegetated sandy woods, all parts of the plant are more conspicuous. The tiny 4-petaled flowers are less than ⅝" wide and are borne singly at the tips of short, erect stalks.

Bloom Season: October–April.

Habitat/Range: Pinelands, dunes, lawns, close-cropped roadsides, and other disturbed sites. Florida, Georgia, and South Carolina.

Comments: This species is often seen listed by its synonym *Hedyotis procumbens*. *Hedyotis* means "sweet ear," the significance of which seems to be lost. The epithet *procumbens* means "prostrate." This species' low growth habit is an excellent field identification character.

PARTRIDGEBERRY, TWINBERRY OR TWINFLOWER
Mitchella repens Linnaeus
Madder Family (Rubiaceae)

Description: This low-growing, vinelike perennial is actually a woody plant, though its habit and form suggest otherwise. The stems are slender, prostrate, and mostly creeping and rooting at the nodes but are sometimes trailing and runnerlike. Leaves are up to about 1" long (often shorter), dark green, opposite, and vary from oval to nearly round in outline. The leaves are evergreen, making the plant easily identifiable throughout the year. Flowers are white, tubular with a flaring apex, and generally produced 2 per node, which explains the common name Twinflower. The fruit is a bright red drupe that appears in the fall. In large populations the showy fruit creates a decorative natural ground cover among the colorful litter of freshly fallen leaves.

Bloom Season: April–June.

Habitat/Range: Deciduous forests, rich woods, mixed hardwood and pine woodlands. Throughout the region.

Comments: The genus name *Mitchella* honors physician John Mitchell (1711–1768), a native Virginian born in Lancaster County and a regular correspondent with the Swedish-born scientist Carl von Linné, or Linnaeus. Linnaeus is credited with formulating the modern system of binomial nomenclature that is used today in the classification of all biological organisms. The epithet *repens* means "creeping" and references this species' ground-hugging growth habit. The common name Partridgeberry refers to the bright red fruit, which are easy prey for ground-dwelling fowl.

ROUGH MEXICAN CLOVER
Richardia scabra Linnaeus
Madder Family (Rubiaceae)

Description: The stems of this herbaceous perennial are sometimes erect and up to about 2' tall but may be spreading and decumbent. Leaves are opposite, mostly lance-shaped, 1–3" long, and rough to the touch along the midrib. Small, white 6-petaled flowers are borne in a dense headlike cluster at the top of the stem. Individual flowers are about ⅜" long. The tiny single-seeded fruit is covered with small protrusions (tubercles) that require magnification to see clearly.

Bloom Season: June–December

Habitat/Range: Vacant lots, roadsides, abandoned fields, and other dry, disturbed sites. Throughout the region.

Comments: Two species of *Richardia* are found in our region, both of which are widely viewed as non-native species introduced to our region from Central and South America. Nevertheless, some authorities consider Rough Mexican Clover to be native to parts of the southeastern United States. The epithet *scabra* means "rough," in reference to the roughened midribs of the leaves. The flowers of *R. brasiliensis* do not exceed ¼" in length.

LIZARD'S TAIL
Saururus cernuus Linnaeus
Lizard's Tail Family (Saururaceae)

Description: The scientific and common names of this species refer to the nodding densely flowered inflorescence. *Saururus* comes from the Greek words *sauros*, "a lizard," and *oura*, "a tail," and the epithet *cernuus* means "nodding." Whether the elongated flowering spike looks like a lizard's tail is conjectural. This is a perennial wetland herb that forms large colonies from underground rhizomes. Stems are erect and about 2' tall. Leaves are 3–4" long with entire margins and long-pointed tips. The 3–8" racemes produce rows of darkened, beadlike fruit, a condition that some observers suggest is more reminiscent of a lizard's tail than is the flowering spike

Bloom Season: May–July.

Habitat/Range: Swamps, marshes, and shaded roadside ditches; generally in wet areas. Throughout the region.

Comments: Lizard's Tail is likely to be confused only with Fairywand *(Chamaelirium luteum)*, a species of flatwoods, savannas, and upland bluffs. Fairywand is usually found only as scattered individuals; its leaves and those of Lizard's Tail bear no resemblance to one another.

HORSE-NETTLE OR BULL-NETTLE
Solanum carolinense Linnaeus
Nightshade Family (Solanaceae)

Description: Horse-Nettle arises from aggressive rhizomes and often forms large colonies. The 1–2½' stem and undersides of the leaves are armed with stout prickles that can pierce the skin. The 1½–6" leaves are alternate, coarsely toothed or shallowly lobed, and borne on stout petioles. Both the stem and leaves are covered with star-shaped clusters that consist of 4–8 hairs and arise from a single point (requires 10X magnification to see clearly). The flower petals are typically white, sometimes tinged with lavender, or are rarely wholly purple. The fruit resembles a tiny ½" tomato and is green at first but turns yellow at maturity.

Bloom Season: May–July.

Habitat/Range: Sandy roadsides, old fields, and other disturbed sites. Throughout the region.

Comments: Although Horse-Nettle is native to the region, its tendency to rapidly colonize disturbed areas has led to it being treated as a troublesome weed in pastures, fields, roadsides, and gardens. Horse-Nettle is in the same family as the tomato, but its fruit is not edible and is poisonous if ingested.

POLYPREMUM, RUSTWEED, OR JUNIPERLEAF
Polypremum procumbens Linnaeus
Tetrachondra Family (Tetrachondraceae)

Description: Plants of Polypremum typically form circular mats of arching and reclining branches, all of which radiate outwards from a central root crown (the epithet *procumbens* means "prostrate"). The mats of robust individuals may be over 2' in diameter. The numerous short, linear ½–1" leaves are opposite with a thickened, lustrous appearance. Tiny, white, 4-petaled flowers are borne singly from the leaf axils. The fruit is a tiny capsule that splits at maturity to expose minute yellowish seeds that are angled or squared in cross section.

Bloom Season: May–September.

Habitat/Range: Fields, lawns, roadsides, sandhills, hammocks, exposed sandbars, stabilized dunes, and moist to wet disturbed sites; adapts to a wide range of habitats. Throughout the region.

Comments: Polypremum is native to this region but displays a weedy habit. It was long included within the Logania Family (Loganiaceae), which some authorities have described as a "garbage can" family due to the wide differences in some of its member genera and species.

LOBLOLLY BAY OR GORDONIA
Gordonia lasianthus (Linnaeus) Ellis
Tea Family (Theaceae)

Description: Loblolly Bay is an attractive wetland tree with showy white flowers. Mature specimens may be 75' tall with a conical shape and attractive deeply furrowed bark. Even though it reaches large proportions, it often produces flowers when very young and shrublike, especially along the sunny edges of depression wetlands. The flowers are about 3" across with 5 white petals subtending a ringed mass of bright yellow stamens. The leaves are alternate, dark green above, paler below, and coarsely toothed along the margins. The fruit is a hard ⅝–¾" capsule.

Bloom Season: July–September.

Habitat/Range: Pocosins, bay swamps, swamp forests, wet pine flatwoods. Florida, Georgia, South Carolina, and North Carolina.

Comments: Sweetbay Magnolia *(Magnolia virginiana)* is also a white-flowered wetland tree and often grows in association with Loblolly Bay. However, the flowers of Sweetbay Magnolia have more than 5 petals and lack the ringed mass of bright yellow stamens.

SILKY CAMELLIA OR VIRGINIA STEWARTIA
Stewartia malacodendron Linnaeus
Tea Family (Theaceae)

Description: The 3" flowers of Silky Camellia are exceedingly beautiful. Five crinkly bright white petals subtend a central mass of purple stamens, creating a very attractive color contrast. The leaves are deciduous, alternate, mostly oval to elliptic in outline, and are arranged along each side of the supporting branch, giving plants a layered appearance.

Bloom Season: May–June.

Habitat/Range: Mesic forest, especially in association with Amercan Beech *(Fagus grandifolia)*. Throughout the region, although in Florida it is associated mostly with the Apalachicola River.

Comments: It is not surprising that Silky Camellia has been adopted by horticulturist for use as a landscape plant. However, it is quite finicky in the garden and can be difficult to maintain. Two species of *Stewartia* occur in the Southeast. Silky Camellia is a species of the coastal plain and outer Piedmont. Mountain Camellia *(S. ovata)* is found mostly in the mountains and inner Piedmont. Silky Camellia is listed as a specialty for Great Dismal Swamp, Virginia.

161

COASTAL BOG ASPHODEL

Tofieldia racemosa (Walter) Britton, Sterns, & Poggenburg
Tofieldia Family (Tofieldiaceae)

Description: Two species of *Tofieldia* occur in the region. Carolina Bog Asphodel *(T. glabra)* flowers from late August to October and is restricted in distribution mostly to southeastern North Carolina but also occurs in 2 counties in adjacent South Carolina. Carolina Bog Asphodel produces a smooth, erect stem (scape) to about 2' tall and has linear "grasslike" basal leaves. The flowers are borne in a terminal raceme with a single flower per node. Coastal False Asphodel *(T. racemosa)* is similar in form, size, and habitat preference, but its scape is rough to the touch due to the presence of a copious covering of short glandular hairs. The flowers of Coastal False Asphodel are typically borne in clusters of 3–7 on the lower and middle portions of the scape,

although there may be only 1 flower per node near the apex of the scape.

Bloom Season: June–August.

Habitat/Range: Wet savannas, seepages, and bog-pocosin ecotones. Throughout the region.

Comments: The common name Asphodel is after the genus *Asphodelus*, especially White Asphodel *(A. ramosus)*, a European lily with edible roots that were used as an ingredient in the making of asphodel bread. White Sunnybell *(Schoenolirion albiflorum)*, which is endemic to extreme southeastern Georgia and Florida, is similar. Its flowers are borne 1 per node at the tips of comparatively long stalks.

CORNSALAD
Valerianella radiata (Linnaeus) Dufresne
Valerian Family (Valerianaceae)

Description: This 8–28" moderately succulent annual herb has an erect stem with opposite branching. The stem leaves are opposite, sessile, mostly spatulate in outline, and 1–2" long; basal leaves are 1–5". Tiny white flowers tip the branches and produce exserted stamens, meaning that the stamens protrude beyond the ends of the petals. The tiny 3-locular fruit typically develops into a single leathery nutlet.

Bloom Season: March–May.

Habitat/Range: Moist roadsides and disturbed sites, bottomlands, woodland borders. Throughout the region (but mostly west of our region in Florida).

Comments: This is a native species with seemingly weedy habits. It is often found in conjunction with common non-native roadside weeds. The genus name *Valerianella* is the diminutive form of *Valeriana*, which is the genus name of Valerian (*V. officinalis*), a common medicinal herb grown throughout Europe and touted for many health benefits. The name likely derives from the Latin word *valere*, "to be healthy." The genus is also sometimes placed in the family Caprifoliaceae.

EASTERN BEARDTONGUE
Penstemon laevigatus Aiton
Speedwell Family (Veronicaceae)

Description: The common name Beardtongue comes from the conspicuous hairy undeveloped stamen (staminode) that is surrounded by 4 shorter fertile stamens. The flowers are tubular, white to purplish, up to about 1" long, and occasionally have faint purple lines in the throat. Plants are erect and 16–40" tall, with opposite 2–5" stem leaves and long-stalked 6–8" basal leaves.

Bloom Season: May–June.

Habitat/Range: Bottomlands and the edges of upland forests, mostly in moist sites. Throughout the region (only at the extreme western edge of our region in Florida).

Comments: Eastern Beardtongue is 1 of 3 common beardtongues likely to be encountered in our region. It may be separated from the other common species, *P. australis* and *P. multiflorus*, by the shape of its flowers, which have a dilated or inflated throat. The rare *P. dissectus*, endemic to Georgia, has bipinnately divided leaves. *P. pallidus*, also uncommon in our region, is restricted mostly to limestone and shale barrens.

163

MANYFLOWER BEARDTONGUE
Penstemon multiflorus Chapman ex Bentham
Speedwell Family (Veronicaceae)

Description: The many-flowered inflorescence of Manyflower Beardtongue easily distinguishes it from other white-flowered beardtongues in our region. Whereas the inflorescences of most members of the genus contain 10 or fewer flowers, the inflorescence of Manyflower Beardtongue may contain 30 or more. This is an erect herb to about 4' tall with opposite, sessile 1–6" stem leaves and white, tubular 2-lipped flowers.

Bloom Season: April–September.

Habitat/Range: Sandhills, sandy roadsides, and flatwoods. Florida and Georgia.

Comments: The genus *Penstemon* is a large and notoriously complex genus with many difficult-to-identify species. The epithet *multiflorus* means "with many flowers," an obvious field identification character that makes Manyflower Beardtongue easy to recognize, even at highway speed. Manyflower Beardtongue often occurs in very large populations that may cover several acres, especially in sandy disturbed sites such as freshly cleared sandhills. It is most abundant in Florida and is the only Beardtongue in our region with a predominantly southern distribution.

PRIMROSE-LEAF VIOLET
Viola primulifolia Linnaeus
Violet Family (Violaceae)

Description: Only 2 white-flowered acaulescent (lacking stem leaves) violets are common and widespread in our region. Primrose-Leaf Violet is distinguished from the similarly flowered Lanceleaf Violet *(V. lanceolata)* by its 1–2½" leaf blades, which are mostly ovate in outline with a broadly tapering, truncate, or nearly heart-shaped base. Flowers are white, ½–¾" wide, striped with purple, and borne on stalks that generally exceed the leaves in length. The fruit is a ⅜" capsule.

Bloom Season: Predominantly March–May.

Habitat/Range: Bogs, savannas, stream and pond edges, pocosins, and moist forests. Throughout the region.

Comments: Violets are noted for their tendency toward cleistogamy, the production of small, generally inconspicuous self-fertile flowers that do not open. In the present species these flowers are borne on erect 1–5" stalks and are enclosed by ¼" sepals that are similar in general appearance to the sepals of the chasmogamous, or "normal" flowers.

YELLOW FLOWERS

This section includes flowers that range from pale to bright yellow. Check the white, green, or red and orange sections if you don't find your plant here.

SAVANNA MILKWEED OR STALKED MILKWEED
Asclepias pedicellata Walter
Dogbane Family (Apocynaceae)

Description: This is our only milkweed with the combination of milky sap, opposite leaves, and yellowish flowers. Butterflyweed *(A. tuberosa)* typically has orange (sometimes yellowish) flowers, clear sap, and alternate leaves. Plants of Savanna Milkweed average 4–18" tall and arise from a thick, elongated, irregularly knobby root with an expanded tuber. The stems are erect, hairy, and purplish near the base. The flowers are erect, about ⅝" long, and borne in 2–8 flowered clusters (umbels) at the tip of a ¼–½" stalk. The terminal umbels are often paired. The ⅜" corolla lobes are erect and greenish yellow. Leaves are sessile, narrowly lance-shaped to linear in outline, and 1¼–3½" long. Seeds are borne in a narrow, elongated 4–6" pod.

Bloom Season: June–August.

Habitat/Range: Wet flatwoods and savannas. Florida, Georgia, South Carolina, and North Carolina.

Comments: Savanna Milkweed is more common in Florida and southern Georgia than the remainder of its range and is considered rare in the Carolinas. It is considered imperiled in Georgia and North Carolina, and critically imperiled in South Carolina. Savanna Milkweed often occurs in small populations of widely scattered individuals. The epithet *pedicellata* and common name Stalked Milkweed refer to the conspicuous flower stalk (pedicel). The low stature makes Savanna Milkweed sometimes difficult to spot in dense flatwoods, even in known locations.

GOLDEN CLUB, NEVER WET, OR BOG TORCHES
Orontium aquaticum Linnaeus
Arum Family (Araceae)

Description: The reason for Golden Club's common name is not difficult to discern. The erect golden yellow 1–2½" clublike spadix (fleshy flower stalk) is a conspicuous adornment to shallow pools or slow-moving streams. The reddish spathe bearing the spadix has a conspicuous white ring just below the inflorescence. The blades of the thick dark green long-stalked leaves are 6–12" long with shiny waxy surfaces. Water droplets stand on the leaf tissue or run off in small droplets, hence the suggestion that the leaves are "never wet."

Bloom Season: February–April.

Habitat/Range: Pools, streams, and swamps. Throughout the region.

Comments: Golden Club often produces large floating colonies on the surface of small pools. All parts of the plant contain calcium oxalate crystals that, when ingested, can cause extensive swelling of the throat, resulting in asphyxiation. Nevertheless, Native Americans processed the roots and seeds for food. One of the best places to see this species in abundance is along the canoe trails and slow-moving backwaters of Okefenokee Swamp at Stephen Foster State Park, Georgia, or in the Okefenokee National Wildlife Refuge. Here, in the subdued light of the swamp's shadowy edges, large floating mats of attractive dark green leaves overtopped by bright yellow flowers give meaning to the name Bog Torch.

LEOPARD'S-BANE
Arnica acaulis (Walter) Britton, Sterns, & Poggenberg
Aster Family (Asteraceae or Compositae)

Description: The epithet *acaulis* means "stemless" or "with very short stems," in reference to the short, erect woody caudex at the base of the plant. The apparent 0.5–2' stem from which the flowers are produced is probably more accurately described as a scape (a mostly leafless flower stalk). The scapes are usually branched but may be unbranched. Basal leaves are 1½–6" long and up to 3" wide. The few stem leaves are much smaller. Up to about 30 bright yellow flower heads are produced in a branched inflorescence, each of which typically contains 10–15, ⅝–1" rays. All parts of the herbage are minutely hairy and glandular. The fruit is a black ⅛–¼" achene.

Bloom Season: April–July.

Habitat/Range: Sandhills, pine savannas, sandy woodlands, and roadsides. Throughout the region, but only along the western edge of the region in Florida.

Comments: The name *Arnica* is of uncertain origin. Leopard's-Bane is not common in our region and is considered imperiled in Florida, where it occurs in only 2 counties. It is listed as vulnerable in both Georgia and North Carolina. At least 7 additional species of *Arnica* (some with numerous varieties) occur in North America, all of which are northern or western species; only the single species *A. acaulis* occurs in the southeastern United States. A tincture produced from the roots of at least 1 species in this genus has reportedly been used as a stimulant and to treat bruises, sprains, and post-surgical swelling.

PURPLE BALDUINA OR PURPLEDISK HONEYCOMBHEAD
Balduina atropurpurea R. M. Harper
Aster Family (Asteraceae or Compositae)

Description: This is a perennial herb with 1 to several erect 4' stems, each topped with a single flower head. Individual flower heads are composed of a ⅝–1" central disk of purplish tubular disk flowers surrounded by 10–20 yellow rays, each with 3–5 apical teeth. The 1–5" leaves are narrow, alternate, stalked, and mostly widest toward the tip. The leaves become smaller and more widely spaced up the stem. The name Honeycombhead refers to the receptacle, which has the appearance of a honeycomb when the flowers are removed.

Bloom Season: August–October.

Habitat/Range: Pitcher Plant bogs, seepage areas, wet pine savannas, and open, wet edges of wet weather drainages. Florida, Georgia, South Carolina, and North Carolina. This is a rare species throughout its range. In our region it is considered critically imperiled in Florida, imperiled in Georgia, and is possibly extirpated in both North and South Carolina. It was previously also reported from Alabama, but may be extirpated there as well.

Comments: Three species of *Balduina* occur in our region, only 2 of which are found primarily in wetland habitats. *B. uniflora,* which is often found in association with Purple Balduina and is vegetatively similar to it, produces flowers mostly in mid-summer and early fall and has a yellow central disk. The 2 species are virtually indistinguishable when flowers are absent.

SHOWY BURR-MARIGOLD OR SMOOTH BEGGARTICKS
Bidens laevis (Linnaeus) Britton, Sterns, & Poggenberg
Aster Family (Asteraceae or Compositae)

Description: About 10 species of yellow-flowered *Bidens* occur in the Atlantic Coastal Plain. Most are wetland species. A few species, such as Showy Burr-Marigold, occur in abundance along natural and human-made lakes and have the propensity to produce stunning floral displays throughout the fall. Showy Burr-Marigold has opposite, sessile, undivided 2–6" leaves, a combination of field characters that serves to distinguish it from other *Bidens* species. Stems are glabrous, erect, and 2–5' tall. The flowers are composed of a dark yellow central disk surrounded by about 8, ¾–1¼" rays. The fruit is a flattened achene with 2–4 barbed awns at its tip.

Bloom Season: August–November.

Habitat/Range: Wet marshes and lake edges, often in standing water. Throughout the region.

Comments: The genus name *Bidens* means "2-toothed," in reference to the stiff, curving tooth-like bristles that adorn the achenes in most species of the genus. These bristles or awns grasp and become imbedded in the fur of passing animals, which explains the common name Beggarticks.

SEASIDE OXEYE
Borrichia frutescens (Linnaeus) Augustin de Candolle
Aster Family (Asteraceae or Compositae)

Description: The combination of saltwater habitat, fleshy gray leaves, erect stature, and showy yellow flower heads distinguishes this woody evergreen from all other species in our region. Stems are 1–4' tall and mostly unbranched. Leaves are thick, simple, opposite, and 1–3" long with a succulent appearance. The grayish color of the leaves results from a dense covering of hairs. Leaf margins are mostly entire, but may be coarsely toothed. Flower heads are borne at the branch tips and are composed of a congested ½" disk surrounded by numerous comparatively short yellow rays.

Bloom Season: May–September.

Habitat/Range: Salt or brackish marshes and shores of saltwater bays and estuaries; confined exclusively to the coastal fringe. Throughout the region.

Comments: Seaside Oxeye spreads extensively by underground rhizomes and often forms large patches at the edges of salt marshes and along low energy shorelines. Its stems are thick, woody, and evident throughout the year. Although considered evergreen, it is much leafier in summer than winter.

LARKSPUR COREOPSIS
Coreopsis delphiniifolia Lamarck,
Aster Family (Asteraceae or Compositae)

Description: The stem leaves of this stiffly erect 1½–3' herb are divided into very narrow segments that are mostly less than ¼" wide. Plants often occur in dense colonies with most plants appearing very leafy. Numerous flower heads are borne in a branched inflorescence at the top of the stem and consist of a yellow, ¼–⅜" disk surrounded by bright yellow ¾–1¼" rays.

Bloom Season: Predominantly May–July.

Habitat/Range: Dry woods, moist pinelands, savannas, and sandhills. Georgia, South Carolina, and Virginia (perhaps elsewhere).

Comments: Some experts believe that this species originated as a hybrid between *C. verticillata, C. tripteris,* and perhaps *C. major,* all of which overlap in range and have divided leaves. Of these 3 purported parent species, the present species most closely resembles *C. verticillata,* due primarily to the very narrow leaf segments (those of *C. major* and *C. tripteris* are typically much wider). *C. verticillata* occurs within our region mostly in Virginia, North Carolina, and northern South Carolina.

SLENDER SCRATCH DAISY
Croptilon divaricatum (Nutt.) Raf.
Aster Family (Asteraceae or Compositae)

Description: Long, slender, diffusely spreading branches, each tipped with a bright yellow daisylike flower head help identify this species. Typical plants are erect, to about 3' tall, and produce numerous flowers. Flower heads consists of a small ¼–⅜" disk surrounded by 7–11 short ¼" rays. The leaves are alternate, linear, 1–2½" long, and normally have at least a few small teeth along the margins. The fruit is a tiny achene.

Bloom Season: July–November.

Habitat/Range: Sandhills, sandy fields, pine-oak–hickory woods, and sandy roadsides. Throughout the region.

Comments: Scratch daisy is native to our region but has very weedy tendencies. It often forms extensive colonies along sandy roadsides and in other sandy disturbed areas and can dominate the ground cover during its late summer and early fall flowering period. The specific eipthet *divaricatum* means "spreading or diverging," in reference to the diffusely branched inflorescence.

LANCELEAF BLANKETFLOWER
Gaillardia aestivalis (Walter) H. Rock
Aster Family (Asteraceae or Compositae)

Description: This blanketflower is an erect freely branched annual or short-lived perennial herb that grows to about 2' tall. The upper leaves are sessile, entire, about 1" long, and more or less linear or oblong in outline; the lower leaves are often short stalked, may exceed 2", and are often toothed or lobed. The flower heads are composed of a dark purplish brown ¾–1" disk of tubular flowers surrounded by 6–15 well-spaced ¾" ray flowers. Ray flowers are mostly yellow with reddish to purple bases and 3 lobed at the apex.

Bloom Season: June–October.

Habitat/Range: Sandhills, limestone glades, prairies, and dry, open woods. Florida, Georgia, South Carolina, and North Carolina.

Comments: *G. aestivalis* var. *flavovirens,* which has yellow disk and ray flowers, is recognized as distinct by some authorities. It occurs mostly in the southern part of our region. The flowers of Lanceleaf Blanketflower differ markedly from the mostly red ray flowers of Firewheel *(G. pulchella).* The present species is not likely to be confused with any other sandhill wildflower.

PURPLEHEAD SNEEZEWEED OR SOUTHERN SNEEZEWEED
Helenium flexuosum Rafinesque
Aster Family (Asteraceae or Compositae)

Description: Purplehead Sneezeweed is probably the better common name for this species. The dark-centered flower heads are an unmistakable field identification character. This is a coarse perennial herb to about 3' tall with a branching stem and decurrent leaves, meaning that the tissues of the leaf base and stem are partly fused. Flowers are borne in few to numerous congested flower heads, each composed of a ⅜–⅝" central disk surrounded by bright yellow ⅜–½" rays. The brown to purplish brown disk flowers have 4 lobes.

Bloom Season: May–August.

Habitat/Range: Riverbanks, pastures, disturbed sites, and moist pinelands. Throughout the region.

Comments: Southern Sneezeweed is 1 of 2 sneezeweeds in our region with purplish brown disk flowers. Shortleaf Sneezeweed *(H. brevifolium)* is superficially similar but has few stem leaves and 5-lobed disk flowers, and typically produces a single or only a few flower heads per plant. Shortleaf Sneezeweed is rare in the Atlantic Coastal Plain. Common Sneezeweed *(H. autumnale)* is similar in form and habit but has yellow disk flowers.

SPRING HELENIUM
Helenium vernale Walter
Aster Family (Asteraceae or Compositae)

Description: This erect, mostly single-stalked perennial herb grows to about 3' tall and arises from a tufted rosette of broadly linear to elliptical leaves. The stem leaves are few in number and mostly reduced in size, especially toward the top of the stem. Flowering stems are topped by a single yellow ¾–1¼" hemispheric head of yellow disk flowers surrounded by up to 40, ¾–1" yellow rays. The disk flowers are subtended by a hard seed (achene), which may be covered with small glands (seen when viewed with magnification) but lacks hairs.

Bloom Season: February–May.

Habitat/Range: Wet pinelands, wet roadside ditches, savannas, boggy edges of bays, swamps, and pocosins. Florida, Georgia, South Carolina, and North Carolina (rare in North Carolina and proposed as endangered there).

Comments: Spring Helenium and Southeastern Sneezeweed *(H. pinnatifidum),* both of which are endemic to the Southeastern Coastal Plains, are virtually indistinguishable from one another without close examination. The 2 species have overlapping bloom times, though Spring Helenium tends to bloom slightly earlier. The most reliable way to distinguish them is by tearing open a mature flower head, allowing the disk flowers to dry, and examining the achenes with at least 10X magnification. The achenes of *H. pinnatifidum* are hairy whereas those of *H. vernale* are covered with only glistening glands. Honeycomb Head *(Balduina uniflora)* also resembles Spring Helenium, but it flowers in the fall and has fewer ray flowers, and the receptacles that bear the disk flowers have honeycomb-like ridges.

NARROWLEAF SUNFLOWER OR SWAMP SUNFLOWER
Helianthus angustifolius Linnaeus
Aster Family (Asteraceae or Compositae)

Description: Exceptionally narrow leaves characterize this sunflower (hence the epithet *angustifolius*). However, as with most sunflowers, there is considerable variability. Plants are 3–6' tall with a purplish to greenish herbaceous stem and numerous leaves. The leaves are 2–8" long, predominantly alternate, sessile, and mostly narrowly lance-shaped (in typical plants the leaves are less than ¾" wide) with rough surfaces and revolute (curled-under) margins. Most leaves are borne along the stem, especially at flowering time, but a few stalked basal leaves may be present. Flower heads consist of a central disk of purplish red (rarely yellow) disk flowers surrounded by up to 21 mostly 1–1¼" ray flowers (rays may be longer on some individuals).

Bloom Season: July–December.

Habitat/Range: Moist to wet roadsides and ditches, flatwoods, bogs, and fields. Throughout the region.

Comments: Many of the sunflowers are known to hybridize freely and therefore individual plants with intermediate characters are often encountered. Narrowleaf Sunflower is one of our more widespread *Helianthus*, with numerous opportunities to cross-pollinate with other species. It is known to regularly hybridize with Florida Sunflower *(H. floridanus)*, which is more common in the southern portion of our region. Some authorities consider the Muck Sunflower *(H. simulans)* to have originated as a hybrid between the present species and Maximillian Sunflower *(H. maximilianii)*, which occurs naturally in the plains of the Midwest but is now widespread throughout the eastern United States.

SPREADING SUNFLOWER
Helianthus divaricatus Linnaeus
Aster Family (Asteraceae or Compositae)

Description: As a group, the sunflowers can be difficult to distinguish from one another. Members of the genus often hybridize freely, resulting in plants that can be difficult to assign to species. Spreading Sunflower is most easily identified by its widely spreading leaves, which are completely opposite and commonly diverge at right angles from the 2–4' stem. Leaves are 2–8" long, ½–3" wide, serrate to nearly entire along the margins, and elliptical in outline with roughened upper surfaces that feel like sandpaper. Flower heads are composed of a ½" disk of tubular yellow flowers surrounded by 8–15, ¾–1¼" rays.

Bloom Season: June–August.

Habitat/Range: Moist woods, calcareous hammocks, woodland borders, and dry pinelands. Throughout the region, but only at the extreme western edge of our region in Florida.

Comments: The epithet *divaricatus* means "widely spreading" or "widely divergent," a description that applies equally well to this species' growth habit and to its spreading leaves. Spreading Sunflower is a perennial with elongated rhizomes that aid in the development of large colonies that can be very impressive when flowering. Spreading Sunflower is probably most similar to Paleleaf Woodland Sunflower (*H. strumosus),* which typically has glaucous leaves. The leaves of Paleleaf Woodland Sunflower are sometimes opposite far up the stem with perhaps only the topmost pair being alternate.

VARIABLELEAF SUNFLOWER
Helianthus heterophyllus Nutt.
Aster Family (Asteraceae or Compositae)

Description: The erect nearly leafless stem topped by a flower head that, with rays included, can be up to 4" wide easily distinguishes this species from all of our other dark-centered sunflowers. Most of the leaves are less than 6" long and borne in a persistent tuft at the base of the plant (a few may extend a short ways up the stem) and are very rough to the touch with the feel of sandpaper. The appearance of the basal rosette is easily learned and identifies the plant at almost any time of year. The flowers are composed of a comparatively large 1–1¼" reddish purple disk surrounded by 10–22 (18 is about average) bright yellow ray flowers that may be 2" long or more. Flower size is variable within any given population; smaller flower heads are often encountered.

Bloom Season: August–October.

Habitat/Range: Bogs, wet roadsides, moist to wet flatwoods, and savannas. Florida, Georgia, South Carolina, and North Carolina.

Comments: Only the Rayless Sunflower *(H. radula)*, which typically lacks ray flowers and has a much smaller inflorescence, has a similar form. Variableleaf Sunflower displays a strong response to fire or disturbance and may produce large populations with simultaneous flowering of numerous individuals. Large concentrations of basal leaf rosettes noted in spring are sure to produce a showy display in the fall, especially following a winter or spring fire. This species is endemic to the Southeastern Coastal Plains.

DUNE CAMPHORWEED

Heterotheca subaxillaris (Lamarck) Britton & Rusby

Aster Family (Asteraceae or Compositae)

Description: This is an erect to somewhat spreading 1–6' tap-rooted annual or biennial herb. Stem leaves are 1–3" long, simple, alternate, and toothed, with the uppermost leaves often clasping the stem. The common name Camphorweed comes from the camphorlike odor of the leaves when they are crushed. Numerous flower heads are borne in a branched inflorescence at the top of the stem. Individual heads consist of a ½" yellow disk surrounded by 20–45 short, bright yellow rays.

Bloom Season: July–December.

Habitat/Range: Coastal dunes, sand flats, sandhills, and sandy roadsides, most often in xeric conditions. Throughout the region.

Comments: This species is often associated with coastal habitats, especially dunes and sandy roadsides, but has very weedy tendencies and readily invades vacant lots and other disturbed sites. In North Carolina it is common inland in the Fall Line Hills. Despite its weedy habit most experts consider camphorweed to be native to our region, although some consider it not native to regions farther north.

OPPOSITE-LEAF DWARF-DANDELION

Krigia cespitosa (Rafinesque) K. L. Chambers

Aster Family (Asteraceae or Compositae)

Description: This is our region's only leafy-branched *Krigia* (the leaves of other species are closely set at the base of the flowering stem). The stem of Opposite-Leaf Dwarf-Dandelion produces numerous erect 4–12" branches, each with numerous leaves that are borne 2 or 3 to a node. Compact ¼–⅜" heads of yellow, golden, or more or less orange ray flowers are borne singly at the end of short axillary stalks at various levels on the upright branches, giving a many-flowered appearance to most individuals.

Bloom Season: March–June.

Habitat/Range: Roadsides, fields, and other disturbed sites. Throughout the region.

Comments: The epithet *cespitosa* derives from *cespitose* (also sometimes spelled *caespitose*), which means "growing in tufts." The extremely short stems of Opposite-Leaf Dwarf-Dandelion produce tuftlike clusters of branches, giving the appearance of a cespitose growth habit. The flower heads lack disk flowers, making them similar in form and appearance to the true dandelions of the genus *Taraxacum*.

BUTTERWEED OR YELLOWTOP
Packera glabella (Poir.) C. Jeffrey
(Syn: *Senecio glabellus* Poir.)
Aster Family (Asteraceae or Compositae)

Description: This annual herb is a showy and conspicuous spring wildflower. The thickened 1–2½' stem is erect and mostly glabrous along its main extent but often hairy in the leaf axils. Leaves are deeply divided with rounded lobes that are toothed along the margins. Basal leaves are largest (up to about 8"), with the upper leaves becoming progressively shorter and smaller. Flower heads are typically less than 1" wide and consist of a central disk of tubular yellow flowers surrounded by numerous bright yellow rays.

Bloom Season: February–June.

Habitat/Range: Moist woods or open areas, wet roadsides, floodplains, bottomland forests, and marshes. Florida, Georgia, and South Carolina, North Carolina.

Comments: The epithet *glabella* means "somewhat glabrous," an allusion to the mostly glabrous stem. Although native to this region, Butterweed has very weedy tendencies and often occurs in large dense colonies. Fallow fields, floodplains, and wide road shoulders dominated by this species can be spectacular.

PINELAND SILKGRASS
Pityopsis aspera (Shuttleworth ex Small) Small
Aster Family (Asteraceae or Compositae)

Description: Some authorities consider this species to be a variety of Narrowleaf Silkgrass (*P. graminifolia*), which is very similar in form and habit. Both are erect perennial 3' herbs with numerous parallel-veined "grasslike" stem leaves and ½" yellow flower heads. They can be distinguished by the stalks of the inflorescence (peduncles). The peduncles of Pineland Silkgrass are covered with very short glandular hairs that require 10X magnification to see clearly, whereas those of Narrowleaf Silkgrass lack glandular hairs and are instead obscured by a dense covering of longer silky hairs that are easily seen with the naked eye.

Bloom Season: June–October.

Habitat/Range: Sandhills and dry flatwoods. Throughout the region.

Comments: A third species of *Pityopsis* occurs in the southern part of our region and is similar the 2 mentioned here. Narrow-Leaved Goldenaster (*P. oligantha*) has larger flower heads and typically flowers in spring rather than fall. It is primarily a species of the East Gulf Coastal Plain, occurring in our area only in Georgia and Florida.

SANDHILL GOLDENASTER
Pityopsis pinifolia (Elliott) Nuttall
(Syn: *Chrysopsis pinifolia* Elliott)
Aster Family (Asteraceae or Compositae)

Description: The numerous narrowly linear mostly 1½–3" leaves of this profusely flowering perennial distinguish it from all other *Pityopsis* in our region. Individual plants are 8–24" tall and produce many flower heads, each of which terminates a mostly leafless branch. Numerous tubular flowers are borne in a central yellow disk that is surrounded by up to about 13, ¼–⅜" yellow rays.

Bloom Season: August–October, but most abundantly in September.

Habitat/Range: Sandhills and sandy roadsides, especially those of the Fall Line Hills. Georgia, South Carolina, and North Carolina. Considered imperiled in Georgia and vulnerable in North Carolina.

Comments: This is another of those species restricted primarily to the Fall Line Hills. It is abundant and often weedy within its restricted range and often forms large colonies by a combination of underground rhizomes and profuse seed production. The epithet *pinifolia* means "with leaves like a pine tree," in reference to the linear needlelike leaves.

BLACK-EYED SUSAN
Rudbeckia hirta Linnaeus
Aster Family (Asteraceae or Compositae)

Description: Black-Eyed Susan is a popular garden plant that enjoys wide use in both residential and commercial landscapes. Typical plants produce several hairy 18–40" stems, each topped with a showy flower head that is composed of a cone-shaped central disk surrounded by several ¾–1¾" yellow rays. Stem leaves are alternate, hairy, variable in shape and size, and usually rough to the touch.

Bloom Season: May–November.

Habitat/Range: Roadside ditches, open woods, old fields, pastures, and other disturbed sites. Throughout the region.

Comments: Though the common name of this species is Black-Eyed Susan, the color of the central disk is closer to purplish or brown than black. This is a widespread species that occurs nearly throughout North America. It may have originated in the prairies of the Midwest and spread to our region, but it is considered native by many experts. Its expansive range and morphological variation has led to the description of several varieties that differ from one another largely in leaf shape and size.

ST. JOHN'S BLACK-EYED SUSAN OR SHINY CONEFLOWER

Rudbeckia nitida Nutt.
Aster Family (Asteraceae or Compositae)

Description: The comparatively large flowers with floppy 1¼–2½" rays and a conspicuously erect conical ¾–1½" disk help distinguish this species from all other coneflowers in our region. The mostly leafless stem is erect, stiff, ribbed, and up to about 5' tall. The dark green basal leaves are glabrous, stalked, coarsely toothed, and relatively large, measuring 4–20" long and up to 3" wide.

Bloom Season: May–July, with a second flowering period September–October.

Habitat/Range: Wet to moist flatwoods, bogs, savannas, seepage areas, and roadside ditches. Florida and Georgia.

Comments: This is a rare plant throughout its range. Within our region it is listed as imperiled in Florida and vulnerable in Georgia. Outside of our region it is known only from Alabama, where it is critically imperiled, and Texas, where it is imperiled. Once learned, the distinctive cluster of large, lustrous, and glabrous basal leaves help identify the plant, even when flowers are absent. The epithet *nitida* means "glossy."

SOUTHERN BOG GOLDENROD OR GRACEFUL GOLDENROD

Solidago gracillima Torrey & A. Gray
Aster Family (Asteraceae or Compositae)

Description: This 2–5' perennial herb arises from a short rhizome. Numerous very narrow stem leaves are borne alternately and often clasp the stem. Basal leaves are 4–12" long, up to about 2" wide, and are usually much longer than wide. Bright yellow flower heads, each with a central disk surrounded by 3–7 ray flowers, are borne in an elongated raceme at the top of the stem. Often, the flower heads are borne along only one side of the axis.

Bloom Season: September–October.

Habitat/Range: Moist savannas and seepage areas in pinelands. Florida, Georgia, South Carolina, and North Carolina (at the western edge of our region in Florida; perhaps also present in Virginia).

Comments: More than 50 species of goldenrod occur in the southeastern United States, many of which are at least somewhat difficult to distinguish from each other. To complicate matters, numerous similarly flowered species that were once included within the genus *Solidago* are now included within segregate genera. Southern Bog Goldenrod is most similar in our region to *S. stricta*, which has a much longer rhizome.

PINEYWOODS GOLDENROD
Solidago pinetorum Small
Aster Family (Asteraceae or Compositae)

Description: This slender goldenrod may be up to about 3' tall and is often leaning or arching due to its weakly erect stem. It is superficially similar to Sweet Goldenrod *(S. odora),* which occurs in similar habitats but lacks basal leaves. Pineywoods Goldenrod has large basal leaves that bear 3 conspicuous veins (when seen from below) and are often toothed along the margins. Upper leaves are much smaller and either spreading or reflexed. The slender inflorescence is composed of short, downward curving branches. The flowers are borne along only one side of these short branches.

Bloom Season: July–October.

Habitat/Range: Dry pinelands and dry road shoulders. South Carolina, North Carolina, and Virginia.

Comments: The epithet *pinetorum* means "of pine forests," a fitting accolade. Though restricted to the northern part of our region (including rare occurrences in the Virginia mountains), Pineywoods Goldenrod is fairly common in its preferred habitat, especially in Longleaf Pine forests of the Fall Line Hills.

SPRING-FLOWERING GOLDENROD
Solidago verna M. A. Curtis
Aster Family (Asteraceae or Compositae)

Description: *Solidago verna* is easy to identify. It is the only goldendrod of undisturbed pinelands that is likely to be in flower in late spring and early summer. This is a 20–60" perennial herb with short spreading hairs. The basal leaves produce a distinctive collection of ovate to heart-shaped 1–4" blades with long, winged petioles. Conspicuous bright yellow flower heads adorn the upper stem and branches, each of which is composed of a central ¼–⅜" yellow disk surrounded by up to about 12, ¼" ray flowers.

Bloom Season: May–June.

Habitat/Range: Savannas, pinelands, and sandhills. South Carolina and North Carolina.

Comments: The epithet *verna* means "of the spring." The genus name *Solidago* comes from the Latin *solido,* which means "to make whole." Species of this genus were once thought to have healing qualities. Today, the goldenrods are often accused of stimulating hay fever and other allergies. However, goldenrod pollen is too heavy to be transported by wind, suggesting that plants other than goldenrods are the true allergens.

SQUAREHEAD OR PINELAND-GINSENG
Tetragonotheca helianthoides Linnaeus
Aster Family (Asteraceae or Compositae)

Description: Squarehead is an excellent name for this 1–3' perennial herb. The flower heads are subtended by 4 large, closely adjacent ¾–1¼" bracts that form a conspicuous square at the top of the flower stalk. Six to 12, ¾–1¼" ray flowers surround a conspicuous ¾–1¼" head of yellowish green to reddish brown disk flowers. The stem and leaves are hairy and somewhat sticky from the presence of tiny, beadlike glands. Leaves are opposite, coarsely toothed, and comparatively large, measuring up to about 8" long and 4" wide. Leaves vary in shape from mostly elliptic to ovate or diamond shaped (rhombic) but become narrow at the base. Some leaves may appear to have short stalks, whereas others are sessile and clasping.

Bloom Season: April–July.

Habitat/Range: Sandy woodlands, oak–hickory–pine forests, and roadsides. Throughout the region.

Comments: The genus name *Tetragonotheca* is from Greek and means "4-angled case," in reference to the 4 large phyllaries that completely enclose the unexpanded flower head. Unopened heads have the appearance of a capsule and might be confused for fruit by casual observers. The specific epithet *helianthoides* means "resembling *Helianthus*," the sunflower genus. Squarehead is restricted in distribution to the southeastern United States and is considered critically imperiled in Virginia, the northern extent of its range, and vulnerable in North Carolina. Three other species within this genus are found in North America, 2 of which occur only in Texas and 1 of which occurs in Louisiana, Arkansas, and Texas.

COMMON WINGSTEM
Verbesina alternifolia (Linnaeus) Britton ex Kearney
Aster Family (Asteraceae or Compositae)

Description: The epithet *alternifolia* means "with alternate leaves," an excellent field identification character for distinguishing this species from Southern Crownbeard *(V. occidentalis).* Common Wingstem is a robust 3–9' leafy perennial. The stem is often winged due to the extension of the leaf stalk, but plants that lack winged stems are not uncommon. Leaves vary from lance shaped to narrowly elliptic in outline and are up to about 10" long and 3" wide. Plants typically bear alternate leaves, though plants with numerous opposite leaves are not uncommon. Up to 100 flower heads are borne in a branching inflorescence, each with a globular ½" central disk surrounded by several bright yellow rays.

Bloom Season: August–October.

Habitat/Range: Marshes, floodplains, edges of floodplain swamps. Throughout the region (but only at the western edge of the region in Florida and South Carolina).

Comments: The bracts below the flower heads of this species point downward and are often closely appressed to the stalk, another field character that helps distinguish it from Southern Crownbeard. Its leaves are also typically much narrower than those of Southern Crownbeard. Once learned, the two are easily distinguished. This is an excellent garden plant that produces numerous viable seeds. Though typically associated with wet places in nature, it does well in moist gardens and is easy to grow.

SOUTHERN CROWNBEARD
Verbesina occidentalis (Linnaeus) Walter
Aster Family (Asteraceae or Compositae)

Description: This large, coarse, leafy-stemmed perennial is typically 3–6' tall and sometimes grows in extensive colonies in roadside ditches. Leaves are opposite, sharply toothed along the margins, and may be up to about 7" long and 4½" wide. The stem is often conspicuously winged. Numerous flower heads are borne in a compact or open inflorescence. Flower heads are composed of a globular ¼–½" disk surrounded by 2–5 bright yellow rays. As with many species of *Verbesina* the varying numbers of rays often give the flower heads a disheveled appearance.

Bloom Season: August–October.

Habitat/Range: Floodplains, hardwood forests, wet ditches near drainages, and roadsides. Throughout the region (but only at the extreme western edge of the region in Florida).

Comments: Unlike Common Wingstem, which has both alternate and opposite leaves, the leaves of Southern Crownbeard are wholly opposite. The name *Verbesina* was given by Linnaeus and means "resembling the leaves of verbena," the Greek name for Vervain *(Verbena officinalis)*.

ASIATIC HAWK'S-BEARD, ORIEN-TAL HAWK'S-BEARD, OR YOUNGIA
Youngia japonica (Linnaeus) Augustin de Candolle
Aster Family (Asteraceae or Compositae)

Description: As its scientific epithet and common names imply, Youngia is a non-native species, but it is distributed across much of the southeastern United States. Plants are typically about 1' tall but vary considerably. Some individuals may approach heights of 3'. The deeply lobed leaves may be up to about 8" long and 2½" wide and are borne in a conspicuous basal rosette. Flower heads are small and borne in a branched inflorescence and are composed of 10–20 yellow ray flowers. There are no disk flowers.

Bloom Season: All year.

Habitat/Range: Lawns, roadsides, and disturbed sites. Throughout the region.

Comments: Like most weedy species, Youngia is confined mostly to disturbed areas in the coastal plains and is probably more common in Florida than other parts of our region. However, it is reported to be spreading rapidly in the Piedmont of Virginia. Look for it mostly in lawns and mowed roadsides.

COASTAL PLAIN PUCCOON OR HAIRY PUCCOON

Lithospermum caroliniense (J. F. Gmel.) MacMill.
Borage Family (Boraginaceae)

Description: This showy, late spring, tap-rooted perennial sometimes forms large colonies in thin, sandy woods and along sandy roadsides. The hairy stem is erect, branched, and may be nearly 3' tall. Individual plants often flower profusely, producing dense cymes of numerous 1" orange-yellow flowers. Numerous alternate, hairy, linear or oblong 1–2" leaves line the stem.

Bloom Season: April–June.

Habitat/Range: Sandhills, sandy roadsides, and other places with dry, sandy soils. Florida, Georgia, South Carolina, and Virginia (mostly west of our region in Florida). Though there seems to be an abundance of suitable habitat, the distribution of this species apparently skips North Carolina.

Comments: The name *Lithospermum* comes from the Greek words *lithos,* meaning "stone," and *sperma,* "seed," an allusion to the hardened nutlets that are common to the genus. The common name Puccoon is the Virginia Algonquian name for "dye." The roots of this and other species of Lithospermum have a reddish or yellowish sap that was once used as dye by some North American Indians.

SOUTHERN STONESEED

Lithospermum tuberosum Rugel ex Augustin de Candolle
Borage Family (Boraginaceae)

Description: The pale yellow to yellowish white ¼" flowers of Southern Stoneseed are much smaller and less colorful than those of Coastal Plain Puccoon *(L. caroliniense),* a field character that easily distinguishes the 2 species. Southern Stoneseed is a perennial herb with a thickened tuberous root and a slender, erect, branching stem to about 2½' tall. The attractive 2–4" basal leaves are clustered at the base of the stem. The stem leaves are conspicuously smaller.

Bloom Season: March–June.

Habitat/Range: Rich, mixed deciduous forests. Florida and Georgia (also South Carolina and Virginia but not within our region).

Comments: The epithet *tuberosum* means "tuberous," in reference to the roots. This species is widespread across the southeastern United States but is more common in the mountains and Piedmont than in the Atlantic or Gulf Coastal plains. It is considered critically imperiled in South Carolina, where it occurs in only 2 counties along the state's southwestern border.

FALSE GROMWELL OR VIRGINIA MARBLESEED
Onosmodium virginianum (Linnaeus) de Candolle
Borage Family (Boraginaceae)

Description: The flowers of False Gromwell are borne in a distinctive leafy, helicoid cyme, meaning a coiled inflorescence in which all of the lateral floral branches develop from the same side of the inflorescence's main axis. Individual flowers are yellowish or orange, about ⅜" long, and very hairy. The mostly oblong leaves are 1–5" long and borne along a slender erect 12–32" stem. All parts of the herbage are hairy and rough to the touch. The fruit is a tiny, hard, pitted seed, which explains the common name Marbleseed.

Bloom Season: April–September, but mostly in the earlier part of this period.

Habitat/Range: Sandhills, pinelands, dry flatwoods, dry hammocks, and shell middens. Throughout the region.

Comments: The name False Gromwell alludes to the similarity between this species and those of the genus *Lithospermum*. Species of *Lithospermum* are often called Gromwell, a Middle English name that apparently developed as a reference to the hard stony seeds common to plants of the genus. According to the mediaeval "doctrine of signatures," close observation of the morphology of plants often reveals their medicinal value or medicinal "signature." Under this doctrine, the hard seeds common to *Lithospermum* suggest the plant's use in the treatment of gravel, or kidney stones. Since *Onosmodium* is similar to, but not the same as, *Lithospermum*, it was called False Gromwell.

WILD RADISH, JOINTED CHARLOCK, OR WHITE CHARLOCK
Raphanus raphanistrum Linnaeus
Mustard Family (Brassicaceae or Cruciferae)

Description: Wild Radish is a clump-forming, freely branched 1–3' herb with erect stems and numerous flowers. The deeply dissected leaves are largest below (to about 10") but reduce rapidly in size upwards along the stem. The flowers are composed of 4, ½" petals and 4 sepals. The petals are typically yellow or white but may also be lavender, pink, or orange. The fruit is a 1–2½" longitudinally ridged silique with an extended beak and segmented seed compartments (a silique is a narrow fruit common in the Mustard Family in which the 2 halves of the seed compartment separate from the central partition at maturity). When fresh, the fruit bears a superficial resemblance to a hot green pepper.

Bloom Season: March–June.

Habitat/Range: Roadsides, fields, and other disturbed sites. Throughout the region.

Comments: Wild Radish is a very common non-native weed. It is an early and often dominant spring wildflower along country roadsides. The genus name *Raphanus* is Latin for radish and derives from the Greek word *rhaphanis*, the ancient name for this long-known vegetable. Wild Radish was introduced to North America from Mediterranean Europe and is now widely distributed across the United States. Some authorities recognize several varieties of this species. However, its cosmopolitan distribution and considerable morphological variation make it difficult to discern consistent morphological patterns and differences. Wild Radish has been touted for numerous homeopathic remedies.

CAROLINA FROSTWEED OR CAROLINA SUNROSE

Helianthemum carolinianum (Walter) Michx.
(Syn: *Crocanthemum carolinianum* [Walter] Spach)
Rockrose Family (Cistaceae)

Description: The flowers of this attractive perennial herb sometimes seem out of proportion with the rest of the plant. The 5 petals are broad and usually overlap one another, often forming a shallow cup that is adorned near its center with striking orange stamens. The larger (1–2½") leaves are borne in a rosette at the base of the plant and subtend a slender erect purplish stem that may be up to 1' tall. Smaller leaves are borne alternately along the stem.

Bloom Season: March–May.

Habitat/Range: Savannas, sandhills, and dry pinelands. Florida, Georgia, South Carolina, and North Carolina.

Comments: This is a worldwide genus with numerous species. Recent genetic evidence suggests that the genus's eastern North American species differ substantially from those of the Old World and are better placed in the genus *Crocanthemum*. The species within our region can be difficult to distinguish from one another. Carolina Sunrose is recognized by combination of its leaves being generally wider than ⅜" and produced mostly at the base of the plant.

GEORGIA FROSTWEED OR GEORGIA SUNROSE

Helianthemum georgianum Chapman
(Syn: *Crocanthemum georgianum* (Chapman) Barnhart)
Rockrose Family (Cistaceae)

Description: Basal leaves are absent on this erect, multistemmed perennial herb, a character that immediately distinguishes it from Carolina Sunrose *(H. carolinianum)*. Stems vary 4–18" tall and are copiously covered with star-shaped hairs that require at least 10X magnification to see clearly. The numerous ¾–1¼" stem leaves are narrowly elliptic. Numerous flowers are borne in scattered clusters or singly at the branch tips, a field identification character that separates it from *H. corymbosum,* which has flowers borne in dense flat-topped cymes.

Bloom Season: April–May.

Habitat/Range: Sandhills, dunes, dry woods, and maritime forests. Florida, Georgia, South Carolina, and North Carolina (rare in the Carolinas).

Comments: Georgia Frostweed ranges in the United States only from North Carolina to Texas and Oklahoma. It is critically imperiled in North Carolina. The leaves of the similar *H. corymbosum* are often silvery beneath whereas those of Georgia Frostweed are more nearly pale green.

ROUND-POD ST. JOHN'S-WORT
Hypericum cistifolium Lamarck
Mangosteen Family (Clusiaceae, including Guttiferae and Hypericaceae)

Description: At least 30 species of *Hypericum* occur in our region with growth forms ranging from herbaceous perennials to woody shrubs. Round-Pod St. John's-Wort is a small woody shrub to about 2½' tall. Leaves are narrowly elliptic or more often lance shaped and up to about 2" long and ⅜" wide. Numerous yellow flowers are borne in a showy cymose inflorescence at the top of the stem. The flowers have 5, ¼" petals subtending a mass of stamens. The fruit is a conspicuous egg-shaped capsule.

Bloom Season: June–August.

Habitat/Range: Wet flatwoods and savannas. Florida, Georgia, South Carolina, and North Carolina.

Comments: The epithet *cistifolius* means "with leaves like *Cistus*," the Rock-Rose genus. The name *Hypericum* probably derives from the Greek words *hyper* and *eikon,* which combined means "above a picture." Flowers of some species were reportedly placed above images to ward off evil spirits during the feast of St. John, an ancient festival that occurred on June 24. Today, the name St. John's-Wort is a well-known name in herbal medicine. Over-the-counter medications of this name are usually concocted from Klamath Weed *(H. perforatum),* a European herb that is now considered a nuisance weed across much of the United States. Though it has been used for centuries as a medicinal herb and often touted as an effective treatment for depression, the National Institutes of Health warn that clinical studies of its effectiveness are inconclusive and that dangerous side effects can occur when it is used in conjunction with other drugs.

PINELAND ST. JOHN'S-WORT

Hypericum suffruticosum P. Adams & Robson
Mangosteen Family (Clusiaceae, including
Guttiferae and Hypericaceae)

Description: The epithet *suffruticosum* means
"somewhat shrubby," which may seem to be an
overstated description of this low-growing St.
John's-Wort. The stems are indeed woody, but
the plant's stature is typically that of a ground-
hugging herb. Most plants are well under 6" tall
with relatively small ¼–⅜" leaves that are
typically about as long as wide. Yellow flowers
are borne singly near the tips of the branches and
consist of 4, ⅜" petals and numerous stamens.
The subtending sepals are of 2 sizes, with 1 pair
being narrow and needlelike and the other pair,
conspicuous and broadly elliptic. The fruit is a
capsule.

Bloom Season: April–June.

Habitat/Range: Savannas, flatwoods, and
sandhills. Florida, Georgia, South Carolina, and
North Carolina.

Comments: The conserved family name
Guttiferae is an allusion to the guttiferous, or oil-
bearing, glands that are present in the leaf tissue.
When held up to the light with magnification,
these glands look like tiny amber-colored
translucent pouches.

HAIRY ST. JOHN'S-WORT

Hypericum setosum Linnaeus
Mangosteen Family (Clusiaceae, including
Guttiferae and Hypericaceae)

Description: This species is one of our region's
more common herbaceous St. John's-Worts.
Plants produce 1 to several slender, erect,
unbranched 1–2½' stems with numerous strongly
ascending ⅜–⅝" leaves. The leaves are often so
tightly appressed to the stem as to obscure its
surface. Both the leaves and stem are
conspicuously hairy, hence the common name
Hairy St. John's-Wort. Several small, yellow, 5-
petaled flowers are borne in a branching
inflorescence near the top of the stem. The fruit
is a ⅛–¼" capsule.

Bloom Season: May–September.

Habitat/Range: Margins of ditches, wet
flatwoods, mesic pinelands, and savannas.
Throughout the region.

Comments: The epithet *setosum* means "bristly"
or "full of bristles," an apparent reference to the
hairy leaves and stem. At a glance Hairy St.
John's-Wort might be confused with one of our
species of *Linum,* which also have yellow 5-
petaled flowers. Hairy St. John's-Wort can be
easily distinguished by its wider, mostly
appressed leaves that are broadest at the base
and tapered to a point above.

GOPHERWEED
Baptisia lanceolata (Walter) Elliott
Pea Family (Fabaceae or Leguminosae)

Description: The rounded bushy form gives this erect perennial herb a shrublike appearance. Plants are 18–36" tall and sometimes covered with appressed hairs that soften the plant's green color. The leaves may be short stalked or nearly sessile and are divided into 3, 1½–4" lance-shaped leaflets. The yellow flowers are about 1" long and borne 1–3 at a time in the leaf axils or in short 3–10 flowered terminal racemes. The fruit is an inflated ½–1" pod.

Bloom Season: March–May.

Habitat/Range: Sandhills, flatwoods, bogs, and oak-hickory woods. Florida, Georgia, and South Carolina.

Comments: Though its common name suggests otherwise, Gopherweed is a native plant (not a weed) that is endemic to the southeastern United States. It is most easily distinguished from our other yellow-flowered *Baptisia* by combination of its 1- to 3-flowered flower clusters, stalked leaflets, and the strongly incurved keel petal.

CAROLINA WILD INDIGO
Baptisia cinerea (Rafinesque) Fernald & Schubert
Pea Family (Fabaceae or Leguminosae)

Description: Carolina Wild Indigo is an erect or more often low-spreading 1–2½' perennial herb with 3-parted leaves. Leaflets are up to about 4" long, shiny above, thick and leathery in texture, and obovate or narrowly elliptic in outline. Comparatively large bright yellow ¾–1¼" flowers are produced in densely flowered racemes that usually contain numerous flowers (typically 5 or more). The fruit is an ellipsoid ⅝–1½" legume.

Bloom Season: April–June.

Habitat/Range: Sandhills and dry woodlands. South Carolina, North Carolina, and Virginia.

Comments: Carolina Wild Indigo is somewhat similar to Gopherweed *(B. lanceolata),* which also occurs in sandhills and pinelands, but is more common in our region in southern Georgia and Florida. Carolina Wild Indigo is distinguished from Gopherweed by its more numerous and larger flowers, thicker and tougher leaves, and more or less spreading growth form. Gopherweed typically displays an erect, bushlike form, and its flowers are produced in clusters of 3 or fewer.

DOLLARLEAF
Rhynchosia reniformis DC.
Pea Family (Fabaceae or Leguminosae)

Description: Both the common and scientific names of this species refer to its rounded or kidney-shaped leaves, which constitute an excellent field character for distinguishing it from others in the genus. Dollarleaf is a 2–6" erect, colony-forming perennial with hairy stems. The leaves are mostly unifoliolate, meaning compound, but with a single leaflet, although a few leaves on some plants may have 2 or 3 leaflets. Leaflets average 1–2" wide. The flowers are yellow and individually small, but are borne in conspicuous congested clusters with ¼–¾" stalks. The fruit is a hairy, elliptic ½–¾" legume.

Bloom Season: Inconsistently from April–September.

Habitat/Range: Sandhills, savannas, dry woods, and roadsides. Throughout the region.

Comments: No other species of *Rhynchosia* in this region has Dollarleaf's combination of short stature and predominately unifoliolate leaves with rounded leaflets.

LOW RATTLEBOX OR RABBITBELLS
Crotalaria rotundifolia Walter ex J. F. Gmelin
Pea Family (Fabaceae or Leguminosae)

Description: Two species of low-growing *Crotalaria* occur in our region. Coastal Plain Rattlebox *(C. purshii)* is very similar to the present species, but typically displays a more upright growth habit while the upper surfaces of its ½–1" leaflets lack hairs. Low Rattlebox typically displays a prostrate or decumbent growth habit and the upper surfaces of its leaflets are hairy, although it sometimes takes close observation with a hand lens to find the hairs. The middle and upper leaves of Coastal Plain Rattlebox also typically display conspicuous winged stipules at the base of the leaf stalk, a character that is lacking in Low Rattlebox. The flowers of both species are yellow and pealike with an upright standard. The fruit is a 1" legume.

Bloom Season: April–August.

Habitat/Range: Sandhills, dry pinelands, and sandy roadsides. Throughout the region.

Comments: Two varieties of Low Rattlebox are recognized. The stems of variety *vulgaris,* the more widespread of the two, display spreading pubescence, whereas the stem pubescence of variety *rotundifolia* is appressed.

TWINING SNOUTBEAN
Rhynchosia tomentosa (Linnaeus) Hook. & Arn.
Pea Family (Fabaceae or Leguminosae)

Description: Twining Snoutbean is an erect 12–36" modestly branched perennial herb with very hairy stems. The leaves are mostly 3-parted with elliptic 1–2" leaflets, though the lowermost leaves on some plants may be unifoliolate (compound but bearing a single leaflet per leaf). The leaflets are densely hairy beneath and feel like velvet. Individual flowers are small, yellow, and borne in 1 to several clusters that may terminate the branches or arise from the leaf axils. The fruit is an oblong, hairy ⅝–1" legume.

Bloom Season: May–June.

Habitat/Range: Sandhills, edges of hammocks, mixed pine and hardwood forests, savannas, and flatwoods. Throughout the region.

Comments: The epithet *tomentosa* means "with a dense covering of matted hairs" and refers to the velvetlike lower leaf surfaces, an excellent field character to remember for identifying this species.

PENCIL-FLOWER OR SIDEBEAK PENCIL-FLOWER
Stylosanthes biflora (Linnaeus) Britton, Sterns, & Poggenberg
Pea Family (Fabaceae or Leguminosae)

Description: Pencil-Flower is a low-growing prostrate to slightly erect perennial herb. One to several 4–16" stems arise from a stout rootstock. Leaves are alternate and 3-parted with narrow ½–1½" leaflets. The small yellow flowers are typical of many of those in the Pea Family, with an upright standard, 2 lateral wing petals, and 2 mostly fused lower keel petals. The legume is actually 2-parted, but the lower part usually aborts and takes on the form of a stout, whitened stalk.

Bloom Season: June–August.

Habitat/Range: Sandy pinelands, sandhills, moist flatwoods, dry upland forests, rocky glades, woodland borders. Throughout the region.

Comments: This is the only species of *Stylosanthes* likely to be found in our region. Pencil-Flower is a favorite summer food plant for the gopher tortoise *(Gopherus polyphemus),* an ecologically important and endangered native tortoise of the southeastern United States that digs deep burrows in sandy Longleaf Pine-dominated forests.

SOUTHERN CORYDALIS

Corydalis micrantha (Engelmann ex A. Gray) A. Gray var. *australis* (Chapman) Shinners
Fumitory Family (Furmariaceae)

Description: The multiply divided leaves of this erect to reclining herb are reminiscent of parsley and other delicate garnishes. The lowermost leaves are relatively long stalked whereas those above are sessile. Several 4–16" flowering stalks arise from the base of the plant and produce a small raceme of several clear yellow ⅝" flowers, each of which is subtended by 2 leaflike sepals. The upper petal is spurred near the tip, a feature that is characteristic of the genus. The name *Corydalis* is a Greek word that means "lark," a type of bird with spurred legs. The fruit is a very narrow, cylindrical ¾" capsule.

Bloom Season: February–April.

Habitat/Range: Dry roadsides and other disturbed sites. Florida, Georgia, South Carolina, and North Carolina.

Comments: Most authorities distinguish 2 varieties of this species, including variety *micrantha*, which occurs mostly west of this region. Other authorities think this species is more properly named *C. halei*. The epithet *australis* means "southern," a reference to our variety's predominantly southern distribution.

BRISTLESEED STARGRASS

Hypoxis wrightii (Baker) Brackett
Yellow Stargrass Family (Hypoxidaceae)

Description: Bristleseed Stargrass is an herbaceous perennial that arises from an upright corm. The dark brown bases of dead leaves often remain attached to the corm and take on the form of fine bristles. Flowers are yellow, 6 parted, about ½" wide, and typically borne singly at the tip of a 1–4" stalk. Leaves are narrowly linear to nearly filiform and up to 10" long. The fruit is a tiny oval capsule with dark brown seeds.

Bloom Season: March–May, but often flowers after fire.

Habitat/Range: Savannas and wet roadsides. Throughout the region.

Comments: Bristleseed Stargrass is sometimes seen listed in older references under the name *H. micrantha*, a name that is now known to have been misapplied. Numerous species of stargrass occur in the region, many of which can be difficult to distinguish from one another. The genus name is an old Greek name and demonstrates the vagaries of botanical nomenclature. *Hypo* means "under" and oxys means "sharp," neither of which have any obvious meaning for the present genus.

YELLOW BUTTERWORT
Pinguicula lutea Walt.
Bladderwort Family (Lentibulariaceae)

Description: The Yellow Butterwort's 3–6" rosettes of fleshy and sticky basal leaves are evident much of the year. A single 6–12" flowering scape arises from the center of the rosette in early spring and is terminated by a solitary sulfur-yellow 1–2" flower with a long spur. The petals enclose a protruding palate that is densely and conspicuously vested with yellow hairs. The scape is also covered with sticky hairs, which aid in entrapping insects and absorbing their internal fluids.

Bloom Season: February–May.

Habitat/Range: Savannas, wet flatwoods, roadside ditches, seepage bogs, and wet road shoulders. Florida, Georgia, South Carolina, and extreme southeastern North Carolina.

Comments: Yellow Butterwort is the only butterwort in the Atlantic Coastal Plain that has distinctly yellow flowers (white forms are rarely reported). Though it often occurs intermixed with other members of its genus, it is easily distinguished when in flower. With a little practice it may also be distinguished by the size and appearance of its basal rosette. *Lutea* means "yellow," while the genus name derives from the Latin word *pinguis,* or "fat," in reference to the greasy appearance of the leaves. The flower petals of this species usually point outward early in the day, nearly hiding the hairy palate, but open wider as the day progresses, eventually curving back over the corolla tube, leaving the palate well exposed.

GOLDEN COLIC ROOT
Aletris aurea Walter
Bog Asphodel Family (Nartheciaceae)

Description: Two yellow-flowered species of Colic Root occur in our region, both of which are erect herbs and are very similar in form, habit, and habitat. Golden Colic Root has an 8–24" scape with flat 1–3" leaves that are borne near the base of the plant. The flowers are golden yellow and about ¼" long with petals that converge at the apex, making the flower appear rounded at the tip and ellipsoid in outline.

Bloom Season: May–July.

Habitat/Range: Savannas, bogs, flatwoods, and wet roadsides. Throughout the region.

Comments: *A. lutea* is similar in color but is not nearly as widespread in the region. Its flowers are well over ¼" long with petals that spread at the apex. Concoctions from the roots of the genus *Aletris* were used by Native Americans and European immigrants to relieve colic and other stomach ailments. The basal leaf clusters of both species are visible for much of the year. The genus name *Aletris* comes from a Greek word meaning "the female slave who grinds the meal" and is a reference to the mealy appearance of the flowers.

YELLOW COLIC ROOT
Aletris lutea Small
Bog Asphodel Family (Nartheciaceae)

Description: The flowering scapes of Yellow Colic Root are up to about 3' tall and arise from a congested basal tuft of yellowish green leaves. The lance-shaped leaf blades are 2–6" long and ½–¾" wide. The ⅜–½" flowers are urn shaped, golden yellow, cylindrical at maturity, and arranged along the uppermost portion of the stem.

Bloom Season: March–June.

Habitat/Range: Savannas, wet roadsides and ditches, wet flatwoods, and bogs. Florida and Georgia.

Comments: Golden Colic Root *(A. aurea)* is similar in appearance and habitat, but its flowers curve inward at the apex, obscuring the orifice and making the tip of the flower appear closed and rounded. The petals of *A. lutea* are slightly spreading at the apex. Yellow Colic Root is more common south and west of our region and is likely to be encountered in our region only in Florida and extreme southern Georgia. Yellow Colic Root has been previously reported for the Carolinas, but these reports are probably in error.

GOLDENCREST

Lophiola aurea Ker Gawl.
(Syn: *L. americana* (Pursh) Wood)
Bog Asphodel Family (Nartheciaceae)

Description: This erect perennial herb is 1–3' tall. Stems are densely covered throughout with fine whitish hairs. The leaves are alternate, linear, mostly less than ¼" wide, and tapered to a narrow point. The flowers are small but borne in a showy, branched, terminal white-hairy cyme. The flower segments are woolly-hairy, yellow above, maroon near the base, and bearded with yellow hairs, hence the common name Goldencrest. The fruit is an egg-shaped capsule that sheds yellowish white seeds.

Bloom Season: April–June.

Habitat/Range: Bogs, wet ditches, wet prairies, and savannas. Florida, South Carolina, and North Carolina.

Comments: The genus *Lophiola* is a monotypic genus of eastern North America, meaning that it contains a single species. Goldencrest is one of a handful of species, along with Hooker's Milkwort (featured in the blue section of this guide), that is widespread in the East Gulf Coastal Plain with disjunct populations in the Carolinas. It was formerly included in the Bloodroot Family (Haemodoraceae). However, unlike Redroot the roots of Goldencrest are whitish or brown, not red. *Lophiola* is very unlike any other genus, leading to confusion about its taxonomic relationships. Recent anatomical, pollen, and chemical studies suggest that it is best placed in the Liliaceae or Nartheciaceae families, though these families, too, do not seem to be perfect fits. The epithet, *aurea*, means "golden," an allusion to the flower color.

YELLOW FRINGELESS ORCHID
Platanthera integra (Nutt.) A. Gray ex L. C. Beck
Orchid Family (Orchidaceae)

Description: The yellow (to sometimes yellowish orange) flowers of Yellow Fringeless Orchid are arranged in a dense, small-flowered cylindrical 1–3" raceme. The ovary may approach ½" in length, but the petals are generally less than ¼" long. The lip lacks the fringed apex typical of our other 2 brightly colored species of *Platanthera*. The stems are erect and angled. The numerous stem leaves are lanceolate in outline and up to 7" long below but reduce sharply in length upwards.

Bloom Season: Late July–September.

Habitat/Range: Savannas, boggy depressions, flatwoods, and wet pinelands. Florida, Georgia, South Carolina, and North Carolina.

Comments: Some authorities describe the flower color of *P. integra* as deep orange or yellow-orange. While individual specimens may tend toward these extremes, the dominant color seems to be closer to yellow than orange, especially when compared with *P. cristata* and *P. ciliaris*, the other orchids of similar color and form. The present species is considered critically imperiled or vulnerable throughout much of its range.

GIANT ORCHID OR NON-CRESTED EULOPHIA
Pteroglossaspis ecristata (Fernald) Rolfe
Orchid Family (Orchidaceae)

Description: The form of this tall, robust orchid is reminiscent of the lilies or agaves. A single erect 1–4' stalk arises from a cluster of basal leaves and is terminated by a leafy elongated raceme of pale yellow to soft green 1–1½" flowers with purplish markings. The petals and sepals converge to form a hoodlike structure enclosing the column. Basal leaves are up to 28" long, less than 1½" wide, and grow in a bundle adjacent to the flowering stalk. The fruit is a ⅝–¾" ellipsoid capsule.

Bloom Season: July–August.

Habitat/Range: Flatwoods, sandhills, old fields, and sandy woodlands. Florida, Georgia, South Carolina, and North Carolina (more widespread in Florida and South Carolina).

Comments: The epithet *ecristata* means "without a crest," in reference to the crestless lip petal. This species has also been included within the genus *Eulophia*, hence one of its common names. It occurs in the United States only in the Southeastern Coastal Plains and is considered imperiled or critically imperiled throughout this distribution.

SMOOTH YELLOW FALSE FOXGLOVE OR EASTERN SMOOTH OAK-LEACH

Aureolaria flava (Linnaeus) Farw.
Broomrape Family (Orobanchaceae)

Description: Stems of this leggy perennial herb are erect or strongly leaning and may be more than 6' tall. Upper leaves are lance shaped and up to about 5" long and 1½" wide with entire or toothed margins. Lower leaves are often much longer and deeply lobed. Tubular yellow flowers are borne in the leaf axils of a showy, branched inflorescence. Individual flowers are 1–2" long and slightly flared at the apex. Blossoms are a pleasing pale yellow when fresh but are highly attractive to bumblebees, whose visits darken the petals. The fruit capsule lacks hairs and the seeds are winged.

Bloom Season: August–September.

Habitat/Range: Woodland edges and oak-dominated forests. Throughout the region (although mostly outside of our region in Florida and Georgia).

Comments: Several species of *Aureolaria* occur in our region. Downy Yellow False Foxglove *(A. virginica)* is similar but flowers May–July. The lower leaves of Appalachian Oak-Leach *(A. laevigata)* are mostly entire to only slightly lobed. The seeds of the other species within our region are less than ⅟₁₆" long and lack wings.

FERNLEAF YELLOW FALSE FOXGLOVE OR SOUTHERN OAK-LEACH

Aureolaria pedicularia (Linnaeus) Raf. var. *pectinata* (Nuttall) Gleason
Broomrape Family (Orobanchaceae)

Description: The 2 yellow-flowered false foxgloves described in this section are easily distinguished by their preferred habitats and contrasting leaf shapes. As its common name implies, the conspicuously hairy ½–2" leaves of Fernleaf False Foxglove are deeply and delicately divided into numerous narrow segments that give the foliage a fernlike appearance. Fernleaf Yellow False Foxglove is a perennial herb to about 3' tall. The funnel-shaped flowers are yellow and up to about 1¾" long.

Bloom Season: May–October.

Habitat/Range: Sandhills and dry, oak-dominated uplands. Throughout the region.

Comments: This is the only species of false foxglove in our region with hairy, deeply divided leaves. It is very similar to *A. pedicularia* var. *pedicularia*, which also has divided leaves but is essentially glabrous above instead of densely hairy. The epithet *pectinata* means "comblike," in reference to the deeply divided, comblike leaves.

199

EASTERN LOUSEWORT, WOOD-BETONY, OR FERNLEAF
Pedicularis canadensis Linnaeus
Broomrape Family (Orobanchaceae)

Description: Lousewort is a 4–16" perennial herb that often forms extensive colonies of closely adjacent plants. The 2–10" leaves are alternate and deeply pinnately divided with toothed segments and a distinctly fernlike appearance. The flowers are sometimes borne in elongated densely flowered 6–10" racemes but are often crowded into a showy headlike cluster at the top of the hairy stem. Individual flowers have an irregular corolla with an elongated upper petal and are typically yellowish but are often marked with brown, red, lavender, or rust. The fruit is a flattened capsule that produces flat, wingless seeds.

Bloom Season: April–May.

Habitat/Range: Stream banks, moist woodlands, calcareous hammocks, and roadsides. Throughout the region, although mostly marginal to the coastal plains in Georgia.

Comments: This species is probably more common in the Piedmont and mountains than in the coastal plains. It is regularly encountered in the southern Appalachians, including along the road shoulders of the Blue Ridge Parkway. The genus name, *Pedicularis,* comes from the Latin word for louse. It was once believed that the presence of this species in fields was responsible for producing lice in sheep. The suffix wort is an old name for plant, hence the common name Lousewort. It has also been reported that American Indians used this species as an aphrodisiac as well as for the treatment of a variety of medical conditions ranging from diarrhea to heart trouble.

TALL MILKWORT OR
TALL PINEBARREN MILKWORT
Polygala cymosa Walt.
Milkwort Family (Polygalaceae)

Description: Tall Milkwort is an erect single-stemmed annual with a leafy stem and branched inflorescence. Small, bright yellow flowers are borne in conspicuous ½–1" congested heads that terminate the branches of a showy 2–6" cyme. Cauline (stem) leaves are numerous, alternate, narrow, stalkless, and ascending to slightly spreading. Lower leaves may be 2–5" long but become smaller upwards.

Bloom Season: May–July.

Habitat/Range: Savannas, flatwoods, roadside ditches, bogs, seepage slopes, depression ponds, and Carolina bays. Throughout the region.

Comments: Tall Milkwort is very similar in general appearance to the Short Milkwort (*P. ramosa*), which occurs in similar places and overlaps in range with Tall Milkwort. As the common names suggest, mature plants of these species may be reliably separated by height. Those of *P. cymosa* are typically 2–4' tall whereas the height of *P. ramosa* rarely exceeds about 18". *Ramosa* means "branched" and *cymosa* means "furnished with cymes," in both cases referring to the inflorescence.

SMALL-FRUITED AGRIMONY
Agrimonia microcarpa Wallr.
Rose Family (Rosaceae)

Description: The small yellow 5-petaled flowers of Small-Fruited Agrimony are borne along an erect hairy stem well above the leaves. The compound leaves have 3–5, 1–2½" coarsely toothed leaflets and are typically crowded near the base of the plant. The relatively long leaf stalks are subtended by conspicuous toothed stipules. The leaflets are usually hairy on both surfaces, though more softly so beneath. The rounded fruit is about ¼" long.

Bloom Season: July–September.

Habitat/Range: Southern mixed hardwood forests and dry to moist woodlands. Throughout the region.

Comments: At least 6 species of *Agrimonia* occur in the Atlantic Coastal Plain, all of which have coarsely toothed compound leaves and small yellow flowers. The axis of the inflorescence of the present species is covered with nonglandular hairs and its leaves usually have 5 or fewer primary leaflets (not including secondary leaflets). Taken together, these 2 characters typically serve to distinguish the species.

YELLOW PITCHER PLANT, TRUMPET-LEAF, OR TRUMPETS

Sarracenia flava Linnaeus
Pitcher Plant Family (Sarraceniaceae)

Description: Though they typically do not persist through especially cold winters, the large trumpet-shaped 1–2½' leaves of Yellow Pitcher Plant can be a conspicuous component of savannas, bogs, and seepage areas throughout much of the year. The leaves are narrow at the base but spread upwards along a continuous angle into a narrow funnel-shaped tube that is open at the apex but shaded by a 1–4" hood with a narrow neck. Most leaves are greenish yellow, but populations of plants with reddish flowers are common and may be the result of hybridization with the Purple Pitcher Plant *(S. purpurea)* or Gulf Coast Purple Pitcher Plant *(S. rosea)*. The flowers are comparatively large with 5 strap-shaped petals and an enlarged modified style that forms an umbrella over the ovary. Petals last only a short time, but the ovary and pistil are evident for an extended period.

Bloom Season: March–April.

Habitat/Range: Savannas, bogs, flatwoods, moist ditches, and sphagnum bogs. Throughout the region (but mostly west of our region in Florida).

Comments: *Flava* means "yellow," in reference to the flower color. The leaves are perfectly adapted for the plant's insectivorous habit. Foul-smelling digestive enzymes exude from the base of the leaf inside and attract a variety of insects. In late summer and early fall, the leaves of some individuals may be filled nearly to the top with hordes of the ubiquitous love bug. Although many insect species are consumed by the plant, others thrive on the enzymes and even breed in them.

HOODED PITCHER PLANT
Sarracenia minor Walter
Pitcher Plant Family (Sarraceniaceae)

Description: The hooded pitchers of Hooded Pitcher Plant explain its common name and provide an excellent feature for immediate field identification. None of our other pitcher plants are so adorned. The pitchers are erect, 5–20" tall, and green. Small white patches surrounded by reddish tissue decorate the hood and constitute part of this species' mechanism for trapping insects. From inside the light filtering through these windowpane-like patches suggests exits to the outside, confusing visiting insects and causing them to miss the opening through which they entered. The flowers have 5 yellow 1–2" petals that dangle below 5 yellowish-green sepals. The 1–2" wide modified style forms an umbrella-like structure that covers and mostly conceals the ovary.

Bloom Season: April–May.

Habitat/Range: Savannas and clearings in wet flatwoods; often occurring in extensive colonies. Florida, Georgia, South Carolina, and North Carolina.

Comments: Hooded Pitcher Plant is very common in northeast and peninsula Florida, southern and eastern Georgia, and southern South Carolina, but it becomes less common northward and is considered rare in North Carolina. The epithet *minor* means "smaller," an allusion to the fact that Hooded Pitcher Plant is typically smaller in stature than other yellow-flowered pitcher plants. Some forms of the Red Pitcher Plant *(S. rubra)* also produce hoods that nearly cover the leaf orifice, but such plants are easily distinguished by flower color.

203

PIRIQUETA OR PITTED STRIPESEED
Piriqueta cistoides (Linnaeus) Griseb. subsp. *caroliniana* (Walter) Arbo
Turnera Family (Turneraceae)

Description: This is an erect 2½' perennial herb that spreads by root sprouts. The leaves are alternate and short stalked or sessile with linear to lance-shaped blades that are ¾–2" long and up to about ¾" wide. Flowers have 5 bright orange-yellow petals that are about ¾" long. In some flowers the stamens are longer than the pistil whereas in others the pistil is longer than the stamens. Plants that exhibit this condition are said to be heterodistylous. The fruit is a rounded 3-valved capsule.

Bloom Season: May–September.

Habitat/Range: Sandhills, sandy roadsides, disturbed sites, and woodland edges. Florida, Georgia, and South Carolina.

Comments: This species has long been known by the Latin name *Piriqueta caroliniana* but has more recently been treated as a subspecies of the somewhat wide-ranging Central and South American species *P. cistoides,* the name used here. The epithet means "resembling *Cistus*," which is the genus name of the Rock-Rose and means "capsule" or "conspicuous in fruit." The Turnera Family is a mostly tropical family of about 120 herbs, shrubs, and a few trees. *Piriqueta* is the only species in the family that is native to the southeastern United States and is perhaps the only member of the family native to North America.

RED AND ORANGE FLOWERS

This section includes red and orange flowers as well as multicolored flowers where the predominant color is red or orange. Since red and orange flowers often become either paler or deeper in color with age, you should check both the yellow and pink sections if you don't find the flower you are looking for here.

FEW-FLOWER MILKWEED
Asclepias lanceolata Walter
Dogbane Family (Apocynaceae)

Description: This tall, smooth, mostly single-stemmed herb is 3–5' tall and topped by a conspicuous cluster of brightly colored flowers. The corolla lobes are bright red and the crowns, orange. Few-Flower Milkweed has 3–6 pairs of opposite leaves that vary from lance shaped to linear in outline, with successive pairs widely spaced along the stem. Mid-stem leaves may be 4–10" long, but the lower 2–3 pairs are often shorter than 2". The leaves and stems exude a white, milky sap when bruised. Seeds are produced in a narrow 4" follicle that splits open to expose the cottony appendages that aid in seed dispersal.

Bloom Season: May–August.

Habitat/Range: Moist to wet pinelands and savannas, fresh and brackish marshes, wet ditches and roadsides, bogs, and the edges of swamps. Throughout the region.

Comments: Few-Flower Milkweed is immediately recognizable by its tall, typically unbranched stem and conspicuous red and orange flowers. It is easy to spot in roadside ditches, even at highway speed, and is readily distinguished from the other 2 reddish to orange milkweeds that occur within the region. Red Milkweed *(A. rubra)* is found in similar habitats. However, its flowers have strongly reflexed dull purplish red to lavender corolla lobes and orange-tinged hoods, and its leaves are typically shorter and wider than those of *A. lanceolata*. Butterflyweed *(A. tuberosa)* occurs in drier sites and is distinguished by its abundant leaves, wholly orange flowers, and clear sap.

BUTTERFLYWEED

Asclepias tuberosa Linnaeus
Dogbane Family (Apocynaceae)

Description: Butterfly gardeners are especially fond of this showy, low-maintenance milkweed. It is a low-growing single- to multistemmed, erect to somewhat decumbent herb to about 2½' tall, but it often looks like a small shrub with a stout stem. The abundant leaves are alternate, 1–4" long, and variable in outline, from nearly linear to narrowly elliptic, obovate, or oblanceolate. The flowers are borne in showy clusters at the branch tips. Both the corolla and crown are typically orange, but they may also be heavily tinted toward either red or yellow. The seed-bearing follicles are up to 6" long.

Bloom Season: May–September.

Habitat/Range: Sandhills, drier flatwoods, sandy roadsides, and open woodlands. Throughout the region.

Comments: This is the only orange-flowered milkweed in the region that produces clear rather than milky sap. It is readily distinguished from other milkweeds by its wholly orange flowers and leafy appearance. The scientific epithet refers to its large, tuberous root while its common name references its attraction to numerous species of butterflies. Zebra Swallowtails and a host of milkweed butterflies, including the Queen and Monarch, use it as a host plant. It is sometimes called Pleurisy-Root because a tea brewed from its root was once used to treat asthma, bronchitis, and other lung infections. Two subspecies of *A. tuberosa* occur in the region. The leaves of subspecies *rolfsii* vary from linear to lanceolate with a hastate (arrowhead-shaped) base. The leaves of subspecies *tuberosa* are widest near the tip with a wedge-shaped base.

FIREWHEEL
Gaillardia pulchella Foug.
Aster Family (Asteraceae)

Description: Firewheel is a diffusely branched, erect to decumbent annual or short-lived perennial to about 30" tall. The reason for its common name is obvious. Both the disk and ray flowers are typically deep purplish red, and the 6–15, ½–1" ray flowers are often tipped with yellow, giving the entire head the appearance of a colorful pinwheel. However, flower color is variable and on some individuals the rays may be wholly yellow. The lower leaves are up to about 4" long and are often pinnately divided or lobed. The stem leaves are sessile or clasping and are usually about 2" long with entire or toothed margins.

Bloom Season: April–October.

Habitat/Range: Beaches, dunes, sandy roadsides, typically along the coast. Throughout the region.

Comments: The specific epithet *pulchella* means pretty, an appropriate appellation. Firewheel is one of our more colorful roadside plants and is widely used in wildflower gardens and coastal landscaping.

CARDINAL FLOWER
Lobelia cardinalis Linnaeus
Bellwort Family (Campanulaceae)

Description: Cardinal Flower is an erect, normally unbranched perennial herb, 2–6' tall with a slender to very stout stem that commonly forms basal offshoots. The spreading leaves are lance shaped and up to about 7" long and 2" wide. The leaf margins are finely to coarsely toothed with most teeth tipped by a tiny callous that is best seen with 10X magnification. The flowers are deep crimson-red, with an upright 2-parted upper lip, a spreading, deeply notched lower lip, and a narrow floral tube. Numerous flowers are crowded along a showy raceme at the top of the stem, above the leaves. The fruit is a ⅜" capsule that splits open at maturity to expose small, bumpy, amber-colored seeds.

Bloom Season: July–October.

Habitat/Range: Swamps, edges of spring runs, floodplain forests, and bogs; normally in shady locations. Throughout the region.

Comments: Cardinal Flower is our only red-flowered *Lobelia*. It has become a popular garden plant and is pollinated by hummingbirds, which use their elongated beaks to probe the narrow floral tube.

CORAL HONEYSUCKLE
Lonicera sempervirens Linnaeus
Honeysuckle Family (Caprifoliaceae)

Description: Coral Honeysuckle is a deciduous twining vine to about 15' long. It takes its common name from the showy clusters of tubular, bright red 1½–2" flowers that terminate the stem and branches. The main stem leaves are whitish below, opposite, short-stalked, and 1–3" long. The 1–2 pairs of leaves nearest the tip of the stem are shorter and connate or perfoliate, meaning that they are joined at the base and completely encircle the stem. The fruit is a red ⅜" berry.
Bloom Season: March–June.

Habitat/Range: Sandhills, upland woods, borders, and fencerows, typically in dry, sunny sites. Throughout the region.

Comments: Coral honeysuckle has become a popular native vine for home landscaping. It is slow growing and showy, attracts hummingbirds, and lacks the aggressive, weedy tendencies of the non-native, white-flowered Japanese Honeysuckle *(L. japonica)*. Japanese Honeysuckle is a troublesome exotic weed that is difficult to control and has the potential to crowd out native ground cover in shaded hardwood uplands. The bright red, tubular flowers and opposite leaves easily distinguish Coral Honeysuckle. Several red-flowered morning glories are superficially similar, including the non-native Cypressvine *(Ipomoea quamoclit)* and Scarlet Creeper or Ivyleaf Morning Glory *(I. hederifolia)*, and the potentially native Redstar *(I. coccinea)*. However, all of the red-flowered morning glories have alternate leaves.

CORAL BEAN, CHEROKEE BEAN, OR REDCARDINAL

Erythrina herbacea Linnaeus
Pea Family (Fabaceae or Leguminosae)

Description: Coral Bean is an erect, prickly, deciduous, multistemmed, predominantly herbaceous perennial to about 4½' tall. The leaves are alternate, 3-parted, and up to 8" long, including the leafstalk. The leaflets are shaped somewhat like arrowheads or spearheads and are up to about 4" long and 4" wide. Flowers are 1–4" long, bright red, tubular, and borne perpendicularly to the axis of an erect, multiflowered raceme. The elongated, often curving legume may be 6" long and is severely constricted between the seed cavities. The legume splits at maturity to expose several bright red seeds.

Bloom Season: April–May, but specimens flowering outside this date range should be expected.

Habitat/Range: Sandy woods, dunes, hardwood hammocks, and pine-oak-hickory woods. Florida, Georgia, South Carolina, and North Carolina.

Comments: The name *Erythrina* comes from the Greek word for red, in reference to the flowers and seeds. The color red is a natural warning sign that often signals danger. In the case of Coral Bean, the raw seeds contain alkaloids, are poisonous to animals and humans, and have been used to poison rats. Coral Bean is more common in Florida and coastal sandhills of Georgia and South Carolina. It occurs in only a handful of the southeasternmost counties in North Carolina. Although it is known as an herbaceous perennial in most of our region, in southernmost peninsula Florida it becomes a woody shrub or small tree to about 8' tall. Some authorities have given the name *E. arborea* to the woody form.

PURPLE SESBAN
Sesbania punicea (Cavanilles) Benxtham
Pea Family (Fabaceae or Leguminosae)

Description: The common name Purple Sesban is often misleading. The color of the flowers is typically much closer to red than it is to purple. Typical plants are erect and 3–9' tall, with a diffusely branched shrublike stature. The 4–12" leaves are alternate and pinnately compound with 10–17 pairs of ½–1¼" leaflets. Up to about 30 red to orange flowers are borne in showy racemes at the leaf axils. The fruit is a 1–3" dark brown, 4-winged pod.

Bloom Season: May–October.

Habitat/Range: Wet roadside ditches, marshes, wet pinelands, and wetland edges. Throughout the region.

Comments: This non-native woody shrub is unmistakable when in flower. It is our only Sesban with red or orange flowers. Similar and related species, most within the genus *Sesbania*, have yellow flowers. Purple Sesban was probably introduced from South America and can become a troublesome weed along wet, sunny fence lines and roadsides.

CRIMSON CLOVER
Trifolium incarnatum Linnaeus
Pea Family (Fabaceae or Leguminosae)

Description: The stems of this 8–20" herb are covered with appressed or softly spreading hairs. The leaves are palmately divided into 3, ½–1½" leaflets. The tiny flowers have red (occasionally white) petals and are borne in compact 1–3" showy heads. The fruit is a 1-seeded egg-shaped legume.

Bloom Season: March–June.

Habitat/Range: Roadsides, fields, and other disturbed sites. Throughout the region.

Comments: Several species of clover in the genus *Trifolium* occur in the region, the majority of which are non-native species. Crimson Clover was introduced from southern Europe and is used in our region primarily for erosion control. It is often planted along interstate highways and other major roadways, especially in Florida, where it produces expansive colonies that dominate the road shoulders. It is included in this guide due to its conspicuous presence. It is not likely to be confused with any other roadside plant.

PINE LILY, CATESBY'S LILY, OR LEOPARD LILY
Lilium catesbaei Walt.
Lily Family (Liliaceae)

Description: Pine Lily's 1–2' stem arises from a ¾" bulb. The 1–4" leaves are alternate, mostly linear in outline, and are so sharply ascending as to be nearly appressed to the stem. The solitary, orange to orange-red flowers are borne at the top of the stem and are marked below with brownish to yellowish spots. Seeds are produced in an oblong 1–2" capsule that remains on the plant for some time after flowering.

Bloom Season: June–September.

Habitat/Range: Savannas, flatwoods, and moist, sunny roadsides. Throughout the region, but uncommon northward and rare in Virginia.

Comments: Pine Lily is easiest to find in sunny, open savannas or wet pinelands with only scattered trees and a dense herbaceous ground cover. Plants often occur as scattered individuals throughout such areas but sometimes form small colonies of several plants. The epithet *catesbaei* commemorates the contributions of the English naturalist Mark Catesby (1682–1749), author of *A Natural History of the Carolinas,* a work that continues to be an important reference to modern-day ecologists.

CAROLINA LILY
Lilium michauxii Poiret
Lily Family (Liliaceae)

Description: The brightly colored 2–3" flower segments of this attractive woodland lily are often so severely reflexed that their apices overlap above the flower. Sterile plants are mostly erect, especially when young, but often lean at flowering time due to the weight of the blossoms. The fragrant flowers are produced mostly 1 or 2 at a time, though occasionally more are seen. Mid-stem leaves are 3–5" long, widest near the apex, and crowded in whorls of 4–15. Leaves of the lower stem are smaller, borne singly at a node, and appear alternate in arrangement.

Bloom Season: July–August.

Habitat/Range: Moist to dry upland forests and slopes. Throughout the region, but only at the western edge of the region in Florida.

Comments: This lily is widely distributed across the southeastern United States but is uncommon in the coastal plains. It is 1 of 3 lilies in our region that bear nodding, reddish orange flowers. It is most easily distinguished from the next 2 species by combination of its habitat, few-flowered inflorescence and fragrant flowers and by leaves that are both alternate and whorled, smooth along the margins, and widest above the middle.

SANDHILLS LILY OR SANDHILLS BOG LILY
Lilium pyrophilum M. W. Skinner & Sorrie
Lily Family (Liliaceae)

Description: The epithet *pyrophilum* means "fire loving," in reference to this species' dependence on a fire-maintained habitat. The common name Sandhills Bog Lily alludes to its restricted range within the Fall Line Hills, a narrow topographic subdivision that separates the Piedmont from the lower coastal plain. One to 5, pendent, nonfragrant flowers are borne at the top of the stem. Individual flowers have 6 often re-curved, 2½–3½" segments that range from yellowish to orange or nearly red. The leaves are 1–5" long, widest near the middle, green above and only slightly paler beneath, distinguishing them from those of *L. michauxii*, which are noticeably paler beneath. The conspicuous 1–2", 3-parted capsule ripens mostly in October.

Bloom Season: July–August.

Habitat/Range: Sandhill seepage bogs and peaty swamp margins in the upper South Atlantic Coastal Plain. South Carolina, North Carolina, and Vriginia. Considered critically imperiled in Virginia.

Comments: Sandhills Lily was first described as a new species in 2002, though its distinctiveness had been suspected for nearly 40 years. It was once thought to represent an extreme range extension of the Panhandle Lily *(L. iridollae)*, a rare species of southeast Alabama and the western part of the Florida panhandle. It is similar to and somewhat intermediate between *L. michauxii* and *L. superbum*, the other 3 orange-flowered lilies that occur in our region. It may be reliably distinguished from *L. michauxii* by its leaves, which are widest near the middle and have roughened margins, and by habitat. *L. michauxii* occurs in dry woodlands, not bogs. *L. superbum* is typically a larger plant with narrower leaves that are mostly more than 5" long.

TURK'S-CAP LILY OR LILY-ROYAL
Lilium superbum Linnaeus
Lily Family (Liliaceae)

Description: Unlike the other 3 orange-flowered lilies treated here, the inflorescence of the Turk's-Cap often produces numerous flowers, many of which may be open at the same time. Typical plants are adorned with 3–30 blossoms, although some plants may produce up to 70. Individual flowers are divided into 6 purple-spotted, reddish orange segments. The bases of the segments have a bright green patch that, when the bases are viewed collectively, have the appearance of a green star. Flowers are not fragrant. Leaves are 3–10½" long, vary from lance shaped to narrowly elliptic in outline, and are borne in whorls of 5–20 along a stout 3–7' stem. Seeds are produced in a conspicuous, chambered capsule.

Bloom Season: July–August.

Habitat/Range: Moist ravines, wet meadows, swamps along black-water streams, edges of wet-weather drains in Longleaf Pinelands. Throughout the region (but only at the western edge of the region in Florida).

Comments: This showy lily occurs in the mountains, Piedmont, and coastal plain. It is probably more common in the mountains and is regularly encountered along the Blue Ridge Parkway, even at higher elevations. Though its wide range might suggest otherwise, most taxonomists agree that representative plants from these regions all belong to the same species. Perhaps future research will result in the description of new varieties, subspecies, or distinct species from this wide-ranging lily. Its height and many-flowered inflorescence help distinguish it.

BRISTLY-MALLOW
Modiola caroliniana (Linnaeus) G. Don
Mallow Family (Malvaceae)

Description: Few members of the Mallow (or Hibiscus) Family resemble this low, branching and creeping perennial herb. Typical plants have numerous branches that radiate outward from the center and often root at the nodes. Stems are mostly procumbent but may be weakly erect and are covered with spreading star-shaped (stellate) hairs that require magnification to see clearly. The ½–1½" leaves are divided into several toothed lobes, somewhat reminiscent of a violet. Cup-shaped flowers arise on ¾–2½" threadlike stalks and have 5, ¼" petals that are reddish orange with a blackish to deep purplish base. Individual flowers produce 20–30 stamens and 15–25 styles. The fruit is a ring of 15–25 carpels (ovaries), each of which produces a smooth, tiny brown seed.

Bloom Season: Primarily March–July, but later flowering dates are not uncommon.

Habitat/Range: Pond and stream margins, seepage slopes, pastures, gardens, roadsides, and lawns. Throughout the region.

Comments: This native herb has weedy tendencies and is often found in lawns, gardens, and weedy fields. Its occurrence at the edges of shallow ponds also qualifies it as a wetland herb. The genus name *Modiola* derives from the Latin word *modiolus*, "the hub of a wheel," an allusion to the fruit, which is composed of a distinctive ring of 15–25 carpels that separate at maturity.

YELLOW FRINGED ORCHID
Platanthera ciliaris (Linnaeus) Lindl.
Orchid Family (Orchidaceae)

Description: The erect, densely flowered racemes of brightly colored flowers make this orchid one of our more conspicuous late-summer wildflowers. Individual racemes are conical in shape, 2–8" tall, and up to about 3" wide. The flowers range in color from bright yellow to deep orange and are equipped with an extended, delicately fringed lip petal. The spur petal often exceeds 1" in length and typically curls upward at the tip; the ovary is only slightly shorter. The lance-shaped leaves may reach 12" in length near the base of the plant, but those nearer the top of the stem are much shorter. Individual plants may reach 3' tall, but heights less than 2' are probably more typical.

Bloom Season: July–September.

Habitat/Range: Bogs, wet flatwoods, savannas, Longleaf Pinelands, and the edges of wetland drains. Throughout the region.

Comments: The Latin epithet *ciliaris* means "like an eyelash," an allusion to the conspicuously fringed lip from which this species takes its common name. *Platanthera* means "flat anthers." Yellow Fringed Orchid may be distinguished from the Crested Fringed Orchid, its nearest look-alike, by its larger size, brighter orange color, conical inflorescence, and much longer spur petals. The 2 species often grow together.

CRESTED FRINGED ORCHID
Platanthera cristata (Michx.) Lindl.
Orchid Family (Orchidaceae)

Description: Crested Fringed Orchid is a single-stemmed herb arising from fleshy roots. Individuals may reach heights of 3', but most plants are less than half this height. The flowers are yellow-orange to deeply orange and borne in a densely flowered, very showy raceme at the top of the stem. Individual flowers are about ¾" long with a long ovary and an extended fringed lip. The spur petal is about ⅔ the length of the ovary, much shorter than the spur petal of *P. ciliaris*. The leaves are lance shaped and up to about 10" long below but are much shorter above.

Bloom Season: June–September.

Habitat/Range: Bogs, wet flatwoods, savannas, and Longleaf Pinelands. Throughout the region.

Comments: The flowering periods of *P. ciliaris* and *P. cristata* overlap in midsummer. *P. cristata* tends to commence flowering as early as June and complete flowering by mid August, whereas *P. ciliaris* tends to begin flowering in mid to late July and continue flowering into mid September. In locales where they co-occur, the period of overlap can be quite spectacular. A third species, *P. chapmanii,* is similar and likely arose as a hybrid between the two. It occurs sparingly in Florida, Georgia, and Texas and is generally distinguished by the length of the spur petal, which is intermediate in length between the lengths of the spurs of its parent species. Its spur petal is normally equal to or only slightly shorter than the ovary. The shape of its raceme is also intermediate, typically being more compact than the raceme of *P. ciliaris,* but somewhat taller and wider than the raceme of *P. cristata.*

ORANGE MILKWORT OR RED-HOT-POKER

Polygala lutea Linnaeus
Milkwort Family (Polygalaceae)

Description: The bright orange heads of this annual or biennial milkwort are both showy and unmistakable. No other milkwort in our region is similarly adorned. The solitary to sparingly branched stems are 6–15" tall with alternate fleshy leaves that are typically widest near the tip. The flowers are individually small but are borne in conspicuous, compact, ½–1½" racemes that terminate the stems and branches.

Bloom Season: March–September.

Habitat/Range: Flatwoods, bogs, savannas, wet roadsides, edges of cypress ponds, and coastal swales. Throughout the region.

Comments: By its scientific name, Orange Milkwort should be yellow. The epithet *lutea* derives from the Latin word for yellowish. The name was obviously bestowed based on a dried specimen, the flowers of which had faded. The plant is also sometimes called Red-Hot-Poker, for obvious reasons. This is a common species throughout the Southeastern Coastal Plains.

RED BUCKEYE

Aesculus pavia Linnaeus
Soapberry Family (Sapindaceae)

Description: At maturity Red Buckeye becomes a small deciduous tree to about 40' tall, but it often flowers while only a 3–4' shrub. The leaves are opposite and compound, with 3–6" stalks and 5–7 (typically 5) dark green 2–7" leaflets. The leaflets radiate from a single point at the tip of the leafstalk, reminiscent of the fingers of a human hand and are often described as palmate or digitate. The brick-red flowers are ½–¾" long, nearly 1" wide, and borne in showy upright 10" by 5" panicles. The fruit is a distinctive fleshy, golden brown 2½" capsule with 1–6 hard, reddish brown poisonous seeds.

Bloom Season: March–May.

Habitat/Range: Rich slopes, moist woodlands, and the edges of swamps, often in association with limestone. Florida, Georgia, South Carolina, and North Carolina.

Comments: Red Buckeye's attractive and somewhat unique foliage and showy flowering panicle have made it a popular native landscape plant. Its common name comes from the fruit, which is very similar to the more northern buckeyes of the same genus.

REDFLOWER PITCHER PLANT OR SWEET PITCHER PLANT
Sarracenia rubra Walter
Pitcher Plant Family (Sarraceniaceae)

Description: This is one of 3 red-flowered pitcher plants in our region. It is easily distinguished from the others by its 4–28" erect, reddish to greenish leaves that are often suffused above with reddish or purplish veins. The leaves are narrow at the base but gradually broaden above, terminating in a relatively small ¾–1¼" orifice. The flowering scape is 6–30" tall and is terminated by a 1–2", 5-petaled flower that is red on the inside and purplish red on the outside.

Bloom Season: June–July.

Habitat/Range: Seepages, bogs, wet savannas, and pocosins. Georgia, South Carolina, and North Carolina (other subspecies occur in the Florida panhandle, west of our region).

Comments: Redflower Pitcher Plant is an extremely variable species. At least 5 geographically isolated forms are recognized, with distributions that span the Southeastern Coastal Plains. Some authorities treat these forms as subspecies of *S. rubra*, while other authorities treat at least some variants as distinct species.

INDIAN PINK OR WOODLAND PINKROOT
Spigelia marilandica (Linnaeus) Linnaeus
Strychnos Family (Strychnaceae)

Description: Few wildflowers are more arresting than Indian Pink. The scarlet-red petals are fused and tubular for most of their 2" length but divide at the tip to form a 5-parted star that displays their yellowish green interior. The dark green leaves are opposite, mostly sessile, and 2–6" long and range in outline from narrowly to broadly lance shaped. Individual plants vary 12–30" tall.

Bloom Season: March–June.

Habitat/Range: Southern mixed hardwood forests, calcareous hammocks, and rich wooded slopes. Florida, Georgia and South Carolina (also North Carolina and Virginia, but outside of our region).

Comments: The Strychnos Family is famous for strychnine. Indian Pink contains the poisonous alkaloid spigeline and was reportedly used medicinally by American Indians and early physicians to expel worms and parasites from the intestines. This species is very distinctive and is not likely to be confused with any other species in our region. Indian Pink is more common in the Piedmont and mountains, which makes it an exciting find in the coastal plains.

SPOTTED WAKEROBIN
Trillium maculatum Raf.
Trillium Family (Trilliaceae)

Description: Trilliums take their scientific name from the 3 whorled leaves or leaflike bracts that subtend the flowers. The leaves of Spotted Wakerobin are mottled green and beige and are borne at the top of a purplish 6–15" stem. The flowers are erect with 3 deep maroon (or sometimes yellowish) 1¾–2½" petals, and 3 greenish sepals. The petals are perceptibly narrowed at the base (a good field identification character) but wider and somewhat spoon shaped above. The narrow base of the petals allows observers to peer "through" the flower and allow the stamens and anthers to be very conspicuous and clearly visible, even at peak flowering.

Bloom Season: March–April.

Habitat/Range: Rich forests, often with a calcareous base, including coquina limestone and shell middens. Florida, Georgia, and South Carolina.

Comments: Though most trilliums in the southeastern United States are associated with the Appalachian Mountains, at least 5 species are known primarily from the Southeastern Coastal Plains, several of which occur in our region. Carolina Dwarf Trillium *(T. pusillum)* is smaller than Spotted Wakerobin and has spreading, creamy white flower petals that are often blushed with pink. Catesby's Trillium *(T. catesabei)* has recurved pinkish petals on flowers that droop below the leaves. Underwood's Trillium *(T. underwoodii)* and Chattahoochee Wakerobin *(T. decipiens)*, both of which occur in south Georgia and northwest Florida, are similar to Spotted Wakerobin, but their wider petals completely conceal the anthers.

BROWN AND GREEN FLOWERS

This section includes flowers that are predominantly brown or green. Some flowers included here also tend toward yellow, lavender, or pale purple. Check those sections if you don't find what you are looking for here.

FALSE ALOE OR RATTLESNAKEMASTER

Manfreda virginica (Linnaeus) Salisb. ex Rose
Agave Family (Agavaceae)

Description: False Aloe is a rhizomatous perennial that forms large basal rosettes of fleshy swordlike leaves that may be up to 20" long and 2" wide. Each rosette produces a single, stiffly erect 4–6' flowering stalk topped by a loosely flowered inflorescence that dominates the upper ¼ of the stem. Up to 30 fragrant, greenish yellow 1½–2" flowers are borne individually on short stalks along the central axis. The fruit is a rounded ½–¾" capsule.

Bloom Season: May–July.

Habitat/Range: Calcareous glades, pinewoods, rocky places, and the edges of southern mixed hardwood forests. Florida, Georgia, South Carolina, and North Carolina (also Virginia, but not within our region).

Comments: The basal rosette of fleshy leaves is very similar to species of *Agave*, a genus within which False Aloe was previously included. Species of *Manfreda* differ from *Agave* by being both herbaceous and bulbous. Some authorities refer to the present species by the commonly encountered synonym *Polianthes virginica*, the genus name of which means "with gray or whitish flowers." A rinse concocted from the roots of *Manfreda virginica* has reportedly been used to treat snakebites, hence the common name Rattlesnakemaster. Native Americans used a tea made from the roots as a diuretic. Others have reportedly used this plant as a laxative and to treat diarrhea. However, the internal fluids of False Aloe may be a strong skin irritant to some.

LARGEFLOWER MILKWEED
Asclepias connivens Baldwin
Dogbane Family (Apocynaceae)

Description: Few other milkweeds in our region have flowers as large as those of *A. connivens.* Individual flowers can be up to ¾" wide and are borne in groups of 3–6 from the axils of the uppermost, bractlike leaves. The flowers have prominent, conspicuously incurving hoods but no horns. The stem is stout, unbranched, and 12–32" tall. The leaves are 1–3" long, thick, opposite, sessile, and oblong to oval in outline, although those near the base are often small and bractlike. Crushed or broken stems, leaves, and flower stems produce a sticky, milky sap. The fruit is a 5–7" follicle that splits at maturity to expose numerous seeds with cottony appendages (technically a coma).

Bloom Season: May–August.

Habitat/Range: Savannas, bogs, flatwoods, and wet roadsides. Florida, Georgia, and South Carolina.

Comments: At least 4 other green-flowered milkweeds occur in our region. Only Green Antelope Horn (A. viridis), which has alternate leaves, has flowers approaching the size and color of Largeflower Milkweed.

GREEN DRAGON
Arisaema dracontium (Linnaeus) Schott
Arum Family (Araceae)

Description: Green Dragon is a perennial, fleshy herb from a subterranean 1" bulb. Stems reach about 40" in height. The leafstalk arises from a thin papery sheath and terminates in the center of a single, compound, curving blade that is divided into 7–15 elliptical to oblong or lance-shaped leaflets that are 3–9" by 1–2". The yellowish green flowers are embedded in a fleshy spike (spadix) that protrudes from a nearly closed spathe below the leaves. A conspicuous cluster of showy, orange-red ¼" berries follows flowering.

Bloom Season: March–May.

Habitat/Range: Moist to mesic hammocks and the lower slopes of southern mixed hardwood forests. Throughout the region.

Comments: Green Dragon is closely related to Jack-in-the-Pulpit *(A. triphyllum)* but is easily distinguished by its numerous leaf segments and long-tapering spadix that extends well beyond the spathe. Jack-in-the-Pulpit never has more than 5 leaflets, all of which are often oriented horizontal to the ground, and its spadix is flared at the apex.

JACK-IN-THE-PULPIT OR INDIAN TURNIP
Arisaema triphyllum (Linnaeus) Schott
Arum Family (Araceae)

Description: Jack-in-the-Pulpit is a well-known herb of rich, shaded mixed hardwood forests. Typical plants are 8–30" tall with a single, erect flowering spathe and 3-parted leaves with 3–6" leaflets. Mature flowering specimens tend to have 3 leaves, while young plants often have only 1 leaf. The flowers are borne along an erect spadix that is enclosed within a flaring and hooded 3–6" spathe. The spadix usually protrudes from the tube of the spathe and is overtopped by the hood, giving rise to the common name Jack-in-the-Pulpit. The spathe withers after flowering and is replaced by a showy congested cluster of bright red berries.

Bloom Season: March–April.

Habitat/Range: Moist southern mixed hardwood forests. Throughout the region.

Comments: The common name Indian Turnip probably comes from Jack-in-the-Pulpit's tuberous root. A tea brewed from the dried roots of this species and the related Green Dragon *(A. dracontium)* have been used as a folk remedy for colds, coughs, bronchitis, and asthma. However, fresh plants are known to contain calcium oxalate crystals that can be intensely irritating and burning to the mouth and throat and can cause skin irritation if handled roughly. The specific eipthet *triphyllym* means "with 3-parted leaves." However, some plants of Jack-in-the-Pulpit have 5-parted leaves. Some authorities treat such plants as *A. quinatum* ("in fives"), while other authorities treat them as *A. triphyllum* var. *quinatum*. At least 2 other varieties of Jack-in-the-Pulpit have also been described. Suffice it to say that this is a variable species.

LITTLE BROWN JUG, WILD GINGER, OR ARROWLEAF HEARTLEAF
Hexastylis arifolia (Michx.) Small
(Syn: *Asarum arifolium* Michx.)
Pipevine Family (Aristolochiaceae)

Description: One look at the flowers of this low-growing perennial herb explains the origin of its common name. The dark brown ground-hugging flowers lack petals but have a thick, firm ¾–1" calyx that looks like a tiny urn. Flowers are typically produced at the base of the leaves and are often hidden in the leaf litter. The leathery, long-stalked, heart-shaped 2–4" leaf blades radiate from the base of the plant and are dark green with brown mottling. The fruit is a fleshy capsule.

Bloom Season: March–May.

Habitat/Range: Dry to moist deciduous forests. Throughout the region.

Comments: Of the 10 species of *Hexastylis* that occur in North America, *H. arifolia* is the most common and widespread. The common name Wild Ginger derives from the plant's use as a food-flavoring agent. It was once widely sought after and collected. The oils within its leaves and roots are reported to contain high concentrations of safrole, a pale yellow, strongly aromatic oil with the odor of ginger or sassafras. Safrole is a naturally occurring substance that is present in many plants but is probably best known as a component of sassafras oil, which was once used to flavor root beer. Ironically, safrole has also been widely used in the manufacture of insecticides. Many authorities believe safrole to be a human carcinogen and its use as a food agent has been outlawed in the United States since the 1960s. Some studies have shown it to cause liver tumors in mice. At least 2 tribes of American Indians reportedly used the roots and leaves of Wild Ginger medicinally for the treatment of pain, asthma, and whooping cough.

AMERICAN EVERLASTING

Gamochaeta coarctata (Willd.) Kerguélen
(Syn: *Gnaphalium spicatum* Lam.)
Aster Family (Asteraceae or Compositae)

Description: Several erect, leafy 10–30"stems arise from the base of this annual herb. The leaves are 1½–4" long, green above, and dull grayish white below. Both the stems and leaves are typically covered with woolly hairs. Numerous tiny brownish flowers are borne in a dense head near the top of the stem. The phyllaries lack hairs, and this can be used as a good field identification character.

Bloom Season: February–July.

Habitat/Range: Dry fields, roadsides, pastures, lawns, and other disturbed sites. Throughout the region.

Comments: This is a non-native weed that is common throughout our region. It is very closely related to and similar to the native Purple Everlasting *(Gamochaeta purpurea),* of which it was once considered to be a variety. The leaves of Purple Everlasting are silvery below and contrast sharply with the upper surfaces and the outer phyllaries are hairy at their bases. Several species of *Gamochaeta* occur in our region, many of which can be difficult to distinguish from each other.

THREE-SEEDED MERCURY OR SHORT-STALKED COPPERLEAF

Acalypha gracilens A. Gray
Spurge Family (Euphorbiaceae)

Description: Linnaeus named this genus after the ancient Greek name for nettle *(akalēphē),* apparently due to the nettlelike appearance of the leaves. Plants of the genus are not true nettles and do not have the stinging hairs common to many nettle species. *A. gracilens* is an erect, branching herb that grows to about 2' tall. The stalked 1–2½" leaves are elliptic to broadly lance shaped with bluntly toothed margins. Flowers are borne in clusters in the leaf axils and are subtended by conspicuous leaflike bracts. The fruit is a 3-chambered capsule characteristic of the Spurge Family. Seeds are reddish to black.

Bloom Season: June–November (typically dying back at first frost).

Habitat/Range: Dry woodlands, lawns, and disturbed sites. Throughout the region.

Comments: The specific epithet *gracilens* means "slender or graceful," a name that doesn't appear well suited to this species. The common name Copperleaf refers to the coppery color of withering leaves, an accolade that is more accurately describes some of the other species within this genus.

CORKWOOD OR WATER TOOTHLEAF

Stillingia aquatica Chapman
Spurge Family (Euphorbiaceae)

Description: Corkwood takes its common name from the weight of its wood. Fishermen once used sections of the stem as floats. The 2–4' stem is usually solitary and erect but sometimes produces reddish branches near the top. The simple, alternate, narrowly lance-shaped leaves are 1 ¼–3¼" long and well spaced along the stem. Numerous tiny greenish, yellowish, or reddish flowers are borne in a conspicuous cylindrical spike at the tips of the stem and branches. The fruit is a 3-chambered capsule that splits at maturity to forcibly expel the seeds.

Bloom Season: May–September.

Habitat/Range: Wet flatwoods depressions, pond margins, and wet roadside ditches. Florida, Georgia, and South Carolina.

Comments: Corkwood is closely related and somewhat similar to Queen's Delight *(S. sylvatica),* an upland species that occurs primarily in moist to dry pinelands. Queen's Delight is herbaceous, much shorter in stature at maturity, and often produces several stems from the base. Corkwood, on the other hand, is woody and occurs predominantly in or near shallow standing water. The specific epithets of the 2 species suggest their ideal habitats. *Aquatica* means "growing in or near water," whereas *sylvatica* means "growing in woods or forests." The Spurge Family (Euphorbiaceae) is one of the world's largest and most diverse families of flowering plants and includes about 7,000 species in more than 300 genera.

STRIPED GENTIAN
Gentiana villosa Linnaeus
Gentian Family (Gentianaceae)

Description: This is the only green-flowered gentian likely to found in our region. It is a mostly ascending to erect leafy perennial with fleshy roots. Stems are 6–20" tall but often flop over due to the weight of the inflorescence. It is not uncommon to find plants with seemingly prostrate stems covered by leaf litter. The leaves are narrowly to broadly elliptic in outline and up to about 4" long and 1¼" wide; those lower on the stem are decidedly widest above the middle. The flowers are 1¼–1¾" long and borne in several-flowered clusters from the axils of the upper leaves. The corolla varies from green to yellowish white and may be tinted with blue or purple.

Bloom Season: August–November.

Habitat/Range: Pine-oak-hickory woods, upland forests, and sandhill-pocosin ecotones. Throughout the region.

Comments: Striped Gentian is uncommon throughout our region. However, where found it typically occurs in populations of several to many plants. When a single individual is found, diligent searching often turns up others. It is somewhat responsive to fire but seems to occur more frequently in comparatively dense ground cover where it can be difficult to spot. This is one of several gentians in our region. Most of the others have blue flowers. Individuals of Striped Gentian with pale blue flowers may be easily distinguished from other blue-flowered gentians by the shape of the lower leaves, which are widest above the middle. The epithet *villosa* means "covered with soft hairs."

EASTERN FEATHERBELLS
Stenanthium gramineum (Ker Gawl.) Morong
Melanthium Family (Melanthiaceae)

Description: This smooth perennial herb arises from a slender bulb and may be up to about 5' tall. A large, branching 1–3' inflorescence (technically a panicle) tops the stem, each segment of which contains numerous greenish ⅜" flowers with narrow petals and sepals. The leaves are 8–30" long and linear in outline. They are longest at the base of the plant but gradually reduce in length upwards. The fruit is a narrowly egg-shaped ½" capsule.

Bloom Season: May–August.

Habitat/Range: Bluffs, woodland borders, and southern mixed hardwood forests. Throughout the region.

Comments: The genus name *Stenanthium* comes from Greek and means "narrow flower," in reference to the slender sepals and petals. The epithet *gramineum* refers to the linear "grasslike" leaves. This species is in the same family as Death Camas *(Zigadenus* spp.). The closely related Mountain Bells *(S. occidentale)* and numerous others in the family are known to be poisonous if ingested.

SPRING CORALROOT
Corallorhiza wisteriana Conrad
Orchid Family (Orchidaceae)

Description: Only a handful of temperate orchids are achlorophyllus, meaning that they lack chlorophyll and with it the ability to produce food from sunlight. This at least partly explains the yellowish brown to purplish stems and branches of the Spring Coralroot and its close relative, the somewhat less common Autumn Coralroot *(C. odontorhiza)*. Spring Coralroot usually occurs in small colonies of several 2–12" stems that are decorated along the upper third with up to 30 pale, greenish yellow ⅜–¾" flowers with purplish brown spots. The fruit is a ⅜–½" drooping capsule.

Bloom Season: February–April.

Habitat/Range: Hammocks and mixed hardwood forests. Throughout the region.

Comments: Spring Coralroot takes its nourishment in cooperation with a subterranean mycorrhizal fungus and is hence said to be mycotrophic. Mycorrhiza is an association between a fungus and a plant in which the fungus lives on or within the plant's roots, forming either a symbiotic or parasitic relationship.

GREEN-FLY ORCHID
Epidendrum magnoliae Muhlenberg
(Syn: *Epidendrum conopseum* Aiton f.)
Orchid Family (Orchidaceae)

Description: Green-Fly Orchid typically forms tight clumps on the trunks and larger lateral branches of Cypress, Live Oak, Tupelo, and Southern Magnolia trees. The evergreen leaves are 1–5" long, narrow, thick, dark green, and linear to narrowly lance shaped. Green to brown rootlike structures, called pseudobulbs, extend outward from the base of the plant, and are closely affixed to the trunk. The fragrant flowers are creamy green, sometimes minutely suffused with purple, with narrow petals that are about or slightly more than ½" long. The lip is flared and 3-lobed. Single flowering stalks produce up to about 10 flowers each, although smaller numbers of flowers is more common. The fruit is an elliptical, drooping capsule with numerous, very tiny seeds.

Bloom Season: June–July is typical, but flowers may be seen at other times.

Habitat/Range: Epiphytic on Cypress, Southern Magnolia, Live Oak, and Swamp Black Gum (the common hosts) in rich, moist woods, swamps, along stream banks, and above backwaters of large alluvial rivers. Florida, Georgia, South Carolina, and North Carolina.

Comments: Green-Fly Orchid is one of only a handful of epiphytic plants in the Atlantic Coastal Plain. Others include Spanish Moss *(Tillandsia usneoides)*, Resurrection Fern *(Pleopeltis polypodioides* var. *michauxiana)*, and Mistletoe *(Phoradendron leucarpum)*. Green-Fly Orchid is not abundant across its range but is probably overlooked by many observers. It is most easily seen with binoculars by searching tree trunks shrouded in Resurrection Fern. However, it also grows at eye level, especially in swamps and on large, low-hanging branches.

CRESTED CORALROOT
Hexalectris spicata (Walt.) Barnh.
Orchid Family (Orchidaceae)

Description: This is a somewhat stout, fleshy, saprophytic (receiving nutrients from decaying vegetation) orchid with inconspicuous scalelike leaves and belowground rhizomes that resemble coral. Aboveground stems are 6–32" tall and vary from brownish to tan or purplish. The 1–1½" flowers are well spaced along the upper stem and are yellowish brown with brown-purple streaks and a purplish lip. The fruit is a drooping, conspicuously 3-ribbed ¾–1¼" capsule.

Bloom Season: June–August.

Habitat/Range: Rich woods, stream banks, hardwood slope forests, mixed pine and hardwood forests, Shortleaf Pine–oak–hickory forests. Throughout the region.

Comments: Crested Coralroot is considered vulnerable or imperiled in several states and should not be removed from the wild or dug up to inspect its roots. This is 1 of 3 orchids in the region that lack chlorophyll. Others include Autumn Coralroot *(Corallorhiza odontorhiza)* and Spring Coralroot *(C. wisteriana)*. Crested Coralroot is easily distinguished by its stout, light brown stem.

SOUTHERN TWAYBLADE
Listera australis Lindley
Orchid Family (Orchidaceae)

Description: Southern Twayblade takes its common name from the 2 opposite leaves that adorn the lower portions of the 3–15" stem. If named for its flowers, it would undoubtedly be called Mosquito Orchid. The form of the tiny brownish to reddish purple flowers is at least superficially similar to this common, biting insect. The leaves are dark green, ¾–1½" long, and ovate to elliptic in outline. The few-flowered or many-flowered raceme may be up to about 4½" tall.

Bloom Season: February–July.

Habitat/Range: Swamps, wet calcareous hammocks, floodplain terraces, wet woods. Throughout the region.

Comments: The epithet *australis* means "southern," in reference to the location from which this species was originally recognized. Its range actually extends from Quebec, Canada, to central peninsula Florida. Southern Twayblade is an inconspicuous orchid that easily escapes notice without diligent observation and an adequate search image. However, it often occurs in large colonies. When a single plant is found, it is usually not difficult to find others nearby.

GREEN ADDER'S-MOUTH
Malaxis unifolia Michaux
Orchid Family (Orchidaceae)

Description: This diminutive, bright green herb may be up to 20" tall but is usually much shorter. The stem is erect and topped with a congested 1–5" raceme of tiny green flowers that are borne on slender, threadlike stalks. Each plant has only 1 rounded, sessile, clasping 1½–2½" leaf. The specific epithet *unifolia* means "with a single leaf." The fruit is a tiny, ¼" egg-shaped capsule.

Bloom Season: March–August.

Habitat/Range: Rich hardwood forests and forested slopes. Throughout the region, but mostly outside of our region in Florida.

Comments: Green Adder's-Mouth is 1 of 3 species of *Malaxis* in the southeastern United States. Florida Adder's-Mouth *(M. spicata)* is similar in appearance and distribution but has 2–3 leaves per plant. The genus name *Malaxis* is a Greek word that means "softening," an apparent allusion to the soft texture of the leaves of at least some *Malaxis* species. Green Adder's-Mouth is generally considered to be uncommon in our region but often occurs in relatively large colonies.

SMALL GREEN WOOD ORCHID
Platanthera clavellata (Michaux) Luer
Orchid Family (Orchidaceae)

Description: The raceme of the Small Green Wood Orchid is often few flowered and less than 2" long, although robust plants may produce racemes to about 3½" long. The flower petals are greenish white or yellowish white and less than ⅜" long, with a comparatively long, slender, curving spur that extends down and below the ovary. Stems are up to about 16" tall with 1 or occasionally 2 leaves at mid-stem or below.

Bloom Season: June–September.

Habitat/Range: Seepages, bogs, and small boggy stream runs. Throughout the region, but only at the western extreme of our region in Florida.

Comments: Plants of Small Green Wood Orchid seem to get larger and more robust with increasing latitude. This is primarily a northern species; southern plants tend to be shorter in stature with smaller leaves and smaller, less congested racemes. The specific epithet *clavellata* means "shaped like a small club," a reference to the slender, clublike spur.

SOUTHERN REIN ORCHID OR SOUTHERN GYPSY-SPIKE
Platanthera flava (Linnaeus) Lindley
Orchid Family (Orchidaceae)

Description: The flowers of Southern Rein Orchid are more nearly yellowish green than the pure yellow color that is suggested by its scientific epithet; *flava* means "pure yellow." The flowering stems of this erect, robust orchid can be 1–2' tall. The 2–3 leaves are borne mostly at mid-stem or below. Larger leaves are up to about 8" long and 2" wide. The densely flowered raceme is 2½–8" tall and about ¾" wide with conspicuous leaflike bracts subtending the lowermost flowers.

Bloom Season: March–September.

Habitat/Range: Swamp forests, wet shady woodlands, and floodplain swamps. Throughout the region.

Comments: Southern Rein Orchid is widespread across the eastern United States from about Maryland and The Great Lakes southward to central peninsula Florida and west to Texas. Some authorities also recognize variety *herbiola*, which has a more northern distribution and is distinguished from variety *flava* by its longer, more numerous floral bracts and its more densely flowered raceme. Variety *herbiola* is rarely encountered in our region.

WHORLED POGONIA OR PURPLE FIVELEAF ORCHID
Pogonia verticillata (Muhl. ex Willd.) Nutt.
(Syn: *Isotria verticillata* [Muhl. ex Willd.] Raf.)
Orchid Family (Orchidaceae)

Description: This 4–15" upright, terrestrial orchid is easily identified by combination of its leaves, flowers, and stature. The leaves are 1–4" long and borne in whorls of 5–6 at the top of a fleshy, glabrous stem (the epithet *verticillata* means whorled). One or 2 flowers are produced on erect 1–2" stalks. Each flower consists of 3 narrow, 1½–2½" purplish sepals and 3 somewhat broader, yellowish green ¾–1" petals.

Bloom Season: April–July.

Habitat/Range: Moist to dry forests and the edges of streams. Throughout the region, but very rare in Florida and only at the western edge of our region.

Comments: The genus name *Isotria*, within which this species was formerly included, is from Greek for "equal" and "three," an allusion to the 3 sepals, which are equal in size and shape. The name *Pogonia* means "beard." Many members of the genus have a bearded lip petal. Some populations of this species may not flower every year, or may flower at widely varying times from year to year, but usually in spring and early summer.

233

CRANEFLY ORCHID
Tipularia discolor (Pursh) Nutt.
Orchid Family (Orchidaceae)

Description: The leaves of Cranefly Orchid first appear during midwinter, long before the midsummer flowering period, and disappear by the time the flowering stalks are produced. They are 2–4" long, ovate, lay flat to the ground, and are easy to recognize. Their upper surfaces are dark green and bumpy with purplish spots; the lower surfaces are most often deep purple, though green lower surfaces are sometimes encountered. Plants produce only a single leaf but often occur in large colonies where the leaves of separate individuals overlap each other. Flowering stems are erect, to about 20" tall, and pale brown or purplish. As many as 40 delicate yellowish brown to purplish ½–¾" flowers are borne along the upper half of the stem. The fruit is a ⅜–⅝" capsule that may remain on the plant for an extended period and is often visible the following spring when the new leaves are present.

Bloom Season: June–August.

Habitat/Range: Southern mixed hardwood forests, mixed pine and hardwoods, and rich slopes with deciduous woodlands. Throughout the region.

Comments: Though easy to recognize, Cranefly Orchid can be a difficult plant to find. It is well camouflaged in the brown litter of the hardwood forests in which it occurs and is not at all conspicuous. Craneflies are thin, long-legged, brownish insects of the family Tipulidae and genus *Tipula*. The genus name *Tipularia* means resembling *Tipula*, in reference to the similarity between the shape of this orchid's flowers and the shape of its namesake insect. The epithet *discolor* references the contrasting color of the lower and upper leaf surfaces.

AMERICAN SQUAWROOT OR CANCERROOT
Conopholis americana (Linnaeus) Wallr.
Broomrape Family (Orobanchaceae)

Description: The yellowish brown hue of the upright stems and scalelike leaves of this 10" parasitic herb tend to obscure the white color of its flowers. Colonies of Squawroot tend to grow in conspicuous clumps and are sometimes confused with fungi. The tiny white tubular flowers are about ⅜" long and borne in an erect 2–8" terminal spike. Individual plants often flower early in the spring, but the stems tend to remain visible for several months. The fruit is a ½" egg-shaped capsule with shiny brown seeds.

Bloom Season: March–June.

Habitat/Range: Rich woodlands in association with oak trees. Throughout the region.

Comments: Members of the Broomrape Family are well known for their typically parasitic habit. The family once included only a handful of species in the southeastern United States but has now been expanded to include numerous additional species, including a large group that was previously classified in the Figwort Family (Schrophulariaceae). Squawroot lacks chlorophyll and does not photosynthesize. It depends instead on nutrients garnered from the roots of nearby trees, mostly oaks *(Quercus)*. The genus name derives from the Greek words *conos* or "cone," and *pholis,* "scale," in allusion to the plant's resemblance to a pinecone. The common name Squawroot references its use by Native American women to treat the symptoms of menopause. The name Cancerroot references its general medicinal properties. It has been touted as an astringent and as a cure for headaches. There is no evidence of its use in the treatment of tumors or other cancers.

BEECHDROPS
Epifagus virginiana (Linnaeus) W. Barton
Broomrape Family (Orobanchaceae)

Description: The flowers of Beechdrops are actually purplish, but the drab color of the plant gives the overall impression that it is totally brown. To the uninitiated Beechdrops might look like the dead tip of a fallen branch. Stems are 6–30" tall, yellowish brown to purplish, and typically multiply branched. The ½" flowers are purplish veined and borne in a spikelike inflorescence along the branches.

Bloom Season: September–November.

Habitat/Range: Southern mixed hardwood forests, always under American Beech *(Fagus grandifolia)* trees. Throughout the region.

Comments: The genus *Epifagus* includes a single species restricted to eastern North America. The name derives from *epi,* which means "upon," and *fagus,* the genus name for the American Beech; Beechdrops grows on the roots of beech trees. The prefix epi is also the prefix for epiphyte, a plant that grows on another plant but receives its nutrients from the air. Although its name suggests that *E. virginiana* might be an epiphyte, Beechdrops is actually parasitic and receives its nutrients from the roots of its host.

CHAFFSEED
Schwalbea americana Linnaeus
Broomrape Family (Orobanchaceae)

Description: Chaffseed is an erect, perennial herb with a hairy, unbranched stem to about 2' tall. The leaves are alternate, entire, and 1–1½" long. Leaf size decreases from the base of the stem upwards, with the uppermost leaves extending into the inflorescence as floral bracts. The tubular 1" flowers are yellowish suffused with pinkish purple and are borne along the upper ½–⅓ of the stem. The narrow fruit is enclosed in a saclike structure, hence the common name Chaffseed.

Bloom Season: May–June.

Habitat/Range: Flatwoods, savannas, Longleaf Pine sandhills, and sandhill-pocosin ecotones. Throughout the region.

Comments: Chaffseed was previously much more common and once occurred in at least 15 eastern states from Connecticut to Florida, westward to Louisiana and Kentucky. It is on the federal list of endangered species and is critically imperiled in most states where populations remain. Chaffseed is extremely dependent on periodic fire and its maintenance requires a high fire frequency, which probably explains much of its demise.

TOOTHACHE GRASS
Ctenium aromaticum (Walter) A. W. Wood
Grass Family (Poaceae or Gramineae)

Description: Toothache Grass is a fire dependent perennial herb that flowers most prolifically following a fire. Recently burned savannas and pinelands can be so heavily dominated by Toothache Grass that it appears to be one of only a few plants in the ground cover. Flowering stems arise from a short rhizome, may be up to 4' tall, and are terminated by a single, recurved, 1-sided 1½–6" spike. The tan to light brown spikelets are borne in 2 rows and are tipped with a conspicuous awn. Basal and lower stem leaves are present and may be up to about 16" long.

Bloom Season: May–October.

Habitat/Range: Savannas, bogs, pinelands, wet flatwoods, sandhill seepages, and the margins of pocosins. Throughout the region, although rare in Virginia.

Comments: The genus name *Ctenium* derives from the Greek word for "comb," in reference to the 1-sided, comblike spikes. The base of the culm has a pungent taste and a short-lived numbing effect on the tongue, gums, and lips if it is chewed. Chewing the plant was once used to relieve toothache discomfort.

TWOFLOWER MELIC
Melica mutica Walter
Grass Family (Poaceae or Gramineae)

Description: Few members of the Grass Family are included within this guide; many grasses are somewhat nondescript and difficult to identify. In contrast, Twoflower Melic is a distinctive species that can be both conspicuous and abundant in rich hardwood forests in early spring. Plants of this species are tufted, weak-stemmed perennials that are typically 1½–2' tall. The flowers are borne in spikelets near the tip of the culm. Each spikelet ordinarily contains only 2 perfect florets (the ultimate floral unit in the grasses), hence the common name.

Bloom Season: February–May.

Habitat/Range: Rich woods, calcareous hammocks, southern mixed hardwood forests. Throughout the region.

Comments: The genus name *Melica* comes from the Greek name for a sweet grass. The epithet *mutica* means "blunt or without a point," in reference to the blunt spikelets. Twoflower Melic has a particular affinity to areas where limestone is very near the ground surface. The related Threeflower Melic *(M. nitens)* occurs rarely in the mountains of Virginia and North Carolina.

SUGARCANE PLUMEGRASS
Saccharum giganteum (Walter) Pers.
Grass Family (Poaceae or Gramineae)

Description: With heights potentially exceeding 10', this is one of our tallest native grasses. The culm (stem) is strictly erect with tufts of hairs at the leaf nodes and topped by a large, conspicuous 4–12" inflorescence of silvery brown to purplish brown spikelets. At flowering time the spikelets are well separated and have the appearance of branches but expand into a plumelike mass as the grains mature. The leaves are up to 20" long and 1" wide and are rough along the margins.

Bloom Season: September–November.

Habitat/Range: Flatwoods, marshes, ditches, savannas, coastal wetlands, and margins of swamps. Throughout the region.

Comments: The epithet *giganteum* refers to this species' large size. This species was formerly included within the genus *Erianthus,* which means "wool flower," but is now generally included within the same genus as Sugarcane. At least 4 related species occur in our region. Mature panicles of the present species usually much exceed 3" in width, which helps distinguish it from others in the genus.

SEA OATS
Uniola paniculata Linnaeus
Grass Family (Poaceae or Gramineae)

Description: Reintroduction of Sea Oats to beaches and coastal dunes is an important step in beach restoration and conservation. The stems of this perennial grass grow vertically as the dune grows, sending out lateral branches that stabilize shifting sands and help the dunal ecosystem withstand the onslaught of wind and water. Stems on old plants may extend far below the ground surface. Aboveground stems are 3–5' tall with flat 3–4' leaves. The flowers are arranged in a showy, drooping, terminal 1–2' panicle with numerous ½–1½" flattened spikelets, the basic unit of the grass inflorescence.

Bloom Season: May–November.

Habitat/Range: Coastal dunes and beaches. Throughout the region.

Comments: Sea Oats were once more common and widespread prior to the onset of coastal and seaside development. It is unlawful in some areas to remove or disturb this species, and recent efforts have been made to reintroduce it to dune habitats.

COMMON CATTAIL
Typha latifolia Linnaeus
Cattail Family (Typhaceae)

Description: Common Cattail is one of our most easily recognized native plants. Its tall, dense, brown, cylindrical 5–10" spikes of female flowers are conspicuous components of roadside wetlands and ditches. Male flowers are lighter in color and borne in a separate but contiguous spike above the female flowers. The leaves are light green, flat on the back, and up to 1" wide and 10' tall. All species of cattail produce long fleshy rhizomes that aid colonization.

Bloom Season: Predominantly April–July, but flowering spikes or the remains of them are obvious most of the year.

Habitat/Range: Wet ditches, artificial impoundments, fresh and tidal marshes, and riverbanks. Throughout the region.

Comments: Several species of cattail occur within our region. Narrowleaf Cattail *(T. angustifolia)* is shorter (usually not exceeding about 6' tall) and has narrower leaves, and its male and female flower spikes are separated by naked stem. Southern Cattail *(T. domingensis)* resembles Narrowleaf Cattail but usually exceeds 8' in height. All of these species are native but have weedy tendencies, especially in disturbed ponds, drainage canals, and ditches. Once started, they spread rapidly and have proved extremely difficult to control at some state parks and national wildlife refuges. Their rapid colonization of wetlands can crowd out other native plants and reduce wildlife habitat.

GLOSSARY

Achene—A dry, hard, one-seeded fruit.

Acuminate—Long-tapering to a pointed apex.

Alternate—Alternating along an axis; bearing a single leaf at each node (see opposite).

Appressed—Tightly pressed against another organ, as leaves that lay flat to a stem or hairs to the surface of a leaf.

Awn—A stiff, hairlike appendage, usually at the tip of a leaf, petal, or sepal.

Axil—The angle between two organs; often used to denote the angle between a leafstalk and its supporting stem.

Basal rosette—Cluster of leaves borne at ground level at the base of a plant.

Bract—A leaflike structure (typically small in size) that subtends another organ; used mostly in reference to the leaflike structures subtending a flower or inflorescence.

Calyx—The outer whorl of parts in a flower, usually subtending the petals.

Carpel—A simple pistil or a single member of a compound pistil.

Cauline—Pertaining to the stem, as in cauline leaves.

Chasmogamous—Of or related to a normal flower that opens for pollination (see cleistogamous).

Clasping—Partly surrounding another organ; often to describe a leaf base that partly surrounds the stem.

Claw—The conspicuously narrowed lower portion of a petal or sepal in contrast to the wider upper portion.

Cleistogamous—Of or related to a type of self-pollinated flower that usually does not open; as in some of the violets and milkworts (see chasmogamous).

Coma—A cottony tuft of long hairs at the end of a seed; used here mostly in reference to the seeds of the milkweeds.

Compound—Said of a leaf that is divided into multiple leaflets.

Corolla—The petals of a flower when referred to as a unit.

Corymb—A flat-topped inflorescence that typically flowers from the margins inward.

Crown—An outgrowth of the staminal part of a flower in the milkweeds.

Culm—The aerial stem of the grasses and sedges.

Cyathium (pl. cyathia)—A cuplike structure, common in some species of *Euphorbia*, that contains a single naked female flower surrounded by several naked male flowers. The cup is called an involucre and often is adorned along the margin with small petal-like appendages that are often important in identifying the species.

Cyme—A broad, flat inflorescence with the innermost flowers maturing first.

Decurrent—Fused with and extending down a supporting structure, as a leaf base that is fused to and extends down a stem.

Deflexed—Pointing downward.

Dentate—Coarsely toothed.

Digitate—Several structures arising from a common point, similar to the fingers of a human hand.

Disjunct—Having an interrupted geographic distribution in which individual populations of a single plant species are widely separated from each other, often by hundreds of miles.

Drupe—A single-seeded fleshy fruit with the seed enclosed in the hardened innermost layer.

Elliptic—Widest in the middle and tapering more of less evenly and symmetrically to each end.

Entire—Said of a leaf with margins that lack teeth.

Epiphyte—A plant that grows on trees or other plants; plants with this habit are said to be epiphytic.

Epithet—The second word in a Latinized scientific name; as *lanceolata* in *Asclepias lanceolata.*

Filiform—Threadlike.

Follicle—A dry fruit that opens along one seam at maturity, as in the milkweeds and bluestars.

Forb—An herbaceous flowering plant that is neither a grass nor sedge.

Glabrous—Lacking hairs.

Gland—A fluid-secreting appendage or depression (often glistening) on an organ such as a leaf surface, or at the tip of a subtending hair. Glandular depressions are often called glandular dots.

Head—A tightly held cluster of flowers, as in the aster family (Asteraceae).

Helicoid cyme—A coiled cyme.

Hemiparasite—Partially parasitic.

Herb—A non-woody seed plant, often of small stature, that dies back at the end of each growing season.

Hip—Fruit of the genus *Rosa* of the Rose Family (Rosaceae).

Hood—The concave, usually upright, part of the petal in the milkweeds.

Horn—An appendage—often protruding—within the hood of a milkweed flower.

Imparipinnate—Of a pinnately compound leaf with a terminal leaflet.

Indeterminate—Used to describe an inflorescence in which lowermost or outermost flowers open first and no terminal flower is produced.

Involucre—Typically a nestlike cluster of bracts subtending and surrounding a flower cluster or single flower, as in the Aster Family (Asteraceae); also used to denote the cuplike structure in the cyathium of the genus *Euphorbia*.

Keel petal—The lower petal of a typical (papilionaceous) pea flower.

Linear—Narrow, with parallel sides.

Mesic—Moist.

Mucro—A short, often stubby, abrupt point.

Mucronate—Tipped with a short projection, usually a protruding vein.

Oblanceolate—Widest at the tip and narrowing to the base; reverse of lance shaped.

Obovate—Reverse egg-shaped.

Opposite—Said of organs, typically leaves, that are attached opposite to one another at the same node along an axis (usually stem).

Ovate—Egg-shaped in a two-dimensional outline.

Palate—A rounded or cylindrical projection extending from the lower lip of a two-lipped flower; as in the genus *Pinguicula*.

Palmate—Divided into several parts from a central point, reminiscent of the human hand.

Panicle—A compound flower with stalked flowers along an axis; inflorescences with this form are said to be paniculate.

Pedicel—The stalk of a single flower within an inflorescence.

Perianth—The collective name for the sepals and petals of a flower.

Petiole—Leafstalk.

Phyllary—(pl. phyllaries) A bract of the involucre in the asters (Asteraceae).

Phyllode—An expanded petiole that resembles a leaf but lacks a true blade.

Pinnate—Used to describe a once-divided, compound leaf with the general form of a feather.

Polymorphic—Varying in form; usually in reference to plant species that vary widely in morphology from plant to plant.

Pome—A fleshy fruit with a thickened outer layer surrounding a central, capsular core that contains the seeds; an apple.

Procumbent—Prostrate.

Pubescent—Bearing hairs; hairy.

Punctation (pl. punctae)—A small dot or depression on the surface of an organ (typically a leaf, sepal, petal, or stem).

Resupinate—Upside down; usually said of a flower that is twisted one-half turn on the stalk, as many species of orchids.

Reticulate—Forming a network of polygons, as in the veins of some leaves.

Revolute—Rolled under along the margins (opposite of involute).

Rosette—Cluster of leaves borne at ground level at the base of a plant.

Saprophyte—A plant that receives nutrients from nonliving organic matter.

Scape—A leafless flower stalk arising from ground level; such structures sometimes have leaflike bracts.

Secund—Appearing to grow on one side of the stem.

Serrate—Sharply toothed along the margins.

Sessile—Lacking a stalk.

Sheath—An organ that surrounds or envelops another organ; often used in reference to the leaves.

Silique—A narrow, elongated seed capsule common to members of the Mustard Family (Brassicaceae or Cruciferae).

Simple leaves—Undivided leaves; as opposed to compound leaves.

Sinuate—With strongly wavy margins.

Smooth—Said of a structure that lacks hairs or other surface features, including entire or untoothed leaf margins.

Spadix—A thickend, fleshy spike with embedded flowers, as in *Orontium aquaticum.*

Spathe—A large, often fleshy, bract surrounding an inflorescence.

Spikelet—The ultimate floral unit in the grasses and sedges.

Spur—A hollow, tubular, pointed appendage arising from a petal or sepal.

Squarrose—Spreading or recurved above the base.

Standard—The upper petal of the flower in some members of the Pea Family (Fabaceae).

Stipule—An appendage at the base of a leafstalk, usually in the axil; common to many families, but particularly well developed in some members of the Rose Family (Rosaceae).

Tepal—Used to describe the parts of a perianth when the sepals and petals cannot be differentiated.

Ternate—Borne in threes.

Thryse—An elongated panicle-like inflorescence with a determinate main axis and determinate cymose lateral axes.

Truncate—Cut-off.

Tube—Sometimes used to describe the fused lower portion of the corolla.

Unifoliolate—Having a compound leaf with a single leaflet.

Verticillate—Borne in a whorl around another structure, as whorls of leaves around a stem.

Wing petal—The lateral petal in the Pea and Milkwort families.

NATIVE PLANT RESOURCES

Wildflower societies, botanical societies, native plant societies, and natural heritage programs provide excellent resources for finding out more about the flora of the Atlantic Coastal Plain. Several plant societies offer regularly scheduled programs, conferences, and field trips, most of which are led by experts on the local flora. Each state's natural heritage program maintains a database of the state's rare and endangered species, and is an excellent place to report unusual discoveries.

Florida Native Plant Society
PO Box 278
Melbourne, FL 32902-0278
Phone: (321) 271–6702
E-mail: info@fnps.org
www.fnps.org/

Florida Natural Areas Inventory
1018 Thomasville Road, Suite 200-C
Tallahassee, FL 32303
Phone: (850) 224–8207
Fax: (850) 681–9364
www.fnai.org/

Georgia Botanical Society
Anita Reaves, Membership Chair
2718 Stillwater Lake Lane
Marietta, GA 30066
Phone: (770) 827–5186
E-mail: members@gabotsoc.org
www.gabotsoc.org/

Georgia Native Plant Society (GNPS)
PO Box 422085
Atlanta, GA 30342-2085
Phone: (770) 343–6000
E-mail: webmaster@gnps.org
www.gnps.org/

Georgia Natural Heritage Program
2117 US Highway 278 SE
Social Circle, GA 30025
Phone: (770) 918–6411 or (706) 557–3032
Fax: (706) 557–3033
http://georgiawildlife.dnr.state.ga.us/content/displaycontent.asp?txtDocument=87

North Carolina Native Plant Society
North Carolina Botanical Garden
Totten Garden Center 3375
University of North Carolina
Chapel Hill, NC 27599-3375
Phone: (919) 962–0522
Fax: (919) 962–3531
www.ncwildflower.org/

North Carolina Natural Heritage Program
Office of Conservation & Community Affairs
1601 MSC
Raleigh, NC 27699-1601
Phone: (919) 715–8687
Fax: (919) 715–3085
www.ces.ncsu.edu/gaston/environment/ncnatherit.html

South Carolina Native Plant Society
PO Box 21266
Charleston, SC 29413
Phone: (843) 928–4001
www.scnps.org/

South Carolina Natural Heritage Program
Heritage Trust Program
S.C. Department of Natural Resources
PO Box 167
Columbia, SC 29202
Phone: (803) 734–3893
www.dnr.sc.gov/conservation.html

SELECTED REFERENCES

Braun, Lucy. *Deciduous Forests of Eastern North America.* Philadelphia: Blakiston, 1950.

Brown, Paul Martin. *Wild Orchids of Florida, With References to the Atlantic and Gulf Coastal Plains.* Gainesville, Fla.: University Press of Florida, 2002.

Chafin, Linda G. *Field Guide to the Rare Plants of Florida.* Tallahassee, Fla.: Florida Natural Areas Inventory, 2000.

Clewell, Andre F. *Guide to the Vascular Plants of the Florida Panhandle.* Gainesville, Fla.: University Press of Florida, 1985.

Correll, Donovan Stewart. *Native Orchids of North America.* Stanford, Calif.: Stanford University Press, 1978.

Cronquist, Arthur. *Vascular Flora of the Southeastern United States, Volume 1, Asteraceae.* Chapel Hill, N.C.: University of North Carolina Press, 1980.

Duncan, Wilbur H. and Marion B. Duncan. *Wildflowers of the Eastern United States.* Athens, Ga.: University of Georgia Press, 1999.

Foster, Steven and James A. Duke. *Eastern/Central Medicinal Plants and Herbs.* New York: Houghton-Mifflin, 2000.

Gledhill, D. *The Names of Plants,* second edition. Cambridge, U.K.: Cambridge University Press, 1989.

Godfrey, Robert K. *Trees, Shrubs, and Woody Vines of Northern Florida and Adjacent Georgia and Alabama.* Athens, Ga.: University of Georgia Press, 1988.

Godfrey, Robert K. and Jean W. Wooten. *Aquatic and Wetland Plants of Southeastern United States: Monocotyledons.* Athens, Ga.: University of Georgia Press, 1979.

———. *Aquatic and Wetland Plants of Southeastern United States: Dicotyledons.* Athens, Ga.: University of Georgia Press, 1981.

Isley, Duane. *Vascular Flora of the Southeastern United States, Volume 3, Part 2 Leguminosae (Fabaceae).* Chapel Hill, N.C.: University of North Carolina Press, 1990.

Nelson, Gil. *East Gulf Coastal Plain Wildflowers.* Guilford, Conn.: The Globe Pequot Press, 2005.

———. *Florida's Best Native Landscape Plants.* Gainesville, Fla.: University Press of Florida, 2003.

———. *Shrubs and Woody Vines of Florida: A Field Guide and Reference.* Sarasota, Fla.: Pineapple Press, 1996.

Porcher, Richard Dwight. *A Guide to the Wildflowers of South Carolina*. Columbia, S.C.: University of South Carolina Press, 2001.

Radford, Albert E., Harry E. Ahles, and C. Ritchie Bell. *Manual of the Vascular Flora of the Carolinas*. Chapel Hill, N.C.: University of North Carolina Press, 1968.

Sorrie, Bruce A. and Alan S. Weakley. Coastal plain vascular plant endemics: Phytogreographic patterns. *Castanea* 66, no. 1–2 (2001): 50–82.

Stearn, William T. *Stearn's Dictionary of Plant Names for Gardeners*. London: Cassell Publishers Ltd., 1996.

Thorne, Robert F. The vascular plants of southwestern Georgia. *The American Midland Naturalist* 52, no. 2 (1954): 257–327.

Turner, Nancy J. and Adam F. Szczawinski. *Common Poisonous Plants and Mushrooms of North America*. Portland, Ore.: Timber Press, 1991.

Weakley, Alan S. 2004. *Flora of the Carolinas, Virginia, and Georgia. Working Draft March 4, 2005.* www.herbarium.unc.edu/flora.htm.

Wells, B. W. *The Natural Gardens of North Carolina*. Chapel Hill, N.C.: The University of North Carolina Press, 1932.

Wunderlin, Richard P. and Bruce F. Hansen. *Guide to the Vascular Plants of Florida,* second edition. Gainesville, Fla.: University Press of Florida, 2003.

INDEX

ABOUT THE AUTHOR

Gil Nelson is a writer, naturalist, photographer, field botanist, and educator. He is a research associate in botany at the Robert K. Godfrey Herbarium at Florida State University and has written widely about Florida and the southeastern United States. His works include the companion volume *East Gulf Coastal Plain Wildflowers*, three field guides to Florida plants, a guide to native landscape plants, and co-authorship of two Audubon field guides. This is his tenth book, the second for Falcon.

Gil also teaches relational database programming and geographical information systems, with a particular interest in the design, development, and uses of relational database technology and GIS for the management and use of biological and botanical data. His hobbies and interests include hiking, wildflower and landscape photography, phytogeography of the southeastern United States, plant ecology, and the structure and composition of natural vegetative communities.

Gil resides with his wife Brenda in the community of Beachton in southwest Georgia.